ETHNOGRAPHY FOR
MARKETERS

ETHNOGRAPHY FOR
MARKETERS
A GUIDE TO CONSUMER IMMERSION

HY MARIAMPOLSKI, PhD
QualiData Research Inc.

SAGE Publications
Thousand Oaks ▪ London ▪ New Delhi

For information:

Sage Publications, Inc.
2455 Teller Road
Thousand Oaks, California 91320
E-mail: order@sagepub.com

Sage Publications Ltd.
1 Oliver's Yard
55 City Road
London, EC1Y 1SP
United Kingdom

Sage Publications India Pvt. Ltd.
B-42, Panchsheel Enclave
Post Box 4109
New Delhi 110 017 India

Printed in the United States of America

Library of Congress Cataloging-in-Publication Data

Mariampolski, Hy.
Ethnography for marketers: A guide to consumer immersion / Hy Mariampolski.
       p. cm.
Includes bibliographical references and index.
ISBN 0-7619-6946-2 (cloth) — ISBN 0-7619-6947-0 (pbk.)
   1. Marketing research. 2. Consumer behavior. 3. Consumers' preferences.
4. Business anthropology. I. Title.
HF5415.2.M3164 2006
658.8′34—dc22   2005003610

This book is printed on acid-free paper.

06   07   08   09   8   7   6   5   4   3   2

Acquisitions Editor:	Al Bruckner
Editorial Assistant:	Maryann Vail
Production Editor:	Diane S. Foster
Copy Editor:	Jacqueline A. Tasch
Typesetter:	C&M Digitals (P) Ltd.
Proofreader:	Mary Meagher
Indexer:	Teri Greenberg
Cover Designer:	Michelle Lee Kenny

Contents

33 76

Introduction

The greatest challenge for market research nowadays is to deliver value by linking findings to the strategic business decisions that confront corporate decision makers. Ethnography responds to this challenge by observing consumers in their "natural" environments and then turning these consumer encounters into ideas that transform brands and product categories.

Ethnography takes research out of the laboratory and into the homes, offices, stores, and streets where people live, eat, shop, work, and play. It permits a more holistic and better nuanced view of consumer satisfactions, frustrations, and limitations than any other research approach. Ethnography can offer insights into consumer language, myths, and aspirations, insights that will meet the toughest challenges brought up by strategic thinkers and brand planners.

Ethnography has rocketed to the top of the market research agenda in recent years because it allows those who create and sell products and services to encounter consumers in new ways. Also referred to as *on-site, naturalistic, observational,* or *contextual research,* ethnographic methods allow marketers to delve into the actual occasions and situations in which products are used, services are received, and benefits are conferred.

This book reviews the theoretical perspectives at the root of ethnography and suggests analytic approaches that yield high-value information for product marketing and communications decisions. In addition, by examining such issues as the "limitations of asking," this work offers a critique of prevailing epistemologies in marketing research, which are superseded by naturalistic and contextual research. We also offer an overview of several new market research applications—in such areas as niche marketing to regional and ethnic subcultures, retail environmental planning, and user interface design for computer technologies—that are benefiting from the use of ethnographic approaches.

Above all, this work is designed to serve as a training and reference resource for the benefit of students, companies, agencies, and research consultants embarking on ethnographic studies. In this context, the material is expected to serve the following ends:

- Promote a common language for discussing project planning, execution, and reporting
- Create a consistent step-by-step system for implementing projects
- Promote a specific management structure so that multicity and multinational projects can be run in a precise and consistent manner; given details of the management system, unanticipated problems can be handled promptly and efficiently
- Share a common set of principles for conducting ethnography and analyzing the collected data while allowing for a high degree of flexibility and accommodation to local conditions and unique project demands
- Provide clients with a common set of expectations that they can use to monitor and control research suppliers as they participate in the life history of the project

This book does not spend a great deal of time discussing the discipline of ethnography in abstract terms; these needs are immeasurably satisfied already by existing works in the literature. Instead, we assume that readers are considering or about to embark on an ethnographic study and can benefit from concrete, practical advice and guidance.

The text itself is divided into four components: Part I describes the background of the discipline; Part II offers implementation steps and provides overall orientation to conducting an ethnography; Part III provides guidance in managing all of the elements associated with a site visit, including data collection and interpretation; Part IV develops guidelines for the effective representation of ethnographic data. Throughout the text, we review decision points that are encountered in every ethnographic study and offer guidelines for resolving fieldwork and data collection issues. The discussion is enhanced by a review of case studies illustrating how substantive and tactical problems were resolved.

Acknowledgments

My work here is the outcome of a constant and collective process, driven, first of all, by the high expectations of clients commissioning research studies; then, by efforts to continuously improve our processes and procedures for conducting ethnographic studies. This book's approach to fieldwork has also been strongly influenced by humanistic concerns about the cooperating study participants, who share their practices and thoughts with sometimes naïve and clumsy visitors (see also, Mariampolski, 1988, 1998, 1999).

After nearly 20 years of experience with scores of research studies and nearly 30 years of teaching and training, I have a very wide circle of influencers and fellow thinkers who deserve acknowledgment.

I conducted my first ethnographic as participant observation exercises during my graduate studies in Purdue University's Department of Sociology and Anthropology. Inspired by the prospect of combining this approach with my interest in international research, I undertook two years of ethnographic study in Israel during 1973 and 1974 to analyze ideological shifts in the kibbutz, the system of collective farming communities first introduced around the beginning of the 20th century. This experience ingrained an appreciation of the promise as well as the problems associated with ethnography. Professors Walter Hirsch and Dean Knudsen, my mentors and advisers during this period, were consistently compassionate and considerate in offering support.

I began teaching ethnographic methods after my appointment as Assistant Professor on the graduate faculty at Kansas State University. Some of the earliest components of this volume go back to this period when I was helping students overcome practical dilemmas in conducting studies for coursework, theses, and dissertations.

In the early 1980s, I made the decision to leave academia for the greener pastures of professional market research by founding QualiData Research Inc. It took quite some time following this transition to begin convincing clients about the advantages of ethnography as an applied research technique for marketers. The focus group was then the main qualitative research approach being used, and this technique was growing in applications and appreciation. By now, thankfully, an entire subindustry has emerged to meet demands for consumer engagement through ethnographic research. Early QualiData clients who were pioneer proponents— Alex LaChance, Bill Stack, and Claudia Schwartz—deserve grateful acknowledgment.

Many of the ideas at the root of this text have emerged over the course of many years of teaching, training, and lecturing in ethnographic methods on behalf of several market research associations. The Qualitative Research Consultants Association (QRCA) has been my second home for many years and has given me numerous opportunities to share my points of view. ESOMAR, the World Association of Research Professionals, has showcased our worldwide workshop, "Ethnography and Observational Research: Applying Cultural Analysis Tools in Consumer Research." I am grateful to my copresenter, Philly Desai, as well as to Anna Alu and Victoria Steven for untiring support. The Advertising Research Foundation has also provided a forum for my evolving ideas about ethnographic methods.

Lecturing outside the United States not only has been personally enriching but also has allowed me to challenge myself and be challenged under the purview of other cultures. In addition to working with ESOMAR, I have traveled and taught ethnographic methods under the auspices of the South Africa Market Research Association, the Market Research Society of Australia, the New Zealand Market Research Society, and the China Market Research Association. China Market Research Association. My conscience and collaborator in World-Class Qualitative Research TM, Pat Sabena has been my companion and co-presenter on some of these voyages.

I have served on the board of advisers for the masters of marketing research program at the University of Georgia's Terry College of Business for more than a dozen years now. I am grateful for advantages far out of proportion to what I have given over this period time. The program's students have come to be as conversant in ethnography and other qualitative methods as they are in data mining and multiple regression—admittedly a significant accomplishment. Professor Ellen Day deserves much of the credit for turning out such fine "quallies" and has been extremely helpful in shepherding this text. Valuable guidance has also been provided by Professor Cara Lee Okleshen Peters, who is now at Winthrop University.

Research assistance for sections of the text was generously provided by Veronica Criswell and Lisa Hardy.

Sharon Wolf, my partner in life and business, has always been my rock and firmament. I am grateful for her feedback on this text and for keeping the business running during all those times when I sequestered myself to write at our country cottage.

PART I

Background

1

Introducing Ethnography to Marketers

D rawn from nearly a century of anthropological and sociological studies, ethnographic research brings marketers, designers, and planners as close to the consumer as possible in order to solve important business problems. Site visits and observational encounters with consumers in their accustomed habitats are the core component of marketing ethnography. They help corporate research managers and their internal colleagues acquire insights into consumers' needs and wishes by decoding behaviors observed and opinions expressed during direct contact with consumers in their natural environments. Both formal and spontaneous interactions with consumers form the underlying data of marketing ethnography.

Ethnography is effectively used in marketing when little is known about a targeted market or when fresh insights are desired about a segment or consumer-related behavior. Received facts about the marketplace have a very short effective life. Change is ubiquitous in contemporary societies, and, worldwide, citizens are continuously adapting to the advances in technologies, economic structures, and political institutions. Life courses on, and people adjust to new realities about their health, family composition, community roles, and relationship to work and leisure.

This dynamic model of the marketplace suggests that we frequently need to be reintroduced to our customers. Much may have changed since we last settled into truths about them—a new baby has turned night owls into diaper changers; having started a new business, a former employee now prowls through office-supplies superstores.

Multinational and cross-cultural studies are well-suited to ethnographic approaches. Populations are in motion throughout the world, following opportunities for employment and freedom; and the globalization of production and consumption proceeds unabated. Consumers everywhere are seizing new opportunities for productivity and lifestyle enhancements. As we attempt to discover new marketplace realities, ethnography becomes a helpful tool for documenting consumer practices, whether these relate to products that they are accustomed to using or first learning to apply.

The categories that call for ethnography tend to be very process intensive, such as home cleaning, personal care, purchase decisions, and food preparation. Alternatively, the category may be interaction focused, such as infant care, sales negotiation, patient–physician relationships, and game playing. This focus on interactivity may involve not only people but also machines, whether they are simple or highly technical; some typical areas are computer navigation, financial transactions, and use of medical devices. Because ethnography concentrates on the natural locations where behavior takes place, these studies are well-suited to environmental and behavioral assessments in retail environments, homes and businesses, and public accommodations such as airports, hospitals, and schools.

Origins

Ethnography was developed at the turn of the 20th century, as scholars began to study social life and institutions on a scientific basis. Indeed, by going to the source and becoming immersed in the life worlds of traditional societies in the Pacific Northwest or the South Seas, such luminaries as Franz Boas, Bronislaw Malinowski, Margaret Mead, and Ruth Benedict[1] were influential in promoting an approach that, by now, has investigated every corner of the Earth. The intent of these pioneers was to turn discovery tools used in the natural sciences—direct observation, careful measurement, classification, and critical inquiry—to the study of diverse human societies. Their purpose was not social or (heaven forbid!) commercial intervention. On the contrary, they were seeking fundamental truths about human nature, social affiliation, and the conduct of daily life.

As the ethnographic approach succeeded in gaining adherents, applications of this approach gradually shifted from the study of so-called exotic and primitive people to the analysis of everyday life in distinctly contemporary urban settings. The perspective shifted from a static to a dynamic model of social life. In other words, social groups were looked on not as isolated and unchanging curiosities but as entities caught up in constant cultural shifts through adaptation, diffusion, and conflict. In the work of sociologists and anthropologists such as Herbert Gans (1967), Oscar Lewis

(1965), and Elliot Liebow (1967) during the 1960s and 1970s, ethnography began to shed light on cultural issues relevant to regional planning and poverty policies. The application of ethnography to contemporary urban studies began with the work of the Chicago School in the 1920s (Wirth, 1928/1956; Zorbaugh, 1929/1976).

The new urban ethnography also recognized that contemporary societies comprise a multiplicity of diverse, sometimes contentious, cultural groups. These collectivities may be linked not only by ties of family and nationhood but also by such characteristics as social class, age, sexual orientation, and consumption patterns.

By the 1980s, ethnographic techniques and related cultural perspectives were increasingly applied to consumer and marketing research. Within the marketing sciences, ethnography evolved as one of a family of tools for gaining insights into consumer roles and for learning about how consciousness and identity are bound into product and brand usage.

At this point, the manner in which ethnographic approaches were applied became markedly different. In the applied research realm, ethnography does not necessarily require becoming a long-term resident in a community, adopting a role, personally interviewing or interacting with numerous residents, and so on. Laurence Wylie's *Village in the Vaucluse* (1976) is an excellent exemplar of the classical approach that brought this sociologist and his family to a southern French town for long periods. Over many years, he was able to chart the transformation of village life as a consequence of industrialization. Kornblum (1974) similarly spent nearly 3 years in a South Chicago community making observations about political sentiments among his working class neighbors.

Classical ethnography requires analytic induction based on the subjective experience of the individual researcher. The applied approach, in contrast, began to rely on teams of researchers making focused observations over relatively short periods of time—often no longer than a few hours for each respondent. The process of analytic induction was transformed to account for relatively discrete spheres of experience, such as shopping in department stores or doing the laundry. Sponsors of ethnographic studies for marketing demanded quick turnaround and rapid assessment of consumer environments.

The reasons for this adaptation were clear. Ethnographic techniques had started to provide the basis for intervention strategies: the groundwork for new product development and strategic marketing. Learning about consumer behavior, emotions, consciousness, and language in relation to brands and product categories offered a point of departure for the marketing adventure. (Hirschmann, 1989; Mariampolski, 1988).

Moreover, analyzing such issues as the sources of product satisfaction, ease-of-use, points of entry, and the dynamics of influence and susceptibility was not a grand cynical strategy for public manipulation. On the contrary, these insights were intrinsic to new consumer-centered approaches to marketing and product development. Theodore Levitt (1983) insisted that "the purpose of a business is to create and keep a customer." Don Norman (1990) demanded that we concern ourselves with "user needs" and "user friendliness" in designing useful things. The result has been a marketplace in which business tries to anticipate consumer needs, strive for total satisfaction, communicate clear benefits, and, above all, make the buyer a partner in the enterprise. Ethnography became another approach for guaranteeing that the customer's voice is represented when business investments are made.

Contemporary Definition

Ethnography generally has one of two complementary meanings when discussed in a marketing context. The definitions are based on the distinction between ethnography as an intellectual approach or analytical framework and ethnographic methods as a model of applied practice.

THEORY

Ethnography can be taken as a theoretical perspective that focuses on the concept of culture and its relation to observed behavior as the principal analytic tool for classifying and explaining consumer dynamics. In this context, culture is not some reified entity; rather, it is the foundation of a worldview and value system, with both stable and dynamic components, which gives meaning to people's concept of self and their roles in daily life. Culture is a major constituent of the material and intellectual environment that frames personal consciousness, ideals, and aspirations.

The sociocultural perspective on behavioral causation is generally contrasted to psychodynamic perspectives, which emphasize the motives, drives, needs, and impulses that shape behavior in the marketplace. In practice, a comprehensive paradigm for explaining consumer choices should not rest on purely psychological grounds while excluding sociocultural and situational perspectives. Shoppers' impulses may arise in some need state for personal gratification, but these dynamics are mediated by social structures and cultural norms that influence, support, modify, or thwart satisfaction of those drives. Motivations and drives may bring customers into the store, but satisfaction will be thwarted if brand image, signage, and merchandising are inconsistent with expectations. This encompassing concept of culture reinforces the holistic insights that qualitative researchers strive to achieve.

METHOD

Ethnography is also understood as a methodological orientation that emphasizes direct contact and observation of the consumer in the natural context of product acquisition and usage. This standard of direct engagement with the "real world" is commonly contrasted with other laboratory-based, probabilistic, and statistical approaches to market analysis, which rely on such techniques as telephone surveys or shopping mall intercepts. Ethnography may also be contrasted to other qualitative techniques such as focus group studies, with which it shares a spirit of consumer engagement without their reliance on synthetically created groups of respondents.

Ethnographic methodology, however, is not entirely hostile toward quantification and is sympathetic toward alternative ways of gaining knowledge. Studies may sometimes include statistical measurement or group interviewing as triangulation and validation techniques.

Ethnography as Qualitative Research

Sometimes also called *field research, observational research,* or *participant observation,* ethnography is the original form of the research tradition that today is categorized as qualitative research.[2] In the constellation of marketing research techniques, its qualitative extremity embraces the more humanistic, naturalistic, creative, and intuitive ways of acquiring knowledge and making sense of the world. In this context, ethnography shares many features with—but can also be strikingly contrasted to—such research approaches as intensive interviewing, focus groups, life history analysis, semiotics, and text analysis. It remains an insurgent tool in marketing research, where qualitative research has been most strongly identified with focus groups since the 1960s. In contrast, academic researchers in sociology, anthropology, and many applied disciplines have taken ethnographic studies to be the exemplar of the qualitative orientation.

The principal features of ethnography as a qualitative approach include some combination of the following orientations to knowledge and practical steps in conducting research—all of which are oriented toward revealing reality from the subject's perspective through the process of induction.

Engagement. Applied practice is based on intensive face-to-face involvement with the research subjects. Ethnographers tend to disparage the presumption that people can be thoroughly understood by having junior researchers speak to a sampling of consumers over the phone for a half hour, the conversation structured by a strict survey questionnaire and the results compiled by statistical analysis. Each of these steps, they argue, incrementally removes the researcher from the respondent's reality. In contrast, doing as much as possible to engage people in their own terms and their own space is the basis of the ethnographic approach.

Context. Ethnographers place high significance on encountering research subjects in their own environment: the home, neighborhood, workplace, store, and so on. In this respect, this discipline differs from related laboratory-based interviewing and observation approaches. The assumption operative here is that this authentic context represents the highest level of grounded reality as experienced by subjects in their day-to-day lives.

Subject-centered. Ethnographers attempt to understand subjects on their own terms while radically suspending their own assumptions and analytic categories. They strive to apply Malinowski's (1922) injunction "to grasp the native's point of view, his relation to life, to realize his vision of his world" (p. 25) or as Powdermaker (1966) has written:

> To understand a society, the anthropologist has traditionally immersed himself in it, learning, as far as possible, to think, see, feel, and sometimes act as a member of the culture and at the same time as a trained anthropologist from another culture. (p. 9)

This dynamic tension between the insider and outsider perspectives produces a level of understanding that extends the researcher's ability to see patterns, types, and models. Instead of using subjects to confirm preexisting hypotheses and validate established theories, the ethnographer uses the absorption into respondents' life worlds to generate what Glaser and Strauss (1967) called "grounded theory."

Ethnographic approaches used by rapid assessment teams are not as effective in entering the participants' worlds as the classical stands exemplified by Malinowski; nevertheless, it is an ideal and a goal to which they aspire.

Improvisational and flexible. Ethnography is based on a combination of both formal and improvisational interviewing and observation procedures. Ethnographers enter the field with a plan but allow emerging discovered realities to modify the issues, questions, and approaches being used. This flexibility allows the researcher to adapt when emerging discoveries and surprises challenge expectations in the field. This ability is in contrast to rigid questionnaire approaches, which require complete faithfulness to the plan but may miss essential truths when emerging findings challenge starting assumptions.

Triangulation. Ethnographers take a critical approach to their emerging knowledge. They obtain support and validation by double- and triple-checking, or what is known as triangulation: using multiple subjects, observers, and methodological tools (e.g., intensive interviewing, nonobtrusive observation, etc.) to confirm and establish facts.

Holistic. Ethnography tries to be comprehensive and inclusive. It aims for a thorough, contextual understanding of the typical respondent's worldview rather than a statistical accounting of attitudinal statements.[3] Basing themselves in the sociological and anthropological concept of culture, ethnographers strive to piece together elements of the inner and outer worlds that shape respondents' behaviors in everyday life.

Comparisons and Benefits

Ethnographic or observational approaches, when compared with related qualitative methods such as focus groups or individual in-depth interviewing, present unique opportunities for generating strategic insights. Ethnographic methods are similar to other qualitative approaches in that they focus on holistic understanding as a research objective and open-ended, respondent-driven interviewing tactics (e.g., Merton et al., 1990). However, several differences add value to ethnography as an information-gathering strategy.

Reality-based. Focus groups and depth interviewing tend to be laboratory-based, whereas ethnography takes place within the context of respondents' lives as they are engaged in product usage, purchase, and other everyday activities. Moreover, because the research is grounded in the respondents' own homes, workplaces, or familiar public places, there is no need for respondents to accommodate themselves to an artificial situation and unknown fellow respondents. Focus groups are collectivities of convenience; respondents have no intrinsic relationships with or feelings about each other. In contrast, ethnographers can gain insights by observing consumers surrounded by their own family members and friends. Focus group respondents may talk about what they feed their children in the morning, but ethnographers present at the breakfast table get to see exactly what happens.

Use of observation. Ethnography not only applies traditional discussion and question-and-answer tactics but also uses *looking* as a data collection device. Thus, it does not rely only on consumer reports and recollection but supplements that with direct observation of behavior. Because consumer self-disclosure can be idealized, obscured, corrupted by interpersonal influence, or poorly recalled, one can argue that observation provides a necessary way to discover and validate behavioral patterns.

Improvisational. Ethnographic site visits tend to be less structured and directed by the researcher than other interviewing styles. The consumer typically has more latitude in shaping the sequence of events during an ethnographic encounter, and the observer relies on inductive strategies to gain insights rather than seeking confirmation of preconceived hypotheses. Respondent-stimulated observations allow researchers to make unanticipated discoveries, which may be obscured by the closed categories and expectation sets that shape conventional research.

Comprehensive. Ethnographies try to explore "a day in the life" or an entire product usage, consumption, or purchase cycle. Thus, they are able to capture details and nuances that are largely overlooked or unanticipated in other research approaches.

Contextual. Ethnography tries to account for the entire context and environment associated with product usage. In practical terms, this means that the *site* is the focus of analysis as well as individual consumers. Product usage or purchase decision making commonly involves interaction among household members or reflects interaction with a particular context and situation. Ethnographic analysis attempts to account for these *in situ* variables.

Engagement. All qualitative strategies attempt to engage the respondent, but ethnography is the closest that the market researcher can get to the consumer. As few barriers as possible mediate the relationship between ethnographer and respondent.

Spontaneity. Ethnography is the least directive of research methods, thereby permitting a highly unfiltered view of the consumer.

Culturally grounded. This method takes account of the cultural dimension in product purchase and usage. It does not depend only on psychological categories—for example, whether the respondent is striving or repressed—that may be valid for one but not other cultural groups.

Behavioral. Ethnography provides behavioral as well as attitudinal data. It pays attention to what consumers actually do as opposed to what they say or wish to have done. In focus groups or other interview-based studies, consumer reports may represent an idealized or socially approved set of behaviors. For example, a study by the American Society for Microbiology reported in *The New York Times* compared the results of reports of hand washing following a trip to the bathroom—95% in a telephone survey—to actual observations of people's behavior in well-trafficked bathrooms in five American cities. In actuality, 67% of the women and 58% of the men were actually observed washing their hands, which tends to undermine the validity of what respondents told researchers (Dewan, 2000).

Context sensitive. Ethnography yields information on product usage in its natural context—the home, store, office, and so on—so that the influence of other people or the physical setting can be assessed.

Creative. Observational research offers novel insights into consumer behavior. Changing the lens used to view consumers creates opportunities for surprises and valuable unanticipated findings.

Notes

1. A full accounting of the discipline's history is beyond the scope of this discussion. A classic of the field, which summarizes its early approach and protocols, is Ruth Benedict's (1934) *Patterns of Culture.*

2. The history of ethnographic methods is rooted by Bogdan and Taylor (1975), in the mid-19th-century investigations of European families and communities by Frederick LePlay. These approaches were melded with the *Wissensoziologie* of Max Weber in the famous Chicago School studies of the 1920s and 1930s and were further developed from the 1940s through the 1970s by researchers working from a variety of perspectives, such as symbolic interactionism and ethnomethodology.

3. Robert Merton's practice of focused interviewing was developed for both laboratory and real world based research. See Merton, Fiske, and Kendall, 1990.

2

The Intellectual Heritage

I t has taken nearly 100 years for the theory and practice of ethnography to spread through the marketing disciplines like a shock wave. Why did it take so long, and what accounts for its recent revival?

The delay can be traced to a huge mental block smoldering under a set of models and assumptions about human beings. Models are intellectual creations, concepts and images that represent the look or operation of something else. A model airplane is a miniaturized and passenger-less version of the real thing. Similarly, models of social processes are ideas that represent how people conduct their daily affairs, whether they are voting in elections, educating their offspring, or selecting a brand of breakfast cereal.

Assumptions are the real or imagined facts that underlie how we think about human affairs. The foundation of cognition and belief, assumptions are like the bottom row of a house of cards: Pull them out and the entire structure collapses. When our opponents challenge our assumptions in a debate, they are attempting to undermine the very basis of our reasoning and credibility and not just take issue with our assertions. One recalls the bumper sticker representing alienated youth: "You're assuming I give a damn."

Marketing Discourse and the Social Sciences

The marketing disciplines have turned to the social sciences for the methods and theories to help them understand consumer-choice dynamics under a world system dominated by mature market capitalism. In doing so, they have inherited a series of debates about epistemological assumptions long smoldering within the academic fields.

Marketing discourse has been somewhat seduced and clouded by a positivist model of how people think and behave.[1] The operating assumption of positivism is that anything that is real can be objectively perceived and counted. Positivist thinkers have also held the corollary to be true; that is, if it cannot be counted, it does not exist. Society is regarded as a closed system with interlocking parts, as easy to comprehend as a colorful Lego® construction sitting in a child's bedroom. Assumptions like these have led to mechanistic and behaviorist models of human actions and consumer choice.

Mechanistic? Behaviorist? Are these terms pejorative and derisive, or do they represent hope for a rational understanding of human dynamics? Most market researchers would probably argue the latter. Mechanistic models allow for clearly patterned arguments of cause and effect. If you are attempting to determine which targeted consumers can be inveighed to buy various car models, the positivists will tell you to simply create a recipe with the correct mix of social status, age, gender, personal fantasies, number of children, commuting time, garage space, and distance to mother-in-law. Do so, and you have captured the essence of the car that will interest one market segment or another.

The logic, as we have said, is quite seductive. Marketing managers have decisions to make, advertising budgets to manage, new product launches to execute. Anything regarded as decision-making support is valued and rewarded. Simplifying the burdens of deep doubt, making compelling arguments to stakeholders (the boss, the client, stock market analysts), protecting marketing investments—the cause-and-effect model offers all this, so it's easy to understand why it produces such allegiance. Market researchers are selling relief from uncertainty.

Qualitative research findings, in contrast, can sometimes disturb the relief that managers seek. By introducing ideas about human volition and choice, emotionality, and context, studies can sometimes replace simplification with complexity.

There is one severe problem; unfortunately, the relief provided by the positivist approach is a chimera—total fantasy. Not only is the approach limited in explaining the complexities of human behavior, it also fails as a predictive tool. At its best, statistical modeling serves well as an audit technique, but it cannot anticipate the evolution of human meanings and feelings without a deeper perspective delivered via methodological pluralism.

Some would argue that the problem was solved by statistical analysis techniques based on multiple regression (such as factor analysis or conjoint analysis), techniques that proliferated as computing power soared. These methodologies were limited in their application, however, and by themselves also failed to produce the depth of insight and consumer understanding—the meaning behind the numbers—that clients were demanding.

The Evolution of Qualitative Research

Starting with the neo-Freudian revival of the 1950s and 1960s, marketers began to realize that they had to delve deeper into the human psyche to speak meaningfully about consumer wishes, needs, and expectations. People are multifaceted, managers asserted, and fit the mechanistic model very poorly. Statistical reasoning could not substitute for "hard thinking." Humans are rational, calculating beings, marketers realized, and also operate on a deeper level of feelings, drives, and irrationality. This fact needed to be assimilated into the marketing sciences.

Neo-Freudian psychological reasoning as expressed through Ernest Dichter's (1964) "motivational research" approach moved marketers closer to reality. His imaginative deductions about the deeper meanings of prosaic everyday items yielded powerful new insights into consumer choice. Despite the opprobrium leveled against Dichter's work by social critics such as Vance Packard,[2] the revival of qualitative research was at hand.

In the 1960s and 1970s, various maverick social scientists also began reminding leading thinkers that there were alternative assumptions about the human experience dating back to 19th-century German historicism. In the graduate schools, the great argument between Max Weber's[3] *verstehende soziologie* and Emile Durkheim's (1966) positivism of *social facts* was revived. The goal of social inquiry, the Weberians and their offspring argued, was to go beyond statistical relationships to a deeper understanding of human affairs. Several inheritors of this tradition, including Erving Goffman (1959), Harold Garfinkel (1967), and Barney Glaser and Anselm Strauss (1967), began to formulate serious theoretical and methodological tools to substantiate this qualitative approach.

By the 1970s, the "focused group discussion" became the technique de rigueur for expressing the qualitative impulse in consumer research. The humanistic neo-Freudian approach of Carl Rogers (1951, 1961), who was famous for launching a wave of encounter groups, T-groups, and consciousness-raising sessions through the human potential movement, was married to a research technique developed in the 1940s by Robert Merton and Paul Lazarsfeld to help mobilize the homefront during World War II. Rogers's client-centered approach, emphasizing empathy and unconditional positive regard for the patient, dovetailed well with Merton's focused interviewing technique. Both used the feelings and verbal expressions of the respondent as the starting point for investigative inquiry. The focus group—the term that evolved for a small group discussion used for research purposes—became the embodiment of the qualitative approach in consumer research (see Merton, 1987; Merton, Fiske, & Kendall, 1990). The evolution of focus groups was widely welcomed and, indeed, represented a clearly superior method for detecting the human dimension in consumer choice. It complemented the lifeless tables and charts of the survey researcher. The honeymoon, however, lasted only a short time. Many focus group practitioners and the clients who commissioned their studies, it turned out, lacked a fundamental understanding of the nature of qualitative or phenomenological reasoning and research. Their studies often used sequential questioning of respondents with strictly delimited questionnaires; findings were developed through the head count, as in, "How many of you prefer Concept A to Concept B?" or "How many of you would buy the product after seeing this ad?"

Even worse, qualitative studies were relegated to the nether realm of "merely hypothesis generation"—awaiting confirmation through purportedly more "rigorous and scientific" testing. The uses of grounded theory and qualitative verification approaches were largely dismissed (Glaser & Strauss, 1967).

This style of practice was fundamentally neither humanistic nor qualitative. It represented a weak and largely invalid shadow of the mechanistic and behaviorist thinking that qualitative methods were meant to challenge in the first place. It was not surprising that growth in the number of qualitative research studies being commissioned was accompanied by complaints about their overuse, inappropriateness, and insignificance.

Even clients and practitioners who correctly used focus groups as a technique for generating insights into the grounds and meanings behind product usage became highly dissatisfied with the limitations of the group discussion. A substantial number of the field's most sensitive and professional practitioners began to augment group discussion with creative problem-solving techniques, imaginative games, and projective interviewing approaches to prevent this backsliding to behaviorism.

It was in this context that in the mid-1980s, reviving ethnography was proposed as a way to bolster the utility of qualitative marketing research.

Ethnography is being advocated not as a replacement for the focus group but rather as a necessary complement in qualitative market research practice. Nothing can substitute for the logistical convenience and empirical immediacy of a well-designed, structured discussion among peers. Nevertheless, participant observation can address many of the limitations inherent in the focus group technique and deliver a more nuanced and textured view of consumers. Increasingly, astute clients are asking their researchers to combine group discussion and creative exercises with ethnographic observation in studies designed as a consumer familiarization tool or inspiration for new product idea generation.

Notes

1. For additional detail on the contrast between the positivist and what is sometimes referred to as the interpretivist positions in marketing research, see Ozanne, 1989, and other essays in Hirschmann, 1989.

2. For a brief overview of Packard's dispute with Dichter, see Rothenberg's (1997) review of a neo-Packardian text.

3. Although his theoretical principles pervade all of his work, a good place to start is Weber, 1949.

3

The Power of Ethnography

As previously noted, ethnography cannot reasonably be classified as just another single method or technique. In substance, it is a research discipline based on culture as an organizing concept and a mix of both observational and interviewing tactics to record behavioral dynamics. Above all, ethnography relies on entering respondents' natural life worlds—at home, while shopping, at leisure, and in the workplace. The researcher essentially becomes a naïve visitor in that world by engaging respondents during realistic product usage situations in the course of daily life. Herein lies the power of ethnography.

Whether called on-site, observational, naturalistic, or contextual research, ethnographic methods allow marketers to delve into the actual occasions and situations in which products are used, services are received, and benefits are conferred.

Going from focus groups to ethnography is somewhat like moving from black and white to color: The immediacy of the smells, textures, tastes, heat, sounds, movements, and muscular strain all stimulate an enriched level of understanding. If the research objective is to understand consumer-shopping patterns, the ethnographer can tag right along at the supermarket or department store. If we need to understand home-cleaning patterns and products, ethnography allows the researcher to sniff the air around the home or stare at the cat's hairballs on the sofa—to actually see the success or failure of product performance. We share the consumer's look of satisfaction and pride after a job well done. We can feel the disappointment when a dish does not turn out the way the cook expected.

Ethnography takes place not in laboratories but in the real world. Consequently, clients and practitioners benefit from a more holistic and better nuanced view of consumer satisfactions, frustrations, and limitations than any other research approach will provide. A comparison might be made to studies of animal behavior. Observations of animals in laboratories and zoos provide adequate, albeit rarefied, constricted, and limited insights into, for example, primate behavior. When Jane Goodall (1991) went to Africa to study chimpanzees in their wild state, however, it yielded a layer of facts and understandings that were unobtainable in a laboratory or in zoos.

This is also the case with consumer studies. Laboratories—in this case, telephone banks, focus group studios, and the like—are limited in their ability to capture the human dimension. In contrast, naturalistic ethnography can offer insights into consumer practices, language, myths, and aspirations that cannot be deduced elsewhere. The enlarged insight can be sufficient to meet the toughest challenges raised by strategic thinkers and brand planners.

Focus groups certainly have their place. The format is well-suited to evaluating peer group influences and for generating true-to-life descriptive discourse about brands. For example, it is fruitful and engaging to see all participants in a discussion swayed by the challenges of a few skeptics. Although disappointed copywriters and other stakeholders may disparage this phenomenon as the misleading effects of a dominant respondent, experienced qualitative researchers know that fickle respondents can betray an underlying weakness of the concept. The conditions of the research may parallel patterns of interpersonal influence that would be operative among friends and acquaintances.

The power of ethnography also rests on the concept of culture and the use of this idea as an organizing principle for understanding human behavior. The main task of ethnography is not only to watch but also to decode human experience—to move from unstructured observations to discover the underlying meanings behind behavior; to understand feelings and intentions in order to deduce logical implications for strategic decisions. Cultural concepts provide this foundation for analysis.

The Cultural Perspective

Spradley (1979) defines culture as "the acquired knowledge that people use to interpret experience and generate social behavior" (p. 5). It appears cut and dried at first glance, however, our understanding of culture has benefited from the enlarged perspective offered by Edward T. Hall (1959, 1977), who has argued that often "culture hides more than it reveals." Culture exists deep within the core of our brains, where it operates on the basis of feelings, sensations, and emotions. It is deeper than thought.

Culture asserts itself most profoundly when we conduct comparative market research or even just travel from one country to another or even between social classes and ethnic groups within a single nation. In a recent multicultural study of laundry behavior, for example, QualiData ethnographers were quite surprised by several practices in an Islamic country that differed considerably from those in Western Europe. Men's and women's clothing, for example, were washed separately in most households. In addition, homemakers devoted extra care and concern to washing socks. The lens of culture was needed to clarify the reasons and expectations behind these practices, namely, the profound sexual segregation characteristic of Islamic culture and the regard for removal of shoes and cleanliness of the feet in connection with prayer.

Because culture is experienced at this primal level, there normally are no good ways to explain any particular cultural practice. There may be good historical reasons to account for even obscure practices, such as matters of etiquette, but the original justifications may have vanished, and now, any particular cultural norm may seem invisible and difficult to articulate. It just feels right to a member of that culture and perhaps a bit unusual to someone raised elsewhere. Americans and other Westerners characteristically have an ethnocentric tendency toward seeing their own cultures as the only normal and natural ways of behaving. The researchers' goal in this context is to transcend their own culture, but to do that, they must first understand the nature of culture and the role it plays in human affairs.

Although the human capacity for culture is biological, cultural content itself is not innate. It is learned as a set of deep ordering principles for a lifetime of experiences. In addition, the various elements of culture are interrelated, and the whole is larger than the sum of its parts. We have seen above how religious principles have impacts on the most prosaic everyday experiences; changing one piece of a culture has implications for the whole cloth. Finally, culture is shared as the conscious and subconscious blueprint for a group's way of life. It defines the boundaries of the group and articulates the distinctiveness they feel compared with others.

Culture is the source of any group's collective memory and provides a basis for consciousness. The values that people hold dear, their collective sense of self, and their aspirations are rooted in cultural learning. Moreover, the material components of culture—the tools and trappings used in daily life—have deep roots in these ideational aspects. In this way, culture comes to play an important role in product choice, usage, and resistance. Deciding to use and picking a particular brand of children's cough syrup are actions rooted in culturally based ideas and values about health, child rearing, and causality of disease.

Also, humans are capable of continuous learning and adaptation. They react not only to situations but to underlying meanings, expectations, symbol systems, and so on. Cultural change is a constant of the human experience, but we cannot predict its rate, direction, or implicit mutability without intensive study. Behavioral change can occur within cultures but, because of the interdependence of cultural factors, there is often a high price to be paid. Upgrading the weapons of warrior cultures from spears to guns, for example, can unleash a morbid tendency toward carnage without the controls that normally would make killing a rare event in those cultures. Similarly, expecting people in one culture to adopt the foods, leisure practices, cleaning rituals, and technologies of another without question is not warranted.

The medium for locating, negotiating, communicating, and articulating culture is language. Thus, the words we use to describe behaviors and beliefs are not independent of their cultural roots. The problems associated with communicating product features and benefits around the global marketplace are not simply artifacts of good or bad translations. Solutions to marketing problems must take into account the multiple meanings inherent in culturally rooted language systems.

By applying a critical perspective on ordinary language, ethnography can bring us closer to the emotions and intentions that underlie people's actions in the purchase and use of daily commodities.

Language: The Foundation of Meaning

Language is a system of culturally based sounds, symbols, words, and utterances designed to organize inner experience and to communicate with others who share that system of meaning. Even though other animals also communicate in complex ways by signaling to each other through sound or smell, for example, humans are unique in their complex language system.

Language has a profound impact on shaping perception. According to the Whorf (1956) linguistics hypothesis, what we see is actually delimited by what we call things, and these names are circumscribed by cultural patterns. Although English has but a few words for describing snow, for example, Inuit languages have a wider and richer vocabulary because snowfall is a much greater component of their daily experience. This suggests more than simply having more words for the same thing. More significantly, the entire manner of creating categories of perception is culturally defined. Thus, Inuit can experience variations and types of what we call snow in ways that go beyond an American's own perceptual limitations.

The case for the mechanistic power of language should not be overstated. The process of communication does not consist of imprinting words into the brains of others. Characteristically, most of us do not use words well. Our daily expressive vocabulary falls far short of the lexis of our literary experts and poets. Furthermore, communication cannot be understood apart from the process of interpretation. Humans practice a highly selective and critical attention—they compartmentalize words and experience—and commonly see the world in ways consistent with their own anticipation, biases, and presuppositions. As Hall (1977) has argued, "language, the system most used to describe culture, is by nature poorly adapted to this difficult task. It is too linear, not comprehensive enough, too slow, too limited, too constrained, too unnatural, too much a product of its own evolution, and too artificial" (p. 57).

Advertisers are quite sensitive to this problem. Experience has taught them that consumers will not automatically believe any assertion made about a brand: Communication must be grounded and bounded by meaningfulness and credibility.

Humans compensate for the limitations of word systems by using equally complex culturally based patterns of nonverbal communication to articulate many of the connotative components of language. Whether expressed through facial and body gestures or voice stress and sound nuance—or even through our manipulation of territory and time, according to Edward Hall (1977)—understanding nonverbal communication is critical in decoding meaning.

Our communications vehicles have moved us even more profoundly toward complexity. Our interactions are not conducted only face-to-face; they transcend time, space, and language. They are affected by the mode of transmission, the printed page, imagery, television, radio, computers, the Internet.

Marketers and advertisers deeply understand this issue, too. They are aware that brand image is communicated by more than slogans and product claims. Color, typeface, design, packaging, celebrity endorsements, and the manners, interactions, and attitudes of characters in an ad all contribute to impressions received by viewers. Also, consumers are not passive in the process. The art and science of semiotics recognizes that the interpreter is essential in assigning meaning to symbols.

We learn language through both formal and interactive or relational means and thereby acquire the means to understand ourselves within daily life. The medium of instruction is not just words but also gestures, images, and symbols. Experience is also an effective teacher.

Ethnographic practice takes a highly critical attitude toward expressed language. It challenges our accepting words and utterances, searching instead for the meanings and values that lie beneath the surface.

In interviewing situations, typically, this involves looking for gaps between expressed and nonverbal communication elements. For example, if actual practices and facial and physical gestures are inconsistent with a subject's expressed attitudes toward a food product being consumed, we are challenged to discover both the reality behind the given answer and the reasons for the subterfuge.

Ethnographic research is also effective as a tool for learning situational and culturally grounded language—the appropriate words for everyday things as spoken by various age or ethnic groups. Copywriters and strategic thinkers are always pressed to talk about products and brands in evocative and original ways. Ethnography helps act as a tool of both discovery and evaluation.

Looking and the Limitations of Asking

We have already described how language is a highly limited way to account for the totality of interpersonal communication. But the ineffectiveness of language is only the start of the problem. Language also has its Machiavellian uses: It is equally important as a means to contrive, delude, seduce, hide, mislead, and control.

Erving Goffman (1959) has provided many important clues for the interpretation of gestures and utterances, and these must be accounted for in research practice. People behave, he argues, not only as a reflection of inner states but in a kind of interactive living theater where they play roles with reference to a given audience. Much behavior is enacted to manage the impressions people stimulate in others and to "define the situation"—to be in control of the grounds and assumptions on which interactions are based. Authenticity is never automatic because utterances must be understood within the context that governs the communication.

This further supports a need for a highly critical attitude toward verbal expressions within the context of observed reality. As Goffman (1959) argues,

> Knowing that that individual is likely to present himself in a light that is favorable to him, the others may divide what they witness into two parts; a part that is relatively easy for the individual to manipulate at will, being chiefly his verbal assertions, and a part in regard to which he seems to have little concern or control, being chiefly derived from the expressions he gives off. (p. 7)

In the course of research encounters, whether in a telephone interview, in face-to-face intercept research, or in a focus group discussion, we are involved in asking questions and receiving answers that we normally take for granted as representing some accurate feeling state of the respondent. However, asking is a highly limited form of obtaining information because respondents' attitudes are governed by the impressions they are trying to make on the researcher. They may be ignorant while trying to seem knowledgeable; they may be confused while wanting to appear expert; they may have forgotten but contrive recollection; they may be responding with what they believe is expected of them; they may hold a negative opinion but want to be positive; they may not care but wish to portray themselves as involved.

If language and communication can be so profoundly muted by the impulse toward control and manipulation, then research practice requires checks to balance our search for valid and reliable information. Looking is a tool for overcoming the limitations of asking. As the famous quote attributed to Yogi Berra declares, "You can observe a lot just by looking." Ethnography uses observation in two ways: first, to document precise behaviors and to overcome the limitations of flawed recollection and selective attention, and, second, to check the consistencies between verbal and nonverbal communication, to act as a truth serum.

Observation also provides the discipline to bring depth and richness to research findings. Utterances alone are not the source of data; our understanding is enlarged by an appreciation of nuance and context. Graphic and detailed description of behavioral settings and situations adds another dimension to the analysis.

The Importance of Context

Context operates on several levels: the immediate physical and situational surroundings, as well as language, character, culture, and history, which all provide a basis for the meaning and significance attached to roles and behaviors. Can we divorce the ways we buy, use, and talk about products from the cultural and linguistic context within which economic transactions occur? The answer is an emphatic no.

Marketers are sometimes guilty of committing what psychologists and social commentators have called the *fundamental attribution error* (FAE), the tendency to overestimate the importance of personal character traits in determining people's behavior and to minimize the importance of situation and context. Is the likelihood of being altruistic or, conversely, of engaging in violent acts a consequence of upbringing, personal commitment, and belief, or does it depend on situational opportunities? Although genetic and subconscious explanations have their appeal, experiments conducted by social scientists suggest that factors such as time pressures can override personal faith in determining whether people will act as Good Samaritans. Malcolm Gladwell (2000) summarizes this issue in *The Turning Point*, his thoughtful work on how social contagions spread:

> Character, then, isn't what we think it is or, rather, what we want it to be. It isn't a stable, easily identifiable set of closely related traits, and it only seems that way because of a glitch in the way our brains are organized. Character is more like a bundle of habits and tendencies and interests, loosely bound together and dependent, at certain times, on circumstance and context. The reason that most of us seem to have a consistent character is that most of us are really good at controlling our environment. (p. 163)

The marketing disciplines have been hampered by a history of dependence on the FAE. Explaining behavior by character and group membership has been adequate, historically, when marketers aimed at and measured undifferentiated mass markets. However, in an emerging situation of customization and marketing to the individual, reliance on psyche and motivation are limited. To gain new insights, we have to create new ways of understanding the settings and situations in which consumers make purchases and use products and services. Even in our persistent attempts to seek world brands, we have to appreciate the minute details of local context.

The time, place, conditions, and circumstances within which aspirations are conceived, decisions are made, and products are used have an impact on the levels of satisfaction experienced in the aftermath. When consumers react to a question on a survey, are they revealing something about their character or something else? Obviously, research practice that ignores context cannot claim to fully understand and represent consumer behavior.

Unfortunately, much of current marketing practice is woefully ignorant of context. Some marketers pretend to shoot with magic bullets aimed straight at buyers' hearts. Consumers are conceived as isolated individuals whose ganglia can be influenced at the cellular level by clever emotional appeals. Yet, we do not really know if anyone is watching those TV messages with anything approaching full attention nor whether anything that marketers say to consumers actually matters. Antidrug appeals targeted at youngsters are a particularly egregious failure; although hundreds of millions of dollars have been spent, evidence suggests that even hip-sounding messages—to say nothing of the "just say no" variety—have no impact in stopping kids from getting blasted at parties.

Ethnography is an antidote to this conceit. What C. Wright Mills (1967) called *abstracted empiricism* is the tendency to remove selected details of behavior from the larger situations in which they are enacted. Mothers may be looking for a convenient breakfast to give their children in the morning; this fact yields little without a deeper understanding of emerging parental roles, children's food fads, ideas about health and nutrition, and the economic pressures faced by young families.

Does ethnography represent a new orthodoxy waiting for its debunkers and detractors to point out its limitations? Ethnographers are not out to conquer the research industry from their own imperialistic and hegemonic point of view. On the contrary, they seek to absorb useful tools from other forms of research practice. At the same time, they demand a fair hearing on the demonstrated value of their own tools and perspectives. Some of these applications are reviewed in the next chapter.

4

Applications of the New Marketing Ethnography

The new marketing ethnography, we have argued, is an effective way to cultivate a highly detailed and context-sensitive understanding of consumer behavior and choice. This approach has been more than intellectually satisfying; it has become a unique competitive asset in business. In the sections that follow, we will describe several pioneering research applications that have benefited from the use of ethnographic methods. In each area, dynamic engagement with managers, buyers, and users reveals new shades of meaning and expanded opportunities for marketers.

New Product Discovery

Ethnographic approaches are particularly well-suited to new product discovery and development. There is a common misunderstanding that pervades some corporate managers that consumers are eager to tell marketers all about their dissatisfactions with current offerings and needs for new products. Our experience has shown that this is almost never the case.

Certainly, some customers write letters of complaint or register their feelings on the Internet after a particularly egregious instance of service malfeasance or product failure. An even smaller cohort may be effusive with praise after a breathtakingly good experience. These represent a negligible minority. Most consumers adjust to product deficiencies; postpurchase cognitive dissonance assures them that familiar products already provide the best in the marketplace for the price they have paid. Consumers do not spend a great deal of time consciously thinking about how to improve on products or what new products might help them. It is hard for them to think beyond what is already available at the store. Most shoppers lack the insights and ingenuity to imagine practical new product opportunities, and the innovations they imagine, when solicited, often have a hackneyed or unachievable quality. For example, their expressed needs may not proceed beyond lower prices and less disposable packaging.

On the other hand, consumers leave numerous clues and hints to new opportunities, which marketers need to watch for and interpret carefully. Consumers exhibit their expertise by using products and reacting to their features and benefits in natural ways. They express their dissatisfactions and needs through behaviors and may not consciously experience any unhappiness about what they are doing. On the contrary, they may see these adaptations as instances of good commonsense and creative home-making. Here are several examples of normative consumer behaviors that suggest new product opportunities.

Combining products and home remedies. If nothing satisfactory exists or if a current product fails to meet all of the needs consumers bring to a task, they may combine products from different categories; or they may concoct home remedies. In an ethnographic study of home cleaning, for example, we saw consumers mixing liquid dish soap and laundry bleach to create a cleaner for light linoleum floors. Probing revealed that the benefits they sought included stain removal, thorough cleansing, and sanitizing. In other households, ethnographers observed consumers spraying room deodorant following completion of the bathroom-cleaning routine. Again, the benefits sought revolved around the need to perceive olfactory cues for task completion and to provide extra disinfecting. Observing these combinations helped the client company to improve on its existing lines of cleaning agents.

Work-arounds. If consumers are frustrated in achieving a goal, they often improvise and work around a barrier. If they are not aware of or do not understand all of the operations required to complete a task in a database program, for example, they may patch together unique ways of solving problems or, alternatively, perform some task based on their own limited knowledge of the program's functionality. They may be ignorant or innovative, but the problem is that the program has not made a simpler operation available or easy to learn from the available information.

Indifference: Putting up with merely adequate results. When products perform poorly, many consumers just accept mediocre results. They will argue that achieving high-quality outcomes is impossible. For example, we observed users of bathroom cleaners accepting mediocre cleaning results;

it just wasn't important for them to get the tiles completely white, they argued, as long as a decent effort was made to get things "mostly" clean. Further observation and analysis revealed that consumers were reluctant to follow directions that they experienced as confusing. Instructions recommended that users give the product at least 15 minutes to penetrate the surface, but few had the patience to follow that procedure. Consumers were also unwilling to exert much more than token effort, even though a reasonable amount of elbow grease would have produced better results. Respondents in our ethnography verbalized relative satisfaction with the product, but their resigned body language and indifference betrayed an actual dissatisfaction with the time and process necessary for optimal results. These observations led to the development of effort-free bathroom cleaning products, which were structured to deliver enhanced results with minimal effort.

Errors. Products may fail dismally, but consumers will blame themselves for the problem. They have internalized a sense of helplessness and insufficient mastery. They may even joke about their inability to program their VCRs or to get their food processors to whip the eggs for a soufflé. Norman (1990, pp. 35–36) points out that product developers should expect errors and design products accordingly. Nevertheless, users tend to trace a product failure to their own deficiencies in learning proper techniques. They will not blame it on tolerances that are set too tightly or the unavailability of feedback related to a failure.

In an ethnographic study of blood glucose monitoring devices used primarily by diabetes patients, for example, researchers found that users blamed a failure on such extraneous factors as too much humidity in the room or oversaturation of the test strip. Their tendency to accept blame diverted their attention away from the narrow tolerances and poor adaptability of their equipment.

Avoidance. If the right product is not available, consumers may just avoid certain tasks or relegate them to the end of the agenda. In studying home cleaning practices, for example, we found that the backs of electrical appliances and computer equipment attract dense, sticky dust on account of static electricity. Home cleaners were disturbed about this dirt but paid little attention to it while cleaning because they were intimidated by the tangles of wires and the density of the dust that collected in these areas. Although they did not express an explicit demand for such a product, the clear implication of the avoidance was the need for an agent that reduced static and cleaned the backs of home electronics with minimal effort.

In a study of home laundering, similarly, careful observation found that some garments were taken out of circulation for public use after washers failed to eliminate stains caused by greasy foods. These clothes remained viable for leisure and home use but were clearly on the way to the rag pile—an expected and "normal" development in the life cycle of a garment. Persistent evidence of this type suggested a need for better grease-cutting agents as well as an opportunity to promote fabric preservation as a benefit for laundry detergents.

Imagining perfection. When products do not perform as expected, consumers simply assume that the capabilities to meet those needs do not exist. Shoppers tend to postpone satisfaction to some distant future when perfection may be more feasible. Observations and interviews with users of cellular telephones, for example, often reveal that input through voice commands and audible feedback are better suited to uses of the device than pecking away at the keypad. Voice communication is, after all, the basic purpose of the product, and pecking away at small buttons and reading a small screen are inconsistent with the mobility benefits the category promises. Express keys and reduced keystroke functions are a partial solution to consumer needs, but they continue to imagine that some future incarnation will rely on words and sounds.

In another case, a study of shower hardware discovered that when some users were imagining perfection, they envisioned multiple shower heads spraying their bodies from different directions simultaneously. The advantages they were looking for included superefficient cleaning and the luxurious interaction with water that this type of hardware would afford. The popular hand-held shower head could provide some of these benefits and could reach into hard-to-attack body parts—another positive benefit driving the fantasy—and was considered about as good as the technology could get. An understanding of consumers' ideas of perfection was able to drive the manufacturer into a number of alternative product-development directions.

Commercial and Corporate Culture

Ethnographic approaches are useful in studying the internal operations of corporate units, employee groups, and commercial environments. Work groups ranging from small project teams and businesses to major service institutions and multinational commercial enterprises all develop unique corporate cultures. These represent the collective character and personality of the organization and provide the basis of values, ideals, and norms that shape such dynamics as internal communications, hierarchy, and mobility. An organization's leadership style and employees' everyday reality are governed by cultural patterns. Corporate cultures define the ways companies think about customers: as objects to be manipulated, with mistrust, or as valued partners.

Corporate cultures exert an important influence on both the internal and external experience of the organization. They influence such weighty matters as employee satisfaction and retention, worker productivity, operations and governance, successful adaptation of technology, relationships with customers and suppliers, the level of customer satisfaction, relationships to the community-at-large, and corporate social responsibility. Spradley and Mann (1975) and Gubrium (1975), who pioneered using ethnographic methods in the study of service enterprises, for example, found that cocktail waitresses exert a major influence in negotiating the relationship with customers. They influenced what drinks were ordered and how big a tip customers would give at the conclusion of the evening. Similarly, the staff of a nursing home was observed to have many routine problems in implementing the expectations of senior management during their dealings with patients. Nurses and aides sometimes had to compromise the official positions to preserve the trust and cooperation of their charges.

In major organizations, corporate cultures have an impact on a variety of issues that are essential to the profitability and success of the enterprise. Ethnographic approaches can play an important role in studying large or small organizations with a view toward revealing the cultural substructure that may not be apparent in analyses of the organizational chart and interviews with senior human resources executives. Here are some of the substantive organizational issues that could benefit.

Integration of subgroups. The corporate culture of some organizations creates an environment of hostility toward emerging subgroups based on gender, sexuality, ethnicity, age, religion, handicaps, or life decisions such as having children. Formal and informal communication patterns between various employee groups, opportunity structures and the system of rewards, social networks within the organization—all are products of cultural norms that are perpetuated over time. Many companies have been beset by poor employee morale, high turnover, and, even worse, the bad publicity and loss of shareholder value that follows an explosion of litigation and government intervention in corporate affairs when such deficiencies as a hostile climate toward women or the lack of opportunity for minorities are exposed.

Workflow and the adoption of new technologies. When technology changes the way things are done in organizations, the consequent adaptations must have a cultural dimension. Computers change more than the work flow and necessary skill sets needed in the organization; they have an impact on the satisfactions experienced by employees in their daily work, create new forms of hierarchy, and alter the socialization of new employees into the work group. Resolving many of these potential points of friction must occur on the cultural level.

Understanding corporate culture's relationship to work flow can also lead to discoveries of new business opportunities. Several years ago, for example, computerized data storage and retrieval technology was changing the ways that organizations were amassing and compiling information. Many corporate records were kept for legal and regulatory reasons and little else up to that point. On the other hand, an ethnographic study of records management, which we conducted for a major business equipment manufacturer, recognized that enhanced retrieval speeds and data merger capabilities would create new demands and opportunities for records managers. Chief among them was the ability to gather customer information directly relevant to the sales organization, which was then collecting its own data and making little use of corporate records. Our recommendations to the client encouraged emphasizing the sales development implications of the technology—to show it was more than just a tool for automating the records management function—and advocated shifts in corporate culture to advance these enlarged opportunities.

Productivity. A contextually grounded understanding of work flow in organizations leads to more than the discovery of potential problems and opportunities. It can stimulate higher levels of productivity by removing barriers, enhancing communication, improving employee morale and commitment, and speeding up the adoption of new technologies. Interventions in corporate culture can alter the relationships businesses have with their customers. In this respect, cultural analyses can serve as diagnostic and strategic tools continuously advancing the larger objectives of the enterprise and its overall health.

Merging of corporate enterprises. Following a merger or new business acquisition, it may be no surprise that conscious adjustment of corporate culture is necessary. Organizations with highly hierarchical cultures may suddenly need to be merged with those that are more collaborative and teamwork oriented. Companies with a domestic heritage may now have foreign owners eager to integrate the new possession into the global marketplace. A desire for global expansion may lead to new management demands and expectations. These changes need to be shepherded and promoted on the cultural level.

Adaptation to change. After an enterprise has grown as a consequence of sudden success or has contracted following an unexpected change in the economic climate, it needs to incorporate these transitions into its patterns of communication and governance. We have observed departments become paralyzed when key individuals were moved into another area or when specific functions were suddenly eliminated. The problem was that no one anticipated the cultural change that would be evident following the shrinkage.

Corporate social responsibility. Corporate and brand images are increasingly being drawn into the service of social responsibility. It is no longer enough to be the most stylish and cool, technologically jazzed, or best advertised brand in the marketplace. In making decisions about product usage, customers and stakeholders are increasingly looking to such factors as concern for the environment, respect for worker rights and fair pay in developing countries where items are manufactured, democratic corporate governance, and the naturalness and healthfulness of product components. Corporate social responsibility is a cultural issue fostered by a high level of awareness, organizational focus, and communication with internal and external audiences.

Ethnic and Regional Subcultures

Populations are in motion throughout the world, and the idea of multiculturalism has taken root in contemporary societies. Developed countries are increasingly coming to be viewed as colorful mosaics constructed from cross-cutting subcultural groups representing various regional, national, racial, linguistic, gender, sexual-orientation, and class-based identities. The degree to which various nation-states either affirm or suppress their minority cultures and the extent to which differentiated cultures practice tolerance and acceptance rather then conflict and discrimination are highly variable.

Marketers largely have found that regional and ethnic subcultures represent an opportunity. Whether to tailor mass-market products to an identifiable niche sharing common tastes and predilections, or to use an evocative promotional cliché in communicating with a subgroup sharing a separate language or argot, marketers have affirmed that brand loyalty and product trial can be strengthened by effective appeals to subcultures. The correct manner of meeting community needs may be learned through qualitative research. For example, a local bank or a health care center may find that recognizing community celebrations, hiring members of neighborhood subgroups to serve as managers, and investing in local businesses and service providers all serve to reinforce allegiance to the brand.

Ethnic groups are important both as consumers of the larger society's goods and services—some of which may have impelled them to leave their home countries in the first place—and as a fountain of innovation for the larger society. Although the groups' styles and tastes in food, music, and the arts appear exotic and foreign to the larger population at first, they eventually become adopted by the dominant society's avant-garde and then are entirely assimilated. In the United States, for example, salsa's growth has outpaced ketchup as a tabletop condiment.

Marketing efforts that target ethnic subgroups are complicated. Not all ethnics are equally reachable; the degree of visibility and assimilation, language issues, and cultural traits and values vary among immigrants. Dominant communities tend to see ethnic communities as undifferentiated masses; majorities are indifferent and ignorant about the subtle features of ethnic identity. Ironically, the view from within the ethnic group is that it is highly diverse. For example, the established Cuban American populace in South Florida has little in common with newly arrived Mexican American immigrants in Southern California, even though they are both regarded as "Hispanics" by the larger culture. The tendencies toward group homogenization in mass societies are counterbalanced by people's need to create smaller units of identity for themselves.

Societies contain both *established ethnic groups*—a larger and visible population segment sharing an identity based on various ascribed characteristics—and *ethnic subcommunities*. The latter may be defined by dialect rather than language or region rather than nation; many are likely to see themselves as long-term guests rather than as migrants. Hispanics are rapidly evolving into the model of an established ethnic group while substantial ethnic subcommunities in the United States include Iraqi American communities in the Detroit area, South Asian immigrants in Texas, Hasidic and Russian Jews in New York City, and Vietnamese Americans in Los Angeles.

Marketers frequently find occasions that call for direct communication to ethnic subcommunities. Culturally sensitive tactics are the preferred discovery technique for obtaining information about community norms and preferences that yield strategic insights. In-home interviews and encounters at social gathering places or ethnographic observation and interviewing that attempt to comprehend the cultural context of ethnic group behavior all yield useful knowledge. Here are some examples of categories particularly well-suited to this approach.

- Products that appeal directly to the cultural distinctiveness of ethnic subcommunities. These may include greeting cards for Dewali, the Hindu Feast of Lights, or foods and ingredients that are common in ethnic diets.

- Public health messages intended for subcommunities that are differentially affected by particular conditions. The Puerto Rican community of New York City, for example, has rates of asthma considerably higher than other groups; Eastern European Jews are subject to relatively higher rates of genetic conditions such as Gaucher's Disease. Pharmaceutical companies that consider these groups as their target markets appreciate culturally specific research that increases the access and usability of drugs and health-related services among these populations.
- Products and services related to the ethnic subcommunities' ties to the home country; for example, education, travel, telecommunications, and cash remittance services.
- Products and services that benefit from personal selling by fellow members of ethnic subcommunities because sales require high levels of trust or explanation in native languages. These may include security, banking, insurance, and brokerage services.
- Professional services that are required for accommodation to the larger society; for example, immigration law, real estate brokerage, and financial services.
- Categories in which members of ethnic subcommunities represent a significant proportion of the marketing channels, such as Korean and Arab grocers on the East and West Coasts.
- Mass market products that may be beneficially positioned or distributed in respect to the specific needs of ethnic subcommunities.

In some recent ethnographic research conducted by QualiData, for example, we discovered the importance of olfactory signals—the smell of pine, particularly—in informing Hispanic Americans that areas of the home have been successfully cleaned. This is not something that is verbalized as common knowledge, but it is betrayed when respondents gleefully proclaim that their kitchens now smell like their grandmother's home at the end of cleaning day. Representations of this research-based understanding can become powerful motivators for repeat product purchase.

The styles and imagery associated with various ethnic cultures also supply emotional ammunition to marketers appealing to "wannabees" who mimic those patterns as their role models and reference groups. In contemporary France, for example, it can be startling to discover the degree to which the fashions and jargon of American ghetto youth are used to communicate with French teenagers. French teenagers adopt these symbols as a criticism of conventional society and as means of personal expression.

Representing just a few words or styles, nevertheless, is not enough. Marketers risk betraying shallowness and a lack of authenticity—the kiss of death—if their usage is not exact and context sensitive. Japanese youngsters, for example, modeling themselves after American basketball stars, have adopted Nike brand sneakers; however, they treat them as

"formal wear" and carefully remove and store them when playing basketball, switching into off-brand sneakers that they do not care about scuffing
and damaging. Marketers need to know contextual details like these to
develop strategic plans for innovative products.

Wong (1993) has pointed out that sensitivity to culture and context is
essential in decoding the meanings that Asian American consumers attach
to constructs that are taken for granted in the general market. What is
meant by *family, head-of-household*, and *decision maker* can differ markedly
depending on the particular situations and contexts in which questions are
posed. Inattention to this context can only misdirect research findings and
create potentially offensive misunderstandings.

In developing societies, cultural values related to consumption can
become a nationwide phenomenon. The People's Republic of China, for
example, has undergone a shift from Marxist socialism to market socialism,
during which marketing and advertising have gone from strictly forbidden
communications to major sociocultural phenomena. Whereas the previous
era frowned on such capitalist activities as the accumulation of personal
goods and independent economic actions, the recent era has seen the growth
of modern media and mass markets, the proliferation of luxuries, and the
emergence of an entrepreneurial class. Tse, Belk, and Zhou (1989) have
demonstrated through content analysis of advertising messages that underlying consumption-related cultural themes have moved away from strict util-
itarianism to the hedonistic values characteristic of Western societies.

Retail Navigation

A growing trend is for marketers to apply ethnographic methods in natural
retail or other commercial environments. Several objectives motivate these
studies. A very compelling goal is a detailed ecological analysis of sales and
merchandising performance. Researchers now are able to assess how all of the
elements that compose retail store environments—lighting, smells, signage,
displays of goods, the location, point-of-purchase displays, size and orientation of shelving, adjacencies—impact buying behavior. The ethnographer's
role is to decode the meaning and consequences of these ecological elements
with an eye toward maximizing retail performance.

Often, these studies use time-lapse photography as a tool for behavioral observation and data collection over extensive periods of time and
avoid actual interaction with consumers. By these means, Paco Underhill
(2000, p. 76) has found, for example, a natural tendency to steer toward the
right when navigating department stores. Other studies make use of the

accompanied walk-through so that consumers can express the meanings behind their experience of the retail environment (see Mestel, 1998). Most studies combine a mix of active and passive data collection approaches.

In research QualiData recently conducted on behalf of a major bank, for example, the objective was to analyze the consumer's experience of navigating a novel type of bank branch targeted at investments rather than traditional types of banking services such as savings and loans. All of the physical and interpersonal elements of the branch were devoted to facilitating analysis, investigation, and purchase of various investment products, and the client's objective was to evaluate how these features were performing. Our research approach involved taking recruited participants through the branch and carefully observing how they interacted with and verbally reacted toward both the technology and people resources within the branch.

Category management is a discipline associated with retail merchandising that combines systematic data collection with strategic allocation of space and resources to maximize the fit between shoppers and products on store shelves (see Corstjens & Corstjens, 1995; Nielsen Marketing Research, 1993). The basic goal is to tailor category assortments, arrangements of shelf space, pricing, and promotions according to the character of a particular store's customer base. Techniques of retail ethnography, particularly video recordings of shopper behavior, have become very useful data collection tools to support category management efforts. Careful analysis can reveal the ways in which shoppers browse, how they make decisions among brands, and how the design of promotions at the point-of-purchase influence what consumers put into their shopping carts.

Guerrilla Ethnography

There is another emerging though controversial approach to research in public spaces that sometimes goes by the name of *guerrilla ethnography* or *pilot ethnography* or *street research*. It involves spontaneously observing and talking with consumers in their natural habitats without emphasizing the researcher role. This tool is touted by many brand planners and others in creative roles at advertising agencies. The goal is to achieve an unfiltered, unpremeditated, and reality-based encounter with targeted consumers. Researchers may, but commonly do not, identify their occupational role, nor do they formally state the objectives behind their interaction with consumers. Instead, through the normal course of chatting with fellow customers or sales personnel, an attempt is made to glean information about customer preferences, sales cues, consumer language, and so on.

The benefit here, clearly, is that the social distance and formal barriers between researcher and subject are broken down, and interaction is more "natural" and less subject to contrivance. The main objection expressed by critics, however, is the potential invasion of privacy and somewhat manipulative structure of interaction. Without informed consent, critics argue, researchers have no right to involve anyone in a commercially based interaction.

Guerrilla ethnography is often used as a pilot research format to help investigators prepare for focus groups or intercept surveys. A quick trip to the supermarket or chain store can introduce researchers to category dynamics at the shelf. Conversations with buyers at the shelf can reveal motivations and mind-sets that can influence interviewing approaches. Here, the objective is not to draw conclusions about behavior but, rather, to familiarize themselves with a category by interacting with actual customers.

Mystery shopping. QualiData has conducted several studies in which the tactics of mystery shopping—usually used to evaluate service encounters—were merged with observational research objectives. In one case, our goals were to understand the impacts of a new sales kiosk for cellular telephones and also to assess sales associates' biases and predilections in recommending various telephone products and services. In addition to careful observations and documentation of shopper behavior around the merchandising unit, our ethnographers occasionally ventured over, posing as fellow customers, to check on what was being experienced at the kiosk; for example, whether the offer was clear and the sales contract could be understood.

In addition, to test salesperson biases, we presented personnel in a succession of stores with various "usage scenarios," each describing occasions that represented the client's sense of what would appeal to the prospective targeted segment. The proposed solutions to our problems offered by salespeople led to an understanding of their perceptions of customers and competing products and helped the client develop strategies for educating and motivating sales staff.

Contextual Technology: Usability and User Interface Design

The relentless march of technology is emblematic of our age. Inasmuch as computers have become the primary productivity tool of the contemporary era and the Internet is emerging as a major marketing and communications channel, it is inevitable that qualitative and ethnographic research are applied to technological tools. The designers of our telephones, microwave ovens, VCRs, and ATMs have learned to respond to the needs and predilections of average people by conducting research and adapting products as indicated by these studies.

The systematic study of people's interactions with tools has created the applied science of usability. The primary goals of this subdiscipline are to better understand consumer/user problems, barriers, and facilitators while engaged with various technologies and tools. The ways in which we design items that facilitate our everyday lives—the interior environments of our homes and workplaces, the simple tools we use to solve daily problems of personal care, meal preparation, or household maintenance, the familiar geography of our activities, such as entryways and signs—can be problematic or supportive of our intentions and ideals.

The term *contextual inquiry* is often applied to the intensive ethnographic exploration of workplaces and home environments. The goals of contextual inquiry are to better understand the needs and processes around which technologies and other tools can be developed.

The Internet has spawned another emerging use of ethnography: as a discipline to develop technology products and to improve the usefulness, enjoyment, and effectiveness of Web sites (Nielsen, 2000).

Norman (1990) has shown that the principles of usability lie in peoples' mental models, their understandings of how things operate based on their experience or learning. Consumers come to product usage with a natural sense of themselves and others, feelings about human capabilities, ways of perceiving the environment, ideas about causation, cultural habits, and so on. Product designers can either leverage these fundamental principles to improve usability or ignore them at their peril. Although consumers may accept poor product performance and inattention to usability for some time, eventually businesses that follow the rules will gain a competitive edge.

Usability studies consistently find that consumers expect that the functionality of their products will have some level of *visibility;* that is, they will be able to understand the operation of a product without referencing external sources. In essence, users anticipate clues to the way things work and feedback following actions they may take. Consider, for example, a light switch: Users know that something needs to be taken from an *on* to an *off* position or advanced to modulate the amount of light, and they know they are correct when they achieve the desired reaction. Nevertheless, in many product categories and usage environments, a gulf can develop between peoples' innate mental processes, based on their own understanding of how things work, and the actual steps required to complete a process as constructed by the engineers, architects, designers, and chemists responsible for our technology and tools.

In an ethnographic study of household insect extermination behavior, for example, QualiData found problems in the ways consumers misunderstood competing insect management technologies. We viewed this as usability problem and based an experiment we conducted on that idea.

Consumers are aware of and purchase two types of ant killers—the bait and the spray. Baits operate by poisoning a token number of ants, which enter the plastic container when the device is placed close to an ant trail. The poisoned ants remain viable long enough for them to return to their nests and proceed to contaminate the entire nest, including its queen.

Many consumers misunderstand the operation of the baits (of course, they probably have not read or understood the directions), and when they see many ants darting out or avoiding the trap altogether, they assume that the bait is not functioning. Our experiment demonstrated how consumers are then likely to use the toxic chemicals of the spray—useful for acute infestations but not for long-term extermination—which has several undesirable consequences for the effectiveness of either technology. The spray eliminates the sickened ants, which do not return to the nest, and it lays down a toxic field that repels other ants from the bait. The conclusion reached by the customer after ants reappear in a few days is that both products are not working, and he or she needs to switch brands.

Our recommendations included encouraging greater consumer education and discouraging the client from using the term *bait* in connection with the product formulation. That term set up a mental image of product performance that was inconsistent with the way the technology actually worked.

Usability testing can be exclusively laboratory based or, owing to obvious limitations of this rarefied environment, can go to homes and businesses to observe product performance or human–computer interactions in their natural context, on real consumer-purchased and customized machines.

QualiData has applied contextual ethnographic approaches in helping clients design home-banking Web sites and ATMs. Listening to consumers' expressed wishes and observing their interactions with computer technology was coupled with careful examination of their surroundings. We have also used ethnography to better understand how business people use interpersonal, print, and electronic resources while researching computer hardware and software they anticipate purchasing. In another study for a major manufacturer of office products, we spent time in business offices to learn how secretaries and clerks use electronic and other resources in compiling reports. These studies yielded concepts and strategies for new product development and marketing communications. When consumers make use of pencil and paper resources, such as Post-It Notes attached everywhere, and avoid computer functionality, the meanings and opportunities for product and process adaptations are sharply revealed.

Microprocessors are being applied increasingly to more everyday appliances and tools. Technologies such as "Blue Tooth" standards, a system for remotely managing appliances, are changing the ways we activate and control everyday things. Adding functionality to everyday products, however, does not automatically make them more satisfying, exciting, or easy to use. Indeed, added benefits may produce complexity and confusion. Designers alone cannot be trusted to anticipate the needs and predilections of typical users. They become overly devoted to their designs, develop a stake that compromises objectivity, place excessive emphasis on aesthetics at the expense of usability, or otherwise lose the ability to recognize normal human reactions to technology. The need for methods that learn from actual users of everyday products is indispensable.

Synthesis: Culture and Context in the Mind of the Consumer

We have described how ethnography has been revived in response to the limitations of traditional qualitative and survey research practice. We have also pointed to several emerging areas that are enlarging the perspective and utility of ethnographic studies in the analysis of ethnic and other subcultures as well as in retail and technology research.

Above all, we have tried to demonstrate the significance of culture and context in the minds of consumers. Because culturally based consumer aspirations and choices are rooted in the deep structures of the brain, ethnography represents an important step in further understanding consumer behavior. Thus, it is likely that the usefulness and application of ethnography will continue to grow.

In furthering the goal of expanding the use of ethnographic approaches in marketing analysis, the next several chapters will provide a step-by-step orientation to implementing studies. Our goal is to demystify ethnography and facilitate its regular application so its benefits may be shared by all relevant marketers.

PART II

Project Management

5

Varieties of Ethnographies

Various types of marketing-oriented studies are classified as ethnographies. In each variety, the site and the observational encounter are defined quite differently. This chapter reviews the different characteristics of each type of ethnographic study and describes some of their logistical implications.

Marketing-oriented ethnographic studies can be classified according to whether they take place in a public space, such as a supermarket, airport, or public park, as opposed to private space, such as a home or business. They may also be differentiated according to how intensive the ethnographic encounter may be; that is, whether the period of engagement with subjects is delimited and task driven or whether it is existential and relatively open-ended. The accompanying table illustrates how the types of studies may be grouped.

Delimited/Task-Driven Studies in Private Settings

OBSERVED PRODUCT USAGE

Observed product usage studies are conducted to obtain insights into a concrete, regular activity typical of a home or business, such as cleaning the kitchen, cooking a meal, doing the laundry, or changing babies' diapers. The length of time spent at a site would vary by the type of activity; however, time estimates should be long enough to permit observations of effort expended in preparation and concluding an activity. Thus, observations of fixing a meal should include effort allocated to assembling ingredients, preparing the meal, eating it, and cleaning up at the end. In general, observing natural activities can take from 3 to 5 hours.

In a recent study whose objective was to observe usage practices of glucose measurement devices among patients with diabetes, we were

	Private	Public
Delimited/task driven	Observed product usage	Accompanied purchase
	Structured product usage	Structured product usage
	Contextual usability	Guerrilla ethnography
Open-ended/existential	Cultural studies	Observed purchase
	Day-in-the-life	Mystery shopping

challenged to coordinate visits with the various timing habits that are customary in this category. Some patients monitor frequently throughout the day whereas others measure in the morning and evening. Accommodating the latter patients involved repeating the visit twice in the same day. In another study for a manufacturer of paper goods, we were challenged to conduct observations at each of the meals consumed by respondents.

STRUCTURED PRODUCT USAGE

The objectives of a structured activity study are to analyze consumer responses to a new product, an alternative formulation of an existing product, or a new usage routine. These structured activities are typically introduced experimentally into their ordinary location of use, or they may be introduced into a neutral environment, such as a laboratory. The site visit consequently is structured by closely watching consumers use this new or unfamiliar product. Although these may be the briefest of site visits, lasting only an hour or two, time should be allocated to setting up the trial, debriefing the respondent about other products used in the past, and evaluating the trial.

CONTEXTUAL USABILITY

Contextual usability studies generally are oriented toward observing respondents interacting with technology or other tools in their own environments. Respondents may be encouraged to demonstrate how they use their own computers to navigate particular Web sites or handle their software programs.

Open-Ended/Existential Studies in Private Settings

CULTURAL STUDIES

Cultural studies strive for a holistic understanding of a group defined by some affiliation based on common ethnic, socioeconomic, occupational, regional, or affectionate characteristics. It shares many features of traditional organizational or community studies. The impetus for this type of study generally is to yield information relevant to product customization and adaptation. For example, a marketer of insurance products may anticipate that knowledge of financial behaviors and values of recent Asian immigrants may drive the development of special products, marketing strategies, and tactics that better meet the needs of this community.

Findings from cultural studies emerge over time and through continuous contact with representative informants from that culture. The ethnographic encounter may take place in the public arena; for example, in religious institutions, stores, and community centers frequented by the targeted group. More commonly, however, the encounter takes place in private spaces, including the homes and workplaces inhabited by members of the targeted subculture.

DAY-IN-THE-LIFE

Day-in-the-life studies are extended visits in a product usage environment oriented toward discovering norms and expectations for products used by particular types of consumers. When commissioning day-in-the-life studies, clients commonly are looking for insights into the range of activities or problems that may occur in particular settings over a day's time.

Numerous occasions may call for this kind of research. Pharmaceutical marketers, for example, may use this to gain a better understanding of daily challenges faced by particular patients—say, people with diabetes, Alzheimer's disease, or schizophrenia.

QualiData has gained experience in conducting this form of ethnography for several other kinds of marketers. For example, a study for a regional telephone company asked us to explore how small businesses interact with customers and suppliers through a range of communications media: mobile telephony, land lines, computers, and so on. Another study for a marketer of data storage and retrieval products traced the "life history" of paper files within an organization over the course of a day. Observations focused on storage formats, how often files are being accessed, what is done with the document once retrieved, how retrieval is tracked, and so on. Both of these studies were oriented toward discovering new product opportunities.

Studies like these require visiting the site at the start of the day and staying until closing. When visiting consumers' homes, researchers may arrive shortly after the household awakes and stay until bedtime. For respondents' convenience if the location is a workplace, day-in-the-life studies sometimes must be limited to less than a full day. However, if objectives require observing an organization over time, site visits can last up to several days.

Delimited/Task-Driven Studies in Public Settings

ACCOMPANIED PURCHASE

This approach is often called *shop-alongs* or *accompanied shops*. Watching and probing consumers in the act of purchasing a particular brand, product, or category can deliver important strategic information. Studies may be conducted in this manner to evaluate merchandising tactics, to observe how competitive appeals are resolved at the supermarket shelf, and to better understand the inner experience of the consumer within the shopping environment. Using the accompanied purchase approach normally involves going to a supermarket, small shop, or discount store outside the home along with the respondent. Alternatively, the researcher may observe the respondent at home while a purchase is completed by phone or over the Internet. Site visits for shop-along studies normally take two to four hours, from the point of planning to completion. These are sometimes combined with additional data collection; for example, watching the respondent prepare a meal after ingredients have been assembled during the accompanied purchase.

STRUCTURED PRODUCT USAGE

Structured product usage may take place in public as well as private settings. These types of studies are often conducted by governmental agencies seeking information that may be applied to municipal conveniences such as public parks, transportation systems, and information centers. For example, an agency responsible for transportation improvements may accompany prospective users through models of proposed new trains and buses to gain insights into ease of access, effectiveness of signage systems, and other features.

GUERRILLA ETHNOGRAPHY

As an alternative to the systematic and organized effort required in completing a thorough ethnography, clients sometimes want just to "get their feet wet" with several random observations in public settings. This effort to learn quickly about usage situations in public places is often called *guerrilla ethnography*. This approach may be used, for example, to observe drinking situations in public clubs, bars, or pubs or to observe consumers shopping for specific products.

Guerrilla ethnographies tend to be less systematic and of brief duration. Critics complain that they may be vulnerable to errors produced by nonrandom respondent selection and insufficiency of respondents, a criticism that is sometimes leveled against all qualitative research. Nevertheless, they are useful in orienting researchers to patterns of product selection and use in a spontaneous, real-world setting.

Open-Ended/Existential Studies in Public Settings

OBSERVED PURCHASE AND MYSTERY SHOPPING

Research objectives sometimes call for observing the retailing context as a whole, rather than focusing on particular respondents. This approach may require placing observers or video recording devices at specific points within the store and making generalizations on the basis of large numbers of shoppers passing through a retailing experience. This is the research format that Underhill (2000) describes as *retail ethnography*. The objective here is to analyze the merchandising environment as a whole, paying attention to activities regulated by the ecology and arrangement of merchandising space within the store.

Consumers or sales personnel in a particular store may be observed. Client demands here may require being in the field over several days or weeks. A recent study for a technology client in support of a new product introduction, for example, required QualiData researchers to encounter sales personnel with usage scenarios—descriptions of likely users and situations, such as, "I'm looking for a gift for my son who is interested in technological gadgets"—in order to assess whether sales personnel were delivering accurate and motivational information about the client's product.

In Praise of Multiple Methodology

Contemporary market research managers are discovering that conducting studies using multiple data collection approaches yields a level of depth and nuance that is unavailable when any single method is applied in isolation. This strategy, usually called *triangulation* or *bricolage*—suggests that knowledge acquisition can be maximized through the accumulation of independent insights derived through multiple methods rather than relying on any single research technique. From an epistemological point of view, all methods contain inherent limitations that render them capable of producing only a single approximation of the truth.

Ethnography works well with other approaches, whether they are statistical surveys or alternative qualitative techniques, in creating actionable consumer insights. QualiData has merged focus group discussions with ethnographic site visits to consumers' homes to gain insights into emerging patterns of children's play. Andrew Burton (2001) has advocated combining expert panels and ethnography in learning about emerging trends that are significant to marketers.

There is virtually no limit to the imaginative ways researchers are combining other electronic and face-to-face research approaches with ethnographic research.

6

Project Overview

Researchers who are considering the use of ethnography to obtain marketing information need to consider a variety of issues. First, of course, is whether ethnography is the right tool for their project. Ethnography used for marketing is not the same as traditional ethnographic research, and the distinctions may help researchers to decide whether ethnography will work for them. Finally, a host of practical issues arise in the application of ethnography in a market research situation. In this chapter, we examine these issues.

Is Ethnography Appropriate?

No doubt the first decision that should be made when considering an ethnographic approach to solve marketing problems is a determination of whether this approach is appropriate. Managers sometimes select a marketing research method because it is trendy, because they have been "sold" by a research provider, or because they are tired of using commonplace approaches and are grasping for something novel. Ethnography is usually appropriate when research goals include one or more of the following expectations.

Cultural. When research seeks to identify the underlying patterns within an organization or a community, ethnography can be a useful discovery tool. Typically, the search for cultural understanding involves a wish to identify ways to access and communicate better with a group, to learn about the dynamics of stability and change within the culture, or to identify particular category and brand relationships. Understanding culture is usually valued as a component in an intervention strategy or an opportunity assessment.

Environmental. Ethnographic methods are appropriate when the location and context of behavior are considered critical variables. These might include the work environment, the places where products are used and purchased, or the signs and symbols in a place where particular behaviors are guided.

Holistic. Ethnography provides a solution where objectives are holistic: where information about consciousness, lifestyle, hopes, and aspirations is viewed as essential to an understanding of consumers.

Engagement. When the researcher wishes to get as close to the customer as possible, ethnography provides the pathway. There is no higher level of encounter with the customer than being right in the home, store, or workplace. Being "right there" delivers a high level of insights and a rich, unfiltered view of reality that are unavailable in laboratories or through the use of research technology.

Visual documentation. Ethnography unites image-based data, such as photography and video, with consumers' written and verbal reports. These visual components provide an added dimension for analysis and communication of results.

Even though ethnography is normally classified as a member of the qualitative research family, quantification and systematic enumeration are not entirely inimical to its objectives. For example, a study of a retail environment may benefit from a systematic audit of the distribution of men and women or people who shop alone versus those accompanied by other adults or children. Nevertheless, if results from a large sample of geographically dispersed respondents are necessary, ethnography cannot deliver the requisite sample sizes or dispersion in an economical and efficient manner.

Ethnography is also unsuitable in other areas. For example, if specific research results need to be compared over time, similarly, ethnography must be abandoned because it can only offer a general picture of stability and change. In-home or in-office approaches also may not be possible in situations where some degree of isolation is necessary for conducting some projective and elicitation techniques; a laboratory may offer better resources.

Academic Versus Marketing Ethnographies

Marketing ethnographies are quite distinct in focus, perspective, and depth from those that are traditionally completed by academically affiliated researchers. The major differences are reviewed below.

CLIENT FOCUS

Marketing ethnographies are conducted to address issues presented by a sponsoring client, who sets the agenda for what *needs* to be known. Whereas academic research addresses disciplinary, public interest, or theoretical issues, marketing ethnographies are primarily oriented by client-stimulated questions related to consumer behavior or to the functioning of business-related organizations.

Marketing studies normally are initiated by a business unit—a strategic marketing, product development, or productivity enhancement group within a company—and are driven by the need to support decisions about corporate investments and direction. Consequently, both the implementation of research activities and subsequent production of results are handled in a businesslike, confidential, and proprietary manner. The information generated by research studies resides with the sponsor. It is rare for clients to permit public release of findings because generally they relate to the internal affairs and strategic plans of corporate entities.

Sometimes, companies allow their organizations to be studied by academic researchers with the intention of learning about organizational processes in general or about the roles of various subgroups, such as women, within the larger context (e.g., Kanter, 1977). These studies should not be confused, however, with marketing ethnographies, whose purposes are confined to advancing client-driven interests rather than those of a disciplinary, societal, or industry focus.

BUSINESS ISSUES

Marketing ethnographies are designed to address questions that have an impact on brand and business development. These issues include:

- How consumer practices might offer ideas for new products
- Whether unarticulated consumer problems offer product modification opportunities
- How products perform in consumer environments
- How products are handled and managed and what these practices suggest for packaging and storage innovations
- The impact of consumer lifestyles, regional or ethnic subcultures, and age-related behaviors on product usage and needs
- How to enhance the productivity of work routines or to improve communications within an organization
- What the emerging trends are in consumer attitudes and behavior

The unifying concern in all of these issues is advancing the company's profitability and long-term value. This is accomplished by introducing desirable product innovations, enhancing the user friendliness of products, reducing the costs of production and distribution, and increasing the effectiveness of consumer-directed communications about the brand.

Restricted budgets and time frame. Because marketing research projects are decision driven, they must adapt to the restrictive time frames and budgets demanded by sponsors. In the classical approach, researchers have more or less endless time and freedom to acquire a community role and allow relationships with community members to evolve over many months. Marketing ethnographers must work within a drastically curtailed time frame. Cultivating relationships with respondents, obtaining valid and reliable information, and achieving actionable results must take place within weeks or months rather than years.

This limitation requires marketing ethnographers to be extraordinarily economical in their allocation of time and deliberate in carrying out the activities that produce valid and reliable information. At the same time, sponsors must understand that ethnographies may sometimes require more time than a "quick and dirty" phone survey. Project planning should consider the extra time required to organize and implement field visits as well as the time required for data review and thoughtful analysis. Good thinking cannot be rushed.

Interactive management. Client sponsorship also entails tight interactive direction between the researching ethnographic team and client-side managers. Clear process steps, defined stages, and mutual responsibilities must be negotiated and planned before the study enters the field. Even though a large element of spontaneity and improvisation must be preserved, there is always a need to delineate execution details at the outset and to stick with the plan.

This integration of researcher and manager brings risks as well as rewards. The main advantage is that executive, technical, product, and brand managers can bring their extensive knowledge and background to the research team. This can cut the lead time necessary for learning about previous research studies, the history of the brand and category, and technologies that are relevant to product efficacy and profitable production. On the other hand, stakeholders may sometimes become political players among whom self-interest overtakes concern about collective resources; for example, when they demand that "bad news" about a test product be suppressed. In this case, the research partner is challenged to maintain a commitment to objectivity and professionalism.

PROCESS ISSUES

Restricted researcher roles. Most marketing ethnographies require researchers to make their roles transparent to informants. A high degree of respondent preparation is required to preserve the "naturalness" of the interaction; however, the preparation in itself threatens to make the observations "unnatural." Although respondents may be a bit self-conscious at first and overly reflective, they become keen on avoiding obvious sources of falsification.

Because the time frame is limited, there is little tolerance for error. Thus, respondent preparation is necessary to allow them to anticipate the sequence of events during the site visit and the practical aspects of the research, such as the number of observers, the type of recording devices that will be used, and so on.

Some ethnographies, including those of the guerrilla or spontaneous variety, require no respondent preparation inasmuch as researchers are carrying out normal roles in a public social context, such as store patron or bar customer. In these types of studies, overt recording and client co-observation are not part of the data-collection strategy. Thus, the fact of observation presents few complications that jeopardize the naturalness of respondent interactions, and transparency is not a requirement.

Team orientation. To achieve objectives in the most expeditious manner and to facilitate interactive management, marketing ethnographies often use a team approach to executing project details. More bodies and minds working in concert compensate for some of the advantages lost by the need to speed up the process. Working as a team requires training and coordination of people who may not regularly work together.

The team orientation actually becomes one of the most energizing and productive aspects of a marketing ethnography because it permits collective sharing and refinement of observations and conclusions. The overlapping intellectual skills delivered by team members produce something greater than just the sum of its parts.

Implementation Overview

Marketing ethnographies follow a fairly regular matrix of process steps as outlined below.

CLIENT BRIEF

Each project begins when a marketer of goods and services, an advertising or promotional agency, governmental group, or any other organization requests information or undertakes a research study that involves use of the ethnographic approach.

- First, client needs and objectives must be understood and clarified to make sure that the ethnographic approach is the appropriate research method for addressing those needs and objectives. Quite commonly, the client brief must be interpreted and modified to guarantee that project tasks can be completed productively.

- It is important to make sure that clients understand what this approach can and cannot deliver and that they are realistic about the logistical challenges and other contingencies that always threaten this type of research. Ethnography does not serve all information objectives equally well, and inappropriate uses should be avoided.

- Ethnographic projects may be implemented as discrete projects, or they may be coordinated with other research that uses various quantitative or qualitative approaches, such as focus groups or telephone surveys. If the latter is the case, research consultants should make certain that objectives are appropriate to the method.

- The brief must have some relationship to the budget allocated for pursuing the study. Usually, research budgets are set before specific studies are funded. This practice can have negative consequences for ethnographies because deploying a research team into multiple markets requires considerable commitment of corporate resources. Underfunding a study risks collecting information that is incomplete and misleading. Therefore, trying to cut corners and economize on a study should be discouraged.

PROJECT DESIGN

A wide range of tactical questions need to be discussed before work is sent out to the field.

- Which and how many sites should a study cover? A retail ethnography, for example, may be fielded at multiple supermarkets in four metropolitan areas; a study of toilet cleaning habits may visit the homes of 20 or more respondents.

- Which and how many respondents should be located at each of the sites? In the supermarket study, for example, the objectives may require informal interviews with 10 people shopping for disposable diapers.

- How much time in the field is sufficient to accomplish the study's information objectives? This question can be tricky: Some studies need to account for seasonal factors, weekend versus weekday variations, and other factors. Studies QualiData conducts on mealtime habits, for example, generally need to observe family behaviors during the week, when adults and children have work and school responsibilities, and on weekends, when they have relatively more leisure time to enjoy meals.

- How will the ethnographic encounter be defined? How much and what type of interaction with respondents is required to address research issues? Some studies require relatively detached observation whereas others demand deep engagement with respondents.

- What is the ethnographer's role at the site? As we will see, the ethnographer may need to play both overt and covert roles so that information objectives may be met.

- How will ethnographers gain the cooperation of respondents? It is important to motivate respondents to make useful and valid contributions and to orient respondents while not overeducating them.

- How will the site be defined? Some studies require considerable mobility. For example, in a project on telecommunications usage in small businesses, ethnographers were required to accompany salespersons across a number of sales calls. Because their natural day involved considerable mobility around the community, to study salespersons involved staying with them through their visits with customers.

- What methods will be used to collect valid and useful data? The various options available include everything from note taking to concealed video.

- How will clients be involved, and how can their effectiveness be maximized? Some clients want to be part of the site analysis team and make observations of consumer behavior on their own.

- How will the collected information be organized and analyzed so that it best meets marketers' needs? Ethnographic studies produce a high volume of raw data: transcripts of respondent interviews, behavioral observations produced by the researcher, the video record, and so on, often with data from multiple observers. Serious attention must be paid to examining this record objectively and dispassionately. Sometimes, computer-assisted data analysis programs are needed to automate the process.

These and other issues are important to settle at the time of initial discussions about a study. Elsewhere, this book will offer numerous guidelines for responding to all of these questions.

TACTICAL PLANNING

The next procedure is to outline the steps required to complete the project. This involves organizing the requisite material and human resources, both internal staff resources and external subcontractors, setting up a budget for allocating financial resources, and developing an overall schedule of tasks and deliverables. The critical element of the planning process is to make certain that client needs—both substantive information expectations and scheduling deadlines—can be addressed at the highest possible quality point and at the most productive resource expenditure.

Components of each project are interdependent, and tasks must be completed in sequence before others are begun. Thus, everyone involved in a project should understand that adhering to strict deadlines is critical in carrying out project responsibilities. Putting the project plan and calendar in writing makes expectations clear for everyone involved in the study.

Conversely, it is necessary to build enough extra time into the project schedule to accommodate unanticipated contingencies. It is also important to maintain a reserve of people resources to guarantee that the completion of tasks can be accelerated, if necessary.

Training. Sharing of intellectual perspectives and skills in data collection and analysis is an important step in each project. Everyone involved should understand client objectives and be conversant about the category being studied. New personnel must be oriented to ethnographic methods. Furthermore, client representatives who will co-observe at the site visits must be educated so that they can become true partners in the process and avoid making errors that may distort observations and conclusions.

Participant recruitment. Creating a list of respondent specifications is the next critical requirement. Most marketing ethnographies try to learn something global about a fairly narrow range of people representing the client's targeted customers. These may be defined in demographic terms; for example, "working mothers" or "recent Hispanic immigrants"; alternatively, they may be defined as category users, such as "home gardeners" or "charcoal grill devotees."

The definition of the study's targeted respondents should be clear in operational terms to facilitate recruitment. For example, it is not enough to say that we need to speak with "users" of a category. We need to be specific about which exact products are under consideration, what frequency or quantity of usage defines a user, and other relevant issues.

Next, the project manager must consider how to identify and invite people to cooperate in the study. Marketing ethnographies normally rely on the same infrastructure of respondent recruitment as researchers use when employing other methodologies, such as phone surveys. Commercial subject recruitment firms are generally employed to develop the requisite respondent pool. These firms, located in major cities around the world, can be located in directories such as the *Green Book* published by the New York Chapter of the American Marketing Association or the *Blue Book* published by the Market Research Association.[1] Respondent recruitment firms will attempt to locate and obtain the cooperation of consumers or distributors matching the needs of any type of study.

To standardize recruitment, the specifications list must be converted into a respondent screening questionnaire. Study participants must necessarily be described in fairly narrow terms in relation to demographic, product usage, and attitudinal variables because they should reflect the client's targeted consumer. The screening questionnaire permits efficient checking of respondent characteristics. (The Appendix contains an example of a screening questionnaire.)

Scheduling. When and for how long site visits are conducted is another important issue with implications for recruitment. The timing and scheduling of a project should have a direct connection to the way respondents actually use products under consideration, and this information needs to be carefully recorded for each prospective volunteer. Thus, if Thursdays, Fridays, and Saturdays are the days when family laundry is commonly done in the household, researchers on a laundry ethnography should be careful to schedule the majority of their site visits on these days of the week.

Access. Because most ethnographic projects take place at respondents' homes and workplaces or at stores and other public facilities, the logistical problems involved in visiting the home or gaining access to places that are not under the respondents' direct control need to be addressed. For example, if a respondent will be accompanied to her favorite supermarket to observe her decision-making process around breakfast cereals, researchers may have to obtain permission from local managers and national headquarters of the chain being visited if they intend to make a visual record, such as photos or videos.

IMPLEMENTING THE PROJECT

Respecting local customs. When visiting homes, cultural and family structural issues should be considered, such as gaining the cooperation of household members and watching behaviors and practices that in other contexts might be considered private. In some Islamic households, for example, the gender division of territory may place some areas of women's space off-limits to men from outside the family. Understanding these cultural factors should yield strategies for acquiring critical information without appearing naïve or offensive.

Businesses. If visiting a business or place of employment, recruiters need to respect the authority structure of the establishment and avoid problems. For example, employers must cooperate if their employees are to take part in a study. This usually involves explaining the project's purpose and process to the site's managers before recruitment can begin. Failure to follow through and track permissions carefully can yield to frustrating and importune events. In one instance, for example, QualiData researchers were in the process of observing members of an administrative group at a California office whose director believed she had the authority to invite ethnographic observers into the space. Unfortunately, her supervisor stormed into the office and, overruling our host, put a quick end to our site visit. The ethnographer, video technician, and client were unceremoniously escorted out of the office building and forced to mull over the implications of losing a day's productivity.

Public places. If conducting guerrilla research or more planned ethnography in public places, many of the constraints and formal procedures that govern research in private spaces are less operative. Nevertheless, consideration must be given to whether researchers will disclose their role while they are collecting data and whether procedures at the site may be in violation of business ethics or rules governing the protection of privacy. On most occasions—even during spontaneous interviews in public spaces—researchers should identify themselves and make an effort to acquire consent, as long as these activities are not inconsistent with research objectives.

Ethics. It violates ethical and possibly legal principles to enter a citizen's private space by misrepresenting oneself with ulterior motives to collect ethnographic data. Several years ago, Nissan Motors suffered severe embarrassment and public rebuke when it was revealed that a young man posing as an exchange student was engaged in a surreptitious form of ethnography. Takashi Morimoto, a Nissan employee, rented a room from a family named French, who lived in Costa Mesa, California. Local newspapers later reported that Morimoto was conducting market research on American patterns of automobile usage. For a month and a half, he apparently took pictures of the family's property and made notes on their lifestyle. The idea, it seems, was to gather data that would help Nissan build cars better suited to American tastes. Furious, the French family filed suit, although it was later dropped.[2]

Data collection. Because the researchers themselves—through their observations and insights—are the primary data collection instruments, it is important that consistent ethnographic perspectives and observation tools are shared among all the researchers involved in each study.

The principal data collection tool is the observation guide. Developed in consultation with the client for each project, the guide outlines all of the topics and observation points that will be covered during a site visit. Sharing the details of the observation guide ensures that all the researchers will be working off of the same set of expectations. A sample observation guide is provided in the Appendix.

Data collection is supported by any combination of data recording tools appropriate to the study. These may include simple pencil and notebook, audio and videotaping, or still photography. Sometimes, the examination and collection of physical traces is a necessary form of data acquisition.

Quality supervision. Project supervisors have the responsibility for guaranteeing that everyone participating in a study is performing at or in excess of expectations. Because all project elements are interdependent, successive stages of the study require that tasks and deliverables be completed at the highest possible quality level.

DELIVERING THE FINDINGS

Data review and analysis. After data are collected from each site, one or several research managers and analysts should review all recordings, notes, photographs, and materials obtained and organize site-specific findings in a logical and consistent manner. A recommended practice is to develop a *case analysis outline* or *site report format,* a template that acts as an organizing tool for data analysis.

It is often helpful to supplement data review with internal brainstorming sessions that allow everyone on the project team to share their overall impressions of the site visits. Sometimes, client co-observers can also benefit from a brainstorming and review session conducted after the completion of site visits.

Reporting and presentation. The client needs to determine which type of reporting format would be most helpful for their project objectives: a full or summary report, video-report, in-person presentation, or other formats. Regardless of the format or media, it is important to guarantee that all deliverables have the following qualities:

- A focus on *actionable* conclusions, that is to say, besides a recitation of what was said and done, the researcher ought to deliver findings that can support client decisions. To accomplish this goal the researcher needs to share a confidential relationship and learn the client's business priorities. Unfortunately, there is sometimes resistance to treating the research consultant with this level of intimacy.
- An emphasis on strategic implications and recommendations for steps that ought to be taken to achieve the client's marketing goals.
- An attractive, creative, and user-friendly format. Ethnographic projects lend themselves well to reporting that uses video, photographic images, and transcripts of customer dialogue.

At the conclusion of a study, it is worthwhile to conduct a quality review with employees, subcontractors, and clients. A satisfied client is one who is able to achieve clear marketing direction, is pleased with their involvement in the project and with deliverables, and is eager to engage in ethnographic work in the future.

Project Timing

Efficient turnaround is usually demanded in a marketing ethnography because critical decisions are dependent on study conclusions. Nevertheless, clients need to be realistic and allow sufficient time for adequate data to be collected and analyzed. Listed below are the considerations that should be accounted in determining the length of time to allow for study completion.

Project planning and start-up. It normally takes at least 3 to 4 weeks to develop all the instruments and tools that will be used in a project, to assemble and orient staff, to develop the necessary contracts, and to obtain client approval for each item in the project plan. Some flexibility is required here to guarantee that unanticipated contingencies can be handled.

Recruitment and respondent orientation. Recruitment for ethnographies may take somewhat longer than for other qualitative or quantitative projects. This is because the respondent pool willing to accommodate home, office, or store visits is smaller than the pool for other methodologies. Therefore, some extra time should be allocated to recruitment.

Most respondent recruitment companies have acquired experience with recruiting ethnographies and understand the differences between the subjects demanded for these and for other types of research. If an agency is inexperienced with this type of research, its personnel may require some orientation and training.

During recruitment, respondents often want to become informed about various aspects of the site visit, such as how many people will be visiting or how recordings will be made. For this reason, some form of respondent preparation, such as a *respondent information memo,* is helpful; it answers respondents' main questions in a simple, nontechnical manner. Respondents should also be provided with a contact name and phone number in case questions arise between recruitment and the actual visit.

It is important to take all steps to avoid last-minute cancellations because this can be very costly; that is, schedules of videographers, clients, and others must be readjusted, and visits must be rescheduled. Respondent orientation should emphasize the importance of carrying out their commitments to the researchers. Nevertheless, there are inevitable disappointments and contingencies, such as family emergencies, which cause cancellation of some visits. Planning procedures should account for extra time and should include extra recruited participants who can take over if last-minute cancellations occur.

Fieldwork. The amount of time in the field will vary with project scope, number and location of sites, the size of the project team, and the definition of the site visit. It is unlikely that fieldwork can be completed in less than 2 weeks; stretching it beyond 4 or 5 weeks generally takes it beyond the scope of client usefulness. Nevertheless, this has to be planned in relation to category peculiarities and client objectives. A study QualiData conducted on home barbecuing, for example, sought to study both seasonal cooks in the Northeast and Midwest and year-round barbecue fans in the Sunbelt. Consequently, the study had to be staged in two parts at different times of the year to gain insights about these two distinct segments.

Seasonal and cultural factors including the time of year, holiday seasons, religious rituals, family routines, and other factors may influence the schedule for carrying out fieldwork. For example, if observing laundry and fabric care, the researcher should recognize that consumers may have larger than average loads of wash during winter months or before holidays. Factors such as these should be considered, both as timing issues and as substantive concerns that may influence the validity of observations.

Analysis. Time allocated to analysis will always vary with the amount of data collected across the entire project. Because audio and video recordings are made in "real time," project planning should account for analysis time that matches the amount of data that must be reviewed. Qualitative data analysis (QDA) software packages are now available to automate some aspects of the compilation process, but these still require considerable time and attention.

Total project timing. Given all of these issues and concerns, a realistic minimum timetable would look more or less like this:

Planning:	2	to	3 weeks
Training:	1	to	2 weeks
Recruitment:	2	to	3 weeks
Fieldwork:	2	to	6 weeks
Analysis and Reporting:	3	to	4 weeks
Total:	**10**	**to**	**18 weeks**

Notes

1. Information about these resources may be obtained from the New York Chapter of the American Marketing Association and Market Research Association.

2. The precise details of this case and the cynicism or innocence of the automaker have been in dispute. For their part, Nissan claimed that the entire information-collection activity was consensual. For more details of this case and a general characterization of Japanese commercial espionage, see DeBenedictis, 1990, and Duggan and Eisenstodt, 1990.

7

Project Design Issues

Once ethnography has been chosen as the appropriate method for a market research project, the work has only begun. Planning for an ethnographic study presents particular demands and challenges, which we review in this chapter.

Project Design Goals

The practical considerations in designing an ethnography should flow from the study's information objectives. A wide range of tactical questions need to be discussed before work is sent out to the field, including the number of respondents, sites, and nature of the encounter. Budgetary limitations and pressing information needs will bracket all of the decisions that need to be made. Reducing bias, preserving objectivity, preserving authenticity, and showing respect and consideration for respondents should serve as the primary considerations for how all of these tactics are implemented. There are few strict guidelines for guaranteeing that each of these goals will be achieved; they remain ideals that should be continuously raised to confront and challenge ethnographers.

Reducing bias. Keeping an open mind and entering a study relatively free of expectations and assumptions—or at least exposing and understanding them—are the primary considerations in reducing bias. It is also necessary to keep guard at every stage of the study—through respondent recruitment, site visits, and analysis—that no sources of distortion are being introduced.

The culture of commercial market research sometimes promotes a climate of competitiveness among various stakeholders that makes achieving objectivity a challenge. An advertising agency, for example, may wish for findings that do not contradict a decision about how a new soft drink should be positioned. They may in turn discourage alternative perspectives about the young adults for whom the drink is expected to have appeal.

Preserving objectivity. The researcher needs to take a dispassionate point of view and give any guesses or hypotheses a chance to fail. Ethnographies should not begin as an effort to prove something. Political agendas should not intrude into the study. It is legitimate to question whether any ethnographic study can be truly dispassionate and without presuppositions; nevertheless, rather than seeking some ideal of pure objectivity, pragmatic concerns force us simply to expose potential issues and proceed as best as we can.

Preserving authenticity. The structure and process of the ethnographic encounter should not change what is being observed. This is difficult; often, simply the fact of being observed can affect respondents, and they may feel obligated to perform for the camera and to idealize or otherwise modify their behavior if they know that observation and recording are taking place. For this reason, some ethnographers advocate never revealing the fact of observation, as Underhill (2000) insists: "It's crucial to our work that shoppers don't realize they're being observed. There's no other way to be sure that we're seeing natural behavior" (p. 14).

Other ethnographers, including this one, take the position that a participatory philosophy can be useful in preserving authenticity; that is, respondents can be viewed as partners and taught how to be effective respondents by sharing information about the conditions that may introduce falsehoods or subtle contrivances that do not reflect conventional realities. In our experience, turning respondents into allies tends to diminish the likelihood that they will perform in ways that damage data collection.

Respect and consideration for respondents. A humanistic attitude toward respondents is necessary. Potential embarrassments, invasions of privacy, and exploitation should be considered before any particular data collection strategy is employed. Respondents must be given an opportunity to decline to participate or to withdraw at any stage in the encounter.

Internal Versus External Execution

An early decision that needs to be made is whether to conduct the study entirely with internal resources as opposed to engaging a consultant to execute most aspects of the study. Many corporations are now hiring

Ph.D.-level anthropologists and sociologists within their market research or strategic information organizations to serve as the interpreters of cultural trends in a manner useful to their business's sales and marketing objectives. Should these market research managers also be involved in data collection, or should they stick to their traditional role as supervisors and analysts of data collected by outside research providers? These guidelines should inform the outcome of this decision.

Internal execution. Its advantages are greater familiarity with the business issues and internal reality of the sponsoring organization and greater confidentiality. Holding all other factors equal, internal execution can provide some cost savings if no extra personnel are employed and if the job responsibilities of the ethnographic team are not compromised.

A recent article[1] (Erard, 2004) about Dr. Genevieve Bell, an anthropologist employed by Intel Research, suggests another advantage of internal execution of ethnographic studies: the ability to conduct work more intensely and over a longer period of time. Over the last 2 years, she has

> visited 100 households in 19 cities in seven countries in Asia and the Pacific to study how people use technology. Twenty gigabytes of digital photos later—along with 206,000 air miles, 19 field notebooks, two camera batteries, five umbrellas, three hats, two doses of antimalarial drugs, and one pair of her favorite sandals—she has come back with some provocative questions about technology, culture, and design. (p. G5)

External execution. Outside consultants, at first glance, are more likely to offer enhanced skills in project design and execution. Familiarity with other product categories and similar targeted respondents can bring a level of insight and experience that can reduce implementation problems. Consultants can be more objective and careful about introducing bias than internal personnel. They have less of a stake in the outcomes and fewer political entanglements in the organization; consequently, they can better deliver and adapt to bad news. Effective consultants can structure efforts of internal personnel, if desired, and leverage their input to produce cost savings.

Optimizing the Design

WHICH AND HOW MANY SITES?

There are no strict rules for determining the number of sites to visit in a marketing ethnography. External considerations such as budget parameters are likely to have a strong impact on the study scope, and the researcher is responsible for making certain that the work is not so grievously under-funded as to produce questionable or biased results.

The validity of qualitative research, fortunately, does not depend on minimum sample sizes or the formal mathematics of probability. Rather than looking for breadth, phenomenological research approaches such as ethnography seek depth and an intense understanding of the cultural, interpersonal, and contextual dynamics associated with market-based behavior. This research aims for a substantive validity; in other words, its value lies in the clarified conditions and opportunities afforded by an inti-mate knowledge of this market behavior. Norms of sample sufficiency should be grounded in whether findings reach the desired level of depth as evidenced by the use of internal validation techniques, such as triangu-lation, and by reaching redundancy in the impressions communicated by subjects in the study.

Because the study will be speaking on behalf of a distinct cultural entity, however, steps should be taken to guarantee that the sample is broadly representative of targeted markets for the brand or category. Some test of comprehensiveness should be made to determine whether all of the segments of a user cluster have had an opportunity to be included; for example, if supermarkets are frequented by both genders as well as the young and the old, the analysis and recommendations about upgraded signage and merchandising should reflect all the component subgroups of the supermarket's customers.

It is also helpful to structure some level of comparability among respondents so that some within-group comparisons can be made. For example, more than one representative of a supermarket chain's shoppers 65 years or older should be invited to participate in a study to evaluate in-store signage needs. This assures that the small sample size will not over-look some cases or dismiss them as highly idiosyncratic.

At times, on the other hand, the substantive needs of ethnographies favor respondents who may now be outside of the mainstream because they are vanguard users of a category or have a high level of need and consequent heavy dependence on a product. In a study of home bathing practices that QualiData conducted for the Moen Corporation (see ElBoghdady, 2002), for example, we aimed to observe respondents repre-senting a range of gender, age, body type, and cultural group characteris-tics; however, we also believed that very frequent bathers were an important group to study. Representatives of this segment, many of whom were performing artists who needed to bathe frequently after rehearsals and shows, introduced us to consumers with high-level needs and intense identification with the category, and this research informed product development for the entire mass market category.

HOW IS THE SITE DEFINED?

Traditional ethnographies have been based in a geographic location. Researchers have emphasized the nation, scene, neighborhood, or community where statuses and roles are enacted and social exchange takes place.

Marketing ethnographies, in contrast, have not limited themselves to restricted geographic locations. In some cases, the definition of the site can follow the traditional focus on home and neighborhood. More commonly, however, the site refers to the precise context in which a limited number of product-related behaviors take place. These locations may be fixed or mobile. They may involve a relatively microscopic view of specific locations where products are used in the home.

A study of barbecuing that QualiData conducted for a manufacturer of home grilling products, for example, emphasized areas of the home—the kitchen, backyard, garage, balcony—where storage, preparation, and usage of the products involved in the preparation and consumption of barbecued foods took place.

Being mobile may often add incremental insights to analysis of usage patterns. In the infant care category, such as disposable diapers, although most of the activities associated with storage, usage, and disposal will take place inside the home, analysis of product usage while mobile is also important. Accompanying the child's caretaker to places outside the home is likely to add insight to product needs across the full range of usage occasions.

Other categories may involve an entirely mobile concept of the site; for example, cellular telephones or personal digital assistants (PDAs) may be used primarily while in transit. Observations of product usage may productively be made aboard public transportation and in stores as well as at home.

In designing ethnographies that focus on product usage, careful consideration should be given to the variety of environments in which products are used or consumed. Laundry, for example, may be washed in the home, at a shared unit in an apartment complex, or in a commercial Laundromat. Efforts should be made to cover all of these usage contexts meaningfully so that all potential occasions for using washing products can be observed.

Ethnographies may also be primarily site focused. They may take place in a commercial business, such as a supermarket or small office, a public space such as a park or shopping mall, or a relatively confined private space. Location-focused studies may be selective in observing respondents; for example, an accompanied shopping study based in a carpet store may focus on specially recruited couples looking at floor coverings. On the other hand, site-focused studies may be nonselective and observe most or all of the people who enter an environment as would be done in a study of public park usage.

WHICH AND HOW MANY RESPONDENTS OR CASES AT EACH SITE?

The study's objectives, its specific information needs, and the definition of the site will usually determine the degree of respondent saturation at the environment of interest. Within the home or office, efforts should be made to interact with all family or workgroup members who are affected by the product category of interest. For example, in a study of how reports are compiled in various types of businesses, which was conducted by QualiData on behalf of an office products manufacturer, an effort was made to cover the site fairly widely. Ethnographers observed and spoke with people who commissioned and used reports as well as those who did the compilation and duplication. Similarly, in a study of small business operations conducted for a telecommunications company, observers covered both the backstage areas that were off limits to customers and where managers and employees conducted their business affairs as well as the public areas of the business where customer interaction took place.

It is difficult to offer strict guidelines on how many participants need to be included in any type of a qualitative study. The strict probabilistic logic of sampling does not necessarily frame questions of validity in most qualitative studies. Consequently, several other criteria for *sufficiency* need to be applied. At the very least, researchers ought to be following the rule of *comprehensiveness* by making sure that all potential segments of category users are included. They should also allow for some degree of *comparability* by engaging sufficient representatives of those categories to draw meaningful contrasts. They should continue to engage respondents and observe sites until some degree of *redundancy* has been achieved.

How many units are required to produce these goals? For pragmatic reasons—because budgetary limitations must be respected—we recommend to clients that no fewer than 15 sites be included in any study. Nevertheless, this number may not produce sufficiency in all cases.

Environment-based ethnographies, such as studies of retail behavior, usually depend on a large number of cases and should follow standard rules of sampling. If particular representatives within the environment are selected for special attention, an effort should be made to select them without bias. A random selection rule, such as "every nth customer passing by a doorway," is necessary so that selection bias does not affect the validity of observations. In retail environments, seasonal factors, weather, time of day, and day of the week must also be considered so that a full comprehensive overview of the space is achieved. Different inferences may result depending on whether the observations take place in the daytime or evening, and these need to be considered before the client makes major investments in adapting a retailing strategy.

HOW MUCH TIME IN THE FIELD?

The amount of time to spend in the field conducting marketing ethnographies is commonly determined more by pragmatic considerations than by scientific principles. Compromises must be reached between ideal as opposed to realistic ideas about fieldwork. Researchers must consider their clients' decision-making deadlines, budgets, and availability for coparticipation in fieldwork activities. Typically, corporate decision cycles allow for no more than 4 to 8 weeks in the field.

Using teams of researchers normally expedites data collection. Even though team approaches are uncommon in traditional ethnographies, they have been adopted enthusiastically by marketers.

Practical limitations of consultants' availability establish a set of boundaries for time commitments. Marketing ethnographers may be involved in multiple assignments for several clients simultaneously and may have to allocate time judiciously. The interest of subjects and their ability to participate also create time constraints.

Guerrilla ethnographies may take only a week or two. A contextual usability study or observed product usage study may be completed over several weeks. In every case, however, planning for time in the field must begin with the needs and demands of client decision makers, and the commercial ethnographer must adapt to their strict limitations.

WHO IS PART OF THE ETHNOGRAPHIC TEAM?

Who gets to participate in the observations and the roles that they may play at the site are necessary components of project planning discussions. How many people should interact with the respondent? Should any attention be given to matching gender, age, or racial/ethnic characteristics? These are important questions.

Some ethnographers have strong beliefs that only female interviewers can provide the degree of safety and confidentiality necessary for valid disclosures within the home. Others are less rigid about gender but have strong feelings about matching the age and racial/ethnic characteristics of ethnographers and respondents. In some cases, this can be justified. For example, although a middle-aged white male who is trained in ethnographic methods can certainly develop rapport with inner-city youngsters over time, the turnaround needs of most commercial research projects require a more pragmatic and cost-effective approach—that is, to match the respondents with ethnographically trained individuals who are better matched in personal traits.

It is necessary to place strict limitations on the number of people who can participate in a single ethnographic encounter. More than two or three visitors are highly intrusive in most households. The team should be limited to observer/interviewers and data-capture professionals. Because many clients of ethnographic research value the personal encounter with consumers, they often wish to become involved in actual site visits. This typically places extra demands on those considering the visiting team's composition.

Some ethnography users prefer to have their consultants execute the entire study by themselves without client attendance; the client expects only the conclusions and final report. Others insist on a high level of involvement through all study stages, including co-observation in consumer homes.

If clients wish to be deeply involved, they should expect to go through training and orientation so that their on-site roles can be discussed and they can learn how to avoid mistakes that might compromise validity. Consumers can become disoriented if authority roles are not clear at the site. Even such relatively simple injunctions as not wearing company logos need to be discussed prior to site visits. The document "Ten Commandments for Great Ethnography" provided in the Appendix is a resource that we often use to discuss appropriate client roles.

HOW IS THE ETHNOGRAPHIC ENCOUNTER DEFINED?

An important component of planning discussions is determining how the ethnographic encounter will be structured. That is, how much time needs to be spent at the site, and what type of interaction with respondents is required to address research issues?

Encounters can be *task-driven*; for example, observing respondents during meal preparation, car washing, or carpet cleaning. In each of these cases, a determination must be made about when the task actually begins; for example, tasks such as meal preparation usually begin with assembling materials and recipes, determining substitutes, arranging tools and implements, cleaning preparation surfaces, and so on. Focusing on each detail leading up to the actual cooking and serving of the meal reveals a great deal about values, intentions, lifestyles, and mind-sets that are significant in food production and satisfaction.

The ethnographic encounter may also be *existentially based*, as in a day-in-the-life study, which traces a wide range of activities and tasks during the day as they are experienced by the respondent. The purchaser of such a study may be a magazine interested in studying its core readers, such as the young women who enjoy fashion magazines. The primary focus of a day-in-the-life study is on lifestyles, cultural values, and trends that affect a wide range of behaviors in consumer environments. For example, the ethnographer in such a study is likely to pay attention to the manner in which a young woman decorates her home, makes social plans with friends, arranges her cosmetics and toiletries, interacts with financial institutions, and so on.

WHAT IS THE ETHNOGRAPHER'S ROLE AND STANCE AT THE SITE?

The roles to be played by observers within the site are also open to discussion when a project is commissioned. We can distinguish between *participant roles*, in which the observer is also a player in the scene, and *external roles*, in which the observer does not become involved as an individual in the setting but maintains the stance of an outside observer. Having determined their own appropriate role, the ethnographer must consider the degree of engagement with respondents, from intimacy to detachment.

In a study of coffee usage at a café, the ethnographer may change stance from that of an external observer to one of a participant by engaging several people in conversation and then offering to buy some new blend for them to try.

Most often in product usage studies, the observer plays an open but external role; for example, taking notes while the respondent completes tasks at a Web site—the observer has little involvement other than asking questions about intentions and results.

HOW IS THE COOPERATION OF RESPONDENTS ENGAGED?

A strategy for gaining the assent of respondents is another feature that must be planned as the project gets launched. In alternative approaches, ethnographers either treat respondents as active individual participants or as members of an undifferentiated public. In the latter case, assent is usually acquired by identifying the environment's entry as a research setting so that the respondent is providing tacit assent by moving inside the public space that is under observation. For example, the front window of a gourmet store may carry a notification that the shop is "under surveillance for research purposes."

If respondents are viewed as individual participants, they must be motivated to make useful and valid contributions. They need to become oriented to the process without getting so overeducated that they are too sensitive and self-conscious to behave naturally. The recommended practice for producing respondent cooperation and motivation is, first, to create a partnership that is mutually satisfying and beneficial to both researcher and respondent.

It is also common in commercial market research to provide a cash incentive for respondents' cooperation. In the United States and some Western European countries, it is common for participants to look at their research involvement as a form of work that merits cash reciprocation. Thus, their expectations for compensation will be roughly in proportion to their social class standing and feelings about comparable worth for alternative employment. It may sometimes be necessary, for example, in a study of home-cleaning practices, to offer different levels of compensation based on the size of the home and the variety of surface materials used in its construction.

HOW ARE DATA COLLECTED?

Deciding how to collect valid and useful data is another challenge faced during the project planning stage. The various options available include everything from pencil-and-paper note taking, still photography, and audio recording to concealed video.

In determining which data collection tools to use, consideration should be given to how the research output will be analyzed and how the final reporting will be accomplished. For example, in situations that will require heavy analysis of body language and physical space, careful video documentation may be necessary. If video presentation will be used to communicate the study's conclusions to clients, high-quality output will also be required.

Deciding which recording tools to use should consider the situations in which respondents will be observed and sensitivities that may arise. The ethnographer should strive for a data collection process that minimizes self-conscious artificial performance and maximizes naturalness, however difficult this is to achieve. The cameras used should be as small as possible, and available lighting should be used instead of the bright illumination that is common in filmmaking. The recent explosion of hand-held digital video recorders has revolutionized the process of capturing consumer behavior. Most of the equipment on the market is lightweight, unobtrusive, and user friendly.

Special observational situations require imagination and some degree of design skill. In QualiData's work on showering behavior for the Moen Corporation, the client and ethnographers developed a specialized video recording system that recognized the unique problems associated with videotaping in people's own bathrooms. The novel tool could be assembled and disassembled in no more than 15 minutes each. It could be installed in any room with a floor and ceiling no more than 15 feet apart. It did not fog under changing temperatures and was completely waterproof and electrically safe. Most significantly, it was small enough that respondents could conduct their normal showering routine without intrusion.

Imaginative ethnographers have recently expanded the range of video recording options. Some have provided respondents with small digital video recorders or photo cameras to record their daily-life situations or various product-usage routines in private.

Recent advances in technology have now opened possibilities for continuous interaction between respondents and ethnographers via the Web, e-mail, instant messaging, text messaging, and cellular telephones. Technological resources such as geographic positioning (GPS), when they are commonplace, may also become valuable data-collection resources.

HOW IS CLIENT INPUT HANDLED?

As noted previously, some clients of ethnographic research prefer a hands-off approach whereas others appreciate the opportunity to visit consumer environments. The internal corporate culture as well as the personalities and personal interests of client personnel determine the degree of involvement they will seek in particular projects. Ethnographic observations of homes and workplaces are increasingly being used by marketers as consumer immersion exercises to familiarize management firsthand with the needs and expectations of people who buy and use their products.

If clients will be part of the site visit team, plans should be made for maximizing the effectiveness of their co-observation. The form and extent of client involvement should be agreed on as the study is initiated. If a high level of co-observation is desired, the research consultant should expect to invest some time in orienting clients to the specifics of on-site behavior and protocols required during the ethnographic encounter.

There is naturally a reciprocal though asymmetrical relationship between the client and research provider; that is, the client initiates the project, sets its parameters, and pays for the performance of professional services, whereas the provider lends expertise, time, and insight to deliver services according to client expectations. The power in the situation rests with the client; nevertheless, at the site, the researcher's authority cannot be diminished without risk to a study's validity. From the participant's perspective, the researchers must be calling the shots because of their greater expertise and higher commitment to objectivity and analytic detachment. If the respondent senses a power differential between the client and researcher—that the researcher is doing the client's bidding on behalf of an agenda beyond data collection—it can negatively affect the level of honesty and openness experienced at the site.

Consequently, plans need to be made for structuring client roles at the site. It is best for them to become occupied with an aspect of data collection rather than serving as observers exclusively.

Even a fairly hands-off client will usually expect timely updates from the field, including details of how well recruitment is proceeding, the progress of site visits, and problems encountered and solved. They are usually curious about emerging conclusions, and the question, "What are you finding?" is relatively common. The consultant in this case is usually hard-pressed to remain tentative and inconclusive because most of the work is still in the field. At the same time, client interest can be addressed by suggesting emerging hypotheses that await additional confirmation as the data collection proceeds.

HOW WILL DATA BE DISSEMINATED?

Deciding how to organize the collected information so that it best meets marketers' dissemination and distribution needs is another project design consideration. Many corporate purchasers of ethnographic studies have intentions for the research deliverables and results that go beyond simply gaining the strategic insights of the study. They may want to use video footage of consumer behavior in their training of management or sales staff; they may want to retain an archive or library of consumer practices. They may want to commit to later additional analysis of interesting subgroups identified by the study such as heavy users or newly formed households.

Additional potential expectations for the video record of site visits include the following: preparing a video report for senior management or the board of directors, using research results in public relations efforts, and using research results as the basis for additional quantitative work. All of these considerations must be discussed ahead of time because they have important implications for how the research is structured. For example, if public dissemination is expected, prospective respondents must be informed and provide appropriate consent and releases at the time of recruitment. If the client expects a usable archive, the client and the research supplier should discuss storage and retrieval issues well before the data is captured. The table below reviews the implications for production, analysis, and storage based on the clients' dissemination expectations.

HOW WILL THE DATA BE ANALYZED?

The purchaser and provider of ethnographic services need to agree on parameters for how the collected information will be analyzed following the completion of fieldwork. Some clients appreciate the opportunity to participate in this stage through analysis workshops, particularly if they have also participated in data collection at site visits. How thoroughly visual information will be integrated with description and analysis also needs to be discussed because this has implications for how thoroughly the video footage is likely to be processed.

Dissemination Requirements	Implications for Production, Analysis, and Storage
Public reporting of study results	Best-quality video footage Respondent releases Careful selection of video clips Possible use of qualitative analysis software to automate retrieval
Creation of a video report of findings for internal presentation	Video editing software or professional assistance High-quality video
Creation of a retrievable archive of consumer practices	High-quality video Careful coding and labeling of materials Qualitative analysis software for coding
Potential reanalysis of data	Careful coding and labeling of materials Qualitative analysis software for coding

Collected data, including notes, documents, video, and photos, may be analyzed impressionistically with only cursory reference to documentation, or they may be subjected to systematic review. To simplify systematic analysis, it helps to create a *case analysis template* at the outset. This document establishes the format for how every case in the study—for example, every household or work group—will be methodically reviewed for analytic purposes. The final section of this book discusses data analysis in greater detail.

Staffing and Other Personnel Needs

BUILDING THE TEAM

The ethnography team should take a logical and consistent form. If all of the personnel resources described here are not available in a single company, it may be necessary to contract with part-time or temporary project staff to complete necessary tasks.

Because the creation of work products for clients depends on strict adherence to the project schedule, it is important that a project be staffed adequately to meet required turnaround needs.

The responsibilities associated with a typical ethnography study are listed here. Please note that these responsibilities are associated with roles and not necessarily individuals. Any particular person may handle multiple responsibilities as needed. These roles also overlap to a high degree, and more than one function can be addressed by a single individual.

The *project director* is responsible for the client relationship and overall project coordination. The director has ultimate responsibility for delivering all components of the project according to the client's needs and expectations. He or she normally plays a consulting role in project planning and delivery of findings and is responsible for the performance of all subordinates.

The *project manager* is primarily responsible for organizing people, equipment, and tasks in any given market or country. Managers are also responsible for all local logistics, and arrangements, and they are the team's main link to the overall project director.

The *recruitment coordinator* handles all arrangements for recruiting, orienting, and scheduling the study's subjects. The recruitment coordinator is also responsible for obtaining and communicating clear travel directions for every site to the managers, ethnographers, videographers, and client coparticipants who will visit the site.

The *ethnographers* are primarily responsible for data collection during the site visit. They are the key people at the site who interact with respondents.

The *videographers* are responsible for any videotaping at the site.

Translators may work at the site or after data is collected to convert local languages into the primary reporting language, which is usually English.

Case analysts are responsible for organizing all information collected at the site—written notes, videotapes, audiotapes, photos, and so on—and integrating and summarizing them with supporting participant quotes in a consistent manner according to the topics in the analysis template. The case analyst is responsible for making inferences and drawing conclusions about the ethnographic encounter. This role may be accomplished by those collecting the data or by analysis specialists. Underhill (2000), for example, says that his "trackers"—observers who follow customers through stores noting shopping behaviors—are expected to write their own summaries and make inferences.

Analysts and report/presentation writers are responsible for the summary report, which is developed after internal brainstorming and review and analysis of all site reports. The work of analysts may be supported by qualitative analysis (QA) software programs and presentation packages such as Microsoft PowerPoint.

A team approach, emphasizing cooperation and full sharing of information learned during the site visit, usually advances meaningful analysis.

TRAINING AND PREPARATION

To create a functioning team, training and preparation of internal staff and associates, external support personnel, videographers, and clients are essential components of ethnographic studies. It is necessary for all staff on the ethnography team to be working from the same perspective, speaking in the same voice, and aiming toward the same objectives. Here are several guidelines for conducting training.

Project-specific training. Everyone involved in the project should have a thorough grounding in client objectives and substantive information needs. They should also have a comfortable familiarity with the brands and product categories being studied. Clients usually can provide this background information, if necessary. Project staff should also be sufficiently familiar with the observation guide so that they do not have to consult it frequently during the site visit.

Internal staff and associates. Because internal staff and associates will bear primary responsibility for conducting and supervising site visits, they should receive the highest level of training. If they are unfamiliar with this methodology, they should demonstrate considerable prior experience in qualitative research methodology. This experience can be evidenced by university or postgraduate training in a social science discipline or several years of employment as a qualitative research practitioner. Staff and associates should also have a thorough educational and experiential grounding in the marketing and product development disciplines. Reading of case studies and methodological texts in cultural anthropology and ethnographic sociology can sometimes substitute for some actual experience.

The substantive knowledge background that fieldworkers should have acquired prior to undertaking site visits includes:

- Basic social scientific concepts, language, and perspectives
- Understanding of human behavior and motivations, particularly in a cross-cultural context
- Familiarity with interviewing skills and routines, such as the proper way to ask questions and probe for more information
- Skills in making and recording observations of behavior
- An understanding of the creative process and how this can be applied in both data collection and analysis
- Skills in organizing information and analyzing these into meaningful generalizations

Client representatives and coparticipants. Clients accompanying ethnographers on site visits should receive the highest level of preparation possible. Often, clients balk at the added time commitment and expense associated with training; however, they should be encouraged to obtain at least a full or half-day of training. If this is not possible, they should be asked to participate in at least a one-hour orientation session. The Appendix contains a document titled the "Ten Commandments of Great Ethnography," which can serve as a guide to talking points for the one-hour orientation session.

The goal of client training should be to help client observers avoid making errors during the interaction with respondents, errors that might bias observations. The value of their input into the data-collection process should also be maximized. In fact, their familiarity with products and technology generally provides client representatives with a unique perspective during data collection. Consequently, client training should include the following substantive areas:

- The dynamics and flow of a site visit
- Interviewing skills, such as asking questions and probing in an appropriate and objective manner
- The basics of making and recording observations while avoiding rushed generalizations

Videographers. People with skills in documentary videography usually are best qualified to accompany ethnographers on site visits. However, they need to receive orientation to our particular needs. Experience has shown that the following directions need to be shared with videographers:

- Make sure to capture the entire context of behavior. Pan the entire environment in which a behavior is taking place. Record the equipment being used.

- Focus on behavior. Zoom in on any specific technique being demonstrated or product being displayed.
- Avoid close-up head shots unless the subject is being directly interviewed.
- Move frequently from wide angles to close-ups following the flow of the behavior.
- Avoid photographing the interviewers.
- Be as unobtrusive with the video camera as possible.
- Above all, the video should be an exact record of the dynamics of behavior being researched. It should be comprehensive and thorough.

Equipment: The Ethnography Kit

It is helpful for everyone involved in a site visit—ethnographers as well as client co-observers—to bring an ethnography kit to record observations or to use as a backup so that valuable details are not missed. The contents of the kit may include:

- *Notebooks and pens/pencils:* Small-format, spiral bound notebooks (9.5 × 6 in. or 24.1 × 15.2 cm) are the least intrusive and most manageable during the site visit.
- *Audio recorders:* High-quality digital voice recorder (DVR) or stereo Walkman-type recorders work best. Most DVRs can record up to 20 hours of sound. If tapes are used, they should be 120 or 90 minutes in length to avoid having to change them frequently during the site visit. An auto-reverse feature is helpful; otherwise, the tape should be checked often so that it doesn't run out while the respondent is talking.
- *Photo camera:* A small-format digital camera or "one-time-use" disposable camera with indoor flash capabilities for making still photographs is usually useful even if the site is being video-recorded.
- *Measurement devices:* Depending on client objectives, any or all of the following may be needed on a site visit:
  - *Timer:* For measuring the amount of time allocated to an activity, a stopwatch or an inexpensive kitchen timer is usually sufficient.
  - *Weight scale:* For measuring the amount of product used in a particular task, an inexpensive kitchen scale or "hook" scale serves well.
  - *Sample collection devices:* Usually at the client's discretion, ethnographers may be asked, for example, to collect samples of particular soils, stains, or residues. Client co-observers can usually accomplish this task if they are part of the site visit team. If the client is asking for collection of samples, ethnographers should be thoroughly briefed by the client on how to do it properly.
- *Respondent agreements:* It is usually helpful to bring along a copy of the respondent information material as well as a copy of the Statement of Confidentiality, Consent, and Release for the ethnographer and respondent

to sign as the visit begins. These forms are good to help establish rapport in that respondents feel that on signing the form, their role in the study is official. It also helps to reassure them that their rights and privacy will be respected. The respondent agreement should contain assurances that the information collected will be for research purposes only and that all transcriptions, photos, and video will be used for internal reports only and not released to the public without further written consent. It also should circumscribe the responsibilities of respondents to provide accurate information and behavioral representations as well as the right to terminate the visits at any time and decline to answer any questions they find disturbing. A sample confidentiality form is included in the Appendix.

- *Labels for notes, tapes, videos, and other data:* It is imperative to establish a consistent system of labeling for project documentation. Each document or tape entered into the project record *must be neatly labeled* as follows:

Date

Location

Project code name

First name or code name for the participant

Principal demographic or usage category

- Organizing and retrieving information for later analysis becomes complicated if all items have not been correctly labeled from the start of the study.

VIDEO ARRANGEMENTS

Video recording creates numerous opportunities and challenges for an ethnographic study. Videotaping is useful for data recording and review as well as for associated training and orientation. All decisions about videotaping should depend strictly on client objectives and expectations.

It is not necessary that all or any site visits get videotaped. In fact, if cost, cultural, organizational, or other factors dictate against videotaping, other data-collection tools should suffice to achieve the study's research goals. On the other hand, for effective reporting, demonstration, and presentation, there is nothing equal to video. Archived videotapes are also useful for later reanalysis and comparisons over time.

If respondent videos are to be used in any public forum, such as sales meetings or promotional events, cooperating participants should be informed of such usage. They should also be given the opportunity to sign a separate release and receive separate incremental compensation.

The primary concerns around the use of videography in connection with ethnography are related to the need for respondent orientation and avoiding intrusiveness during the site visit.

Respondent orientation. If videotaping will be used, respondents should be informed of that at the time of recruitment, and they should be given an explanation of reasons behind its use. It is usually adequate to describe video simply as the "most efficient recording tool."

Avoiding intrusiveness. At the site visit, we do *not* want the videotaping to hinder respondent cooperation, encourage them to perform for the camera, or engage in nontypical behaviors. Consequently, using the smallest, most discreet, high-quality technology is required.

It is also helpful to give the respondent some time to relax with the camera. The increasing proliferation of video surveillance and growing popularity of reality television programming worldwide have made people media savvy and comfortable with recording devices. Unfortunately, these developments have also spurred a tendency toward exhibitionism. Not calling unnecessary attention toward and dwelling on videotaping is essential; after a brief time with the camera running, most respondents generally ignore its presence.[2]

Recommended technology. Discreet miniaturized digital video cameras have revolutionized documentary videography by allowing the capture of broadcast quality film with minimal equipment. *High-8 format* video cameras and film are also very useful for these reasons. This equipment has the advantages of providing commercial quality recordings without the use of extra lighting, which is very important to avoid. This format also offers time-coding on the recording, which helps during later analysis and video editing.

Alternative video recording. Depending on client objectives, it may be necessary to deploy passive fixed video or other filmed formats.

Passive, fixed-video units may be installed in stores, amusement centers, and other public areas. Some respondents may permit installation of a camera in their homes. Even though a video operator need not always be present, discreet supervision is needed to change tapes and check for the integrity and continuous operation of the device. The advantage of this resource is continuous monitoring of behavior over a lengthy period of time in the same place; consequently, researchers can observe impacts of environmental factors such as the locations of displays, signage, and merchandising.

Time-lapse technology, which speeds up the passage of time as viewed on film, is also very helpful in studying environmental factors involved in product usage and selection. This technique can reveal traffic patterns in parks or airport terminals. William H. Whyte (1980), for example, pioneered the use of time lapse photography to demonstrate that pedestrians behaved in predictable ways while navigating the urban environment.

Feelings of safety and comfort, for example, could be shaped by the barriers and visual impediments along the streetscape, and, in his view, manipulating the landscape had the potential for revitalizing urban areas by altering the subjective experience of public spaces.

Time-lapse photography was critical for Whyte in demonstrating patterns that could be influenced in positive directions.

Notes

1. Michael Erard's (2004) *New York Times* article provides several interesting examples of how the ethnographer's understanding of culture has stimulated several unique products, including a mobile phone with an embedded compass to allow Muslims to locate Mecca.

2. For an opinionated exploration of the new reality-based programs, see Sella, 2000.

8

Respondent Recruitment

R espondent recruitment can be one of the most vexing and problematic aspects of an ethnographic study. Specifying appropriate respondents in a manner that does not bias results, respecting respondent autonomy and self-determination, and motivating respondents in a manner that preserves the integrity of the research site are problems that must be handled wisely. Market research is generally categorized by whether it takes place in private or public settings and whether the respondents are being addressed as individuals or as undifferentiated actors in a public setting.

Recruitment in Public Settings

Studies that require the respondent to reveal personal behaviors not normally conducted in public or that require entry into private space must always follow the rules of formal recruitment and informed consent. For example, observing how homemakers do the laundry or how they make decisions about detergents at the supermarket always requires the cooperation and consent of the individual respondent. The same is true if a respondent is intercepted and asked questions about product preferences at a public shopping mall.

On the other hand, if the ethnography is taking place in a public setting and involves behavior normally enacted in public without any specific expectation of privacy, serious consideration should be given to how individuals and sites will be selected. For example, the management of a supermarket chain wishes to use behavioral data about the ways customers use in-store pet food displays and point-of-purchase resources, such as a coupon dispenser. They determine that the best way to gather data about this behavior is to videotape shoppers at the aisles, to analyze the behavior of customers in general, and to select a segment of these customers for intercept interviews designed to obtain additional insights and consumer reactions to several proposed modifications of in-store designs. Some of the vexing questions associated with this research design include:

- *Should the ethnographer reveal that the environment or the respondent is being watched?* Normally, consumers do not expect privacy in a supermarket; furthermore, they expect security surveillance in most commercial establishments and pay little attention to cameras set up for that purpose. Ethical responsibilities to the respondent nevertheless suggest that, indeed, there should be some noticeable disclosure that surveillance for research purposes is being conducted. (Suggestions for how to handle this responsibility are reviewed below.) When a store is designated this way, people who enter are giving their tacit approval for participation.

- *If a subset of respondents is being selected for further attention, how should they be selected and recruited?* Marketers and merchandisers may want to pay extra attention to customers with specific age-related needs, such as children or seniors, or they may be interested in how to better meet the expectations of a predominant category of shoppers, such as mothers between 18 and 35. These segments may receive extra attention in analyzing the general video record without concern. However, if particular people are selected for extra interviewing, full disclosure should be made that they have already been part of the passive video record. They should be given information about why they have been selected for additional attention; they should receive some consideration—cash or a nonbiasing gift—for their cooperation; and they should be asked to sign a Statement of Confidentiality, Consent, and Release covering any further research activity. At this point, they have been transformed from members of an undifferentiated group of shoppers to individual respondents, and their rights to decline from being a part of even the passive record need to be respected.

- *What exactly should prospective respondents be told about the research?* Respondents should be informed about the auspices and objectives of the study to the highest degree possible without biasing or informing them in a manner that threatens data validity.

- *Can ethnographers preserve the site in its natural state despite observation?* There is some debate about whether the site can be kept free of bias if the fact of research observation is disclosed in a manner that creates respondent self-consciousness and possible performance for the observer. If research conclusions are in doubt because of this problem, additional investigation using other approaches should be conducted to confirm results.

Regardless of how the researcher addresses the issues associated with research in public spaces, the norms of objectivity, integrity, site preservation, and respondent protection must constantly guide the approach.

COVERT RECRUITMENT

Rules of ethical research usually require that respondents be given information about the research, that they are formally or informally recruited to serve as informants, and are given the privilege of declining.

Some types of research in natural environments, such as mystery shopping, however, depend on spontaneous interaction with consumers in natural settings such as discount stores, bars, or banks. In these situations, it is hard to preserve naturalness if the fact that research is being conducted is disclosed. For example, if we are accumulating information on the interaction between customers and service providers in a fast-food restaurant, it would be impossible for staff *not* to be on their best behavior if they knew they were being watched.

In these situations, we must use strategies for approximating informed consent so that the ethical spirit is preserved in its entirety. If researchers may not reveal their role and participants must be recruited covertly, several strategies for limiting the damage of overtness may be employed. These typically involve:

1. Providing a generalized notification that does not distinguish exactly what is being watched

2. Providing notification that does not specify the time frame of observation

3. Gaining the authority to conduct general observation from a responsible third party

If covert recruitment and observation are taking place in an environment, research ethics may be addressed by placing a notification at the entrance to the store or restaurant stating that covert observations for research purposes are taking place. People who elect not to participate have the right not to enter. This information should be displayed with some prominence in a sufficiently large and readable typeface. A typical statement may read as follows:

> NOTICE: Covert observations and videotaping for market research purposes are taking place inside the store today. [OPTIONAL: If you do not wish to participate in this kind of activity or if you believe that this violates your privacy, please do not enter.]

People who enter the store after being given this information can be viewed as tacitly offering their informed consent.

A similar notification might be used at the entrance to a service provider:

> NOTICE: During the month of February, we will be conducting random observation of interactions between customers and agents for the purpose of improving our services to the public. [OPTIONAL: If you do not wish to participate in this kind of activity or if you believe that this violates your privacy, please do not enter.]

Presumably the longer time frame heightens the probability that participants will revert to naturalness and will be off-guard after a few days, thus revealing normal behaviors during customer encounters.

Many organizations that regularly study public encounters with their products or services generally provide clear notification to new hires at the time of employment that covert observation and mystery shopping will be used as marketing and service-assessment techniques. The employee handbook, employment contract, or verbal information transmitted at the time of hiring should formally communicate that the employer reserves the right to review performance by both overt and covert means. A standardized announcement may also be made to the public, putting everyone on notice that they may without other warning become part of a research activity.

FORMAL VERSUS INFORMAL RECRUITMENT

Formal recruitment involves a specific series of steps to inform prospective respondents about the study, seek access to private spaces, gain compliance and cooperation, and motivate and offer incentives to participate.

Informal recruitment, in contrast, is more subtle and likely to take place in studies covering public spaces. Prospective respondents are usually approached after they have shown evidence of some demographic or product-usage criterion and given an opportunity to participate or decline. For example, a study for a multinational brewer about drinking behavior in a bar or pub may look for patrons of a certain age or gender who have spontaneously ordered a particular brand of beer.

A study QualiData conducted for a fast-food chain sought adults who were coming for lunch or dinner together with children under the age of 12. After every nth party that appeared to meet the group composition and product-purchase criteria sat down, the families were approached by an ethnography team member who politely begged their pardon and proceeded to conduct informal recruitment. Here's a sample dialogue:

> We're doing a market research study here and would like to sit with your family and ask some questions while you're having dinner. We'll give you $10 if you let us sit with your family and ask questions and another $25 if you let us videotape your family eating together from now until you leave. It's OK to decline—either way, we'll give you all coupons for a dollar off your meal the next time you visit, just for letting us interrupt you.

This recruitment dialogue fulfills a number of conditions. It clearly defines the attempt to recruit as an interruption and infringement of personal space and provides a reward regardless of agreement to participate. It further specifies the time frame and conditions of observation, giving the respondent information relevant to making a choice.

If, as is likely, there are further recruitment criteria, these may be solicited once the customer stands ready to cooperate. In our restaurant study, agreement to participate was quickly followed by:

> Before we can accept you into the study, we need to know where you live to make sure that your home is within the service area of this restaurant.

Participants who agreed to videotaping were immediately handed a waiver and consent form to sign, allowing the use of their own and their children's images for research and internal presentation purposes.

This informal recruitment approach provided general information about the study, added an extra incentive for a higher level of participation, and allowed the respondent to decline with no penalty. Everyone approached was given coupons. Several restaurant guests approached the researchers, asking us if they could participate, but they were not accepted as these would have violated our standards for sampling.

Formal Recruitment Approaches

Respondent specifications. Formal recruitment requires specific and clear specifications so that the people recruited represent what the client regards as critical segments of its strategic marketing efforts. Specifications may represent demographics, product usage, attitudes about brands or the category, and so on. These characteristics are translated into a screening questionnaire or *screener*, which is administered to restrict participation to those that the client regards as necessary to the study.

Good screening depends on an operationalized definition of targeted respondents. For example, it is not enough to ask for "heavy users"; the precise usage level, such as "six times each month," must qualify respondents;

otherwise, determining a "heavy user" would be arbitrary and individualistic. Unbiased research outcomes require that the information has been collected from the correct participants. Because respondents are expected to represent the client's targeted segments, failure to recruit the appropriate ones will jeopardize the validity of the research.

Prioritized specifications. Because achieving a full spectrum of respondents across all specifications may be logically or practically impossible, it is important for the research user to articulate the two or three most important recruitment specifications for any project. Criteria that are too specific may be hard to actualize and add to time in the field and project costs.

Articulate and cooperative respondents. Having met substantive recruitment goals, it is also important to assemble respondents who are exceptionally cooperative and articulate, regardless of individual characteristics or social strata. People who previously have been effective participants in other forms of market research, such as focus group discussions, as long as they meet screening, past participation, and security restrictions, should be considered as good candidates for the respondent pool.

On the other hand, respondents who seem overly compliant and obsequious should be viewed with some skepticism. People who appear likely to misrepresent themselves or who seem too willing to please a researcher may not provide valid information.

Scheduling, travel directions, and maps. In an ethnographic project, the recruiter plays an important role in project logistics by scheduling the respondent visits and providing the site visit team with clear travel directions and maps. Scheduling should be sensitive to the amount of time required to travel between sites as well as the team's requirements for meals, relaxation, debriefs, and attention to other concerns.

Working outside the respondent's home. When observational research is conducted outside the respondent's residence—for example, in a restricted public space, such as a school, office, or business—the added problem of gaining access to the site must be addressed during recruitment. A separate recruitment step may be required. Also, incentive payments may be required for individuals who must authorize entry into private environments. For example, conducting an accompanied purchase in a department store may require authorization from the store manager; observations of nurses in a hospital setting will require approval by supervising authorities, as well.

Other public spaces, such as parks or playgrounds, may not require this type of authorization. No one's rights are abused if a recruited subject is asked to demonstrate some behavior in a public space. However, the researcher should still respect norms of public courtesy and the rights of others to use public spaces in an unimpeded manner.

Cultural and family structural issues. Norms of hospitality associated with visiting a home, as well as codes of authority that circumscribe gaining the cooperation of household members, should be considered during the recruitment process. These cultural rules may restrict who is to be consulted during recruitment, the gender of visitors to the household, and other features that impact the ethnographic process. In some cultures, for example, it may be inappropriate for men to watch the laundering of female undergarments.

Recruitment Guidelines

Whether responsibilities for recruitment are handled internally or through the services of an independent recruiter or a field service, it will be helpful to follow these guidelines and best practices:

Recruitment approach. Recruitment methods should be consistent with the study's objectives. There are several common sources for individuals who might be willing to cooperate in a study, including professional recruiters' internal databases, lists supplied by survey sampling companies and direct mail suppliers, and publicly available databases, such as telephone directories; random digit dialing may also be used. Screening through these approaches, as well as other resources in which prospective respondents have not opted into a pool of potential research participants, can be costly and time-consuming because securing respondent cooperation may be difficult and rare.

Potential subjects are sometimes recruited after being intercepted in such public places as a shopping street, a shopping mall, or a conference center. Recruitment through intercepts is appropriate if the researcher is reasonably sure that the type of person sought is likely to pass through the intercept point.

Screening. Strict adherence to a recruitment questionnaire that distinguishes the target respondents for a particular study is an important quality control measure. Screeners, as these are called, should be written and translated in a manner that allows for easy administration. All recruiters should be instructed to adhere to the screener script. In particular, recruiters should not prompt respondents beforehand about key screening requirements or inform them about responses that will cause them to be dropped from consideration. Recruiters should not dwell on the respondent incentive in a manner that subtly encourages dishonesty.

Identifying the client sponsor. It is not generally helpful to identify the corporate client sponsor during recruitment because it may bias toward selection of people who hold favorable views of a particular brand or manufacturer. This detail, provided that the client agrees, may be revealed at the conclusion of the research if the subject continues to be curious.

It is not advisable to offer study participants information on study findings as a motivation for participation because results are typically confidential.

Many public service clients feel differently about the issue of disclosure. In many cases, identification with a cause or issue may spur participation. Informing prospective participants that they are going to help authorities improve programs for HIV-positive patients or public transport systems is likely to appeal to social concerns or civic pride in a manner that overcomes the natural reluctance people feel about becoming part of a research study.

Setting the respondent incentive. A cash incentive is generally offered to participants in marketing ethnographies. Sometimes called the "co-op fee," the payment is generally offered at the end of the screening interview. How much to offer a prospective respondent is usually determined by various considerations.

• The offering is usually associated with rarity. Users of high-incidence products, such as soap, laundry detergent, and breakfast cereal, generally receive incentives at the low end of the scale. In contrast, low-incidence respondents, such as users of particular corporate computer programs, luxury automobiles, and business-class fliers, typically receive incentives at the upper end of the scale.

• The going rate in the countries and regions where research is done should be respected. Fees that are too high for local expectations are vulnerable to attracting respondents who will be overly compliant. On the other hand, in the United States and many other cultures, research participation is valued as a form of work, and respondents expect to be paid at a level commensurate with professional services employment. Thus, there is a distinct class bias in the assignment of incentives: Common demographic or occupational categories, such as middle income white-collar workers, receive incentives on the low end of the scale whereas high-income individuals, being harder to find in the general population and expecting a higher rate of remuneration for their services, can command higher incentives.

- Incentive fees are generally higher if some degree of respondent preparation or pretasking is required; for example, if respondents are required to sample a product or keep a diary prior to the site visit.

- The incentive should never be presented as payment for opinions because that tends to bias participants to views favorable to the client or places them in a performance frame of mind. Rather, the incentive should be described as compensation for the time and trouble of participating in the ethnography.

- The incentive may be paid in cash at the end of the site visit. If cash is used, the respondent should be asked to sign an Acknowledgment of Receipt of Cash for documentation purposes. If payment is not made at the time, respondents should be given clear information on the source and timing of payments.

- Never offer products in the category under study as an incentive because this may bias respondents and may also reveal the research sponsor. A token gift given at the end of a visit, along with the promised cash incentive, can be appropriate but is usually not necessary.

Above all, respondents should be recruited by appealing to higher goals and virtues: the opportunity to experience something novel and to help improve commonly used products. Participation in a unique and interesting activity on behalf of improving products for consumers like themselves should be a major draw. Motivating by money alone may yield cynical and manipulative respondents.

Overrecruitment. Because there is a natural attrition of recruited participants prior to site visits, it is generally necessary to recruit one or two more subjects per market than quotas require. If backup respondents are not actually visited in the study, the incentive must not be reduced because that household has already made its time and hospitality available to the researcher.

Managing recruitment. Quality control procedures at every stage of the recruitment process are necessary if problems are to be avoided. Adhering to several best practices will optimize the success of recruitment.

- Establish strict expectations and schedules
- Put everything in writing so that if problems arise, handling the situation will be easier
- Provide regular updates of recruitment progress; problems can be corrected early in the process if the researcher becomes aware of difficulties being experienced

Creating an Effective Screener

Good formal recruitment depends on the screening questionnaire to ascertain that potential respondents match the definition of the targeted consumer. Writing an effective screener is a combination of art and science. (Please note: A sample screener is provided in the Appendix.)

Clear specifications that are operationally defined and measurable in an objective manner form the basis of an effective screener; some examples might be females, mix of ages between 21 and 49, and primary household cleaner. Various types of respondent characteristics can be established through screening, including

- Demographic groups: age, gender, income, household composition, geographic and ethnic segments
- Product usage categories: frequent users, light users, those who have tried and rejected the brand, users of competing brands, and so on
- Attitudinal or psychographic groups: people who consciously or unconsciously share motives or feelings about various brands or categories; for example, those who aspire to a higher social status, who are receptive toward new products, and who express brand loyalty
- Trend-oriented groups: emerging segments such as teenagers, high-fashion oriented, artists and gays

Past participation and security screening. It is necessary to screen out participants who work with competing companies, in trade channels, or with marketing and advertising firms. This is a very important security consideration because the sponsor normally does not want an insider's view but rather an unvarnished consumer perspective. Furthermore, potential competitors can disclose findings; even the fact of conducting research on a particular topic may tip competitors to corporate strategies or concerns.

Past participation limits are usually set at 3 months, 6 months, or a year, at the client's discretion. These limits are set to eliminate respondents who are possibly being overused in research and thus losing the innocence and naiveté about research that ought to characterize the average consumer. On the other hand, a high past-participation limit can increase the cost of a study because, as market research studies are proliferating, average consumers are becoming more savvy about perspectives and methods common in the market research discipline.

Quality control of screener development. The following quality control points will help in designing screeners:

- Be realistic. Do not overdefine the targeted respondents or they will be difficult to find.
- Keep the screener as brief as possible. Avoid asking "nice to know" information questions not directly related to screening criteria.
- Use only one variable per question. For example, avoid questions like, "Do you enjoy purchasing cleaning products and using them regularly?"
- Ask questions directly using active verbs; for example, *use, prefer,* or *buy.*
- Do not frame questions in a leading way or in a manner that alerts the respondent to critical requirements. Leading questions often provide too much information; for example, "We're looking for people who drink at least three cups of coffee per day. Is that your practice?"
- Use plain consumer language. Avoid trade terminology or marketing jargon. Avoid regional or local colloquialisms.
- Be specific on screening and quota requirements.
- Place major disqualifiers at the beginning of the screener. These are questions that could terminate a respondent from consideration if not answered acceptably.
- Place sensitive questions, such as those dealing with income, toward the end of the screener.
- Type instructions to interviewers in bold or upper case so they can be easily differentiated when the screener is being administered.
- Avoid yes/no questions as much as possible.
- Do not always use the first or last response category as your disqualifiers requiring termination. Experienced research subjects often know that the first and last categories ought to be avoided.
- Phrase questions in an open-ended manner as often as possible. For example, instead of asking, "Do you use Gillette shaving gels?" the smart researcher inquires, "What brand of shaving gel do you use?"
- Make the terminating conditions—those that may disqualify a prospect from participation—as clear as possible. Do not leave serious judgments up to the recruiters because they may not have sufficient background or may be too self-interested to disqualify any particular prospect. For

example, if being articulate is a criterion, do not have the interviewer make a judgment about who is articulate or not.

- If a product or brand variant is required, do not rely on your respondent to recall all of the fine points. It may sometimes be necessary to ask them to reach for an actual product so that they can read information off the label.

Follow-up. The key to successful recruitment is consistent follow-up. Here are several steps that should be followed:

- Inform respondents of how the follow-up will be handled. Leave each respondent with a contact name and number. Instruct them to call the recruiter if they are no longer available as scheduled so that a replacement can be found.
- Be culturally sensitive in handling the follow-up. Some participants may find repeated reminder calls disruptive or annoying.
- Send a follow-up appointment confirmation letter along with the respondent information sheet.
- Call respondents at least twice to confirm. The last confirmation call should take place within 24 hours of the site visit.

9

Respondent Orientation

Marketing ethnographers prefer respondents who are collaborators, allies, and partners to those who are naïve or misled. Respondents are cultural experts who are willing to share details of their lives and everyday experience for the benefit of the client. An informed respondent who understands the process ahead of time and has a commitment to research project goals is our most effective partner in research. By *informed*, we are not referring to someone who has been prompted about anticipated research outcomes. Instead, it implies a respondent who understands the steps involved in ethnography and is committed to providing the most accurate and honest depiction of behaviors and attitudes. The key objective here is encouraging *natural* behaviors. A respondent who is too compliant and deferential is as much of a threat to research validity as one who is hostile.

Another objective in orienting respondents is to maintain the integrity of the site. If the act of observation dramatically changes a consumer's practices or behaviors, then the data collected are potentially invalid and misleading. Thus, it is necessary to make certain that the respondent has not gone out to purchase products or equipment for the benefit of the visitors or has not rearranged the house or workplace for the benefit of observers and will adhere to their normal schedules.

Finally, we want to allow respondents to anticipate—as much as possible without biasing results—how the site visit will be conducted. Surprises at the site tend to discourage spontaneity and are experienced as threatening and disorienting by subjects.

Orientation of respondents begins with the recruitment process, continues through follow-up, and gets reinforced when the site visit is initiated. A written *participant information memo*, which outlines the most important conditions of proper cooperation and answers the most frequently asked questions, is a useful information tool. Whether or not printed information is offered to respondents, recruiters and ethnographers should be prepared to provide this information verbally and answer any additional questions that respondents may present.

A sample participant information memo is provided in the Appendix. Reviewed below are the issues and questions that prospective subjects usually bring to the exercise; these should be addressed during the recruitment and orientation.

Who Is Conducting the Study?

It is usually enough to provide the name of the research company and to say that the study is being conducted "on behalf of a well-known consumer products manufacturer" or other client category. Divulging the name of the client at the outset of a project may create conditions for bias because respondents may feel obligated to say something "nice," avoid complaints, or go out and buy that client's products before observers arrive at their homes. Some respondents may also have political objections to the sponsoring client, especially it seems if the client is involved in the manufacture of tobacco products, alcoholic beverages, oil or pharmaceuticals.

Questions About the Study

WHY IS THE STUDY BEING DONE?

It is reassuring for respondents to learn that market research studies are conducted so that manufacturers and marketers can better understand consumers' needs and expectations. This knowledge normally stimulates ideas for new and improved products or better ways of talking about the product.

WHY IS THE STUDY USING AN ETHNOGRAPHIC APPROACH?

Subjects who are familiar with other research methods sometimes need to be sold on the ethnographic approach to data collection. Respondents may be made aware that research studies carried out through other methods have several limitations that can be overcome by having observers visit their own environments and watch them in the act of using the product or category. It is motivating to say that this is a rare and special type of research approach that focuses on subjects' own unique ways of getting things done.

Questions About the Site Visit

WHAT HAPPENS DURING THE SITE VISIT?

Prospective subjects are reassured when informed of the course that the site visit is likely to take. All of the techniques and data-recording devices to be employed in the site visit should be disclosed. Respondents should be told, for example, that the observers will carry along notebooks and tape recorders to make sure they don't miss any valuable details or that observers may take still photos. This is also the time to introduce discussion of the video camera if it is part of the data collection strategy. Respondents should be aware that an oral and visual record of each household will allow the researcher to compare the many ways in which different people complete tasks; this helps researchers to recognize patterns and generalizations.

HOW LONG WILL THE VISIT TAKE?

Researchers should be frank and open about the length of time the visit may take because the respondent has multiple additional responsibilities to manage and needs to schedule time judiciously.

WHO WILL BE VISITING MY HOME?

An accurate description of the research team's composition will be helpful, although describing authority relationships among the site visit team in great detail may intimidate respondents and hinder disclosures. For example, if they are told that an individual is someone else's "boss" or supervisor, respondents may feel that this person requires some extra courtesies. It is our practice to remind respondents that all visitors have been instructed to be good guests—to stay out of their way and to respect their privacy.

WHAT WILL THE OBSERVERS DO?

It should be made clear that the observers are visiting to watch and take notes about how the respondent is carrying out the tasks under investigation. Also, the cooperating participant should be reminded that usage will be observed from the very start to finish of the activity. Subjects should be informed that along with observation, the interviewers will speak with them at length, and possibly with other household members, to gain a better understanding of the context, methods, and ideas behind usage.

BUT I DO THINGS MY OWN WAY—IS THAT OK?

Respondents should be reminded that visitors are coming without expectations and have no judgments about the right or wrong ways to accomplish tasks. They should also be informed that the researchers want to see a range of respondents in their natural environments using products in their own unique routine ways.

HOW SHOULD I PREPARE FOR THE HOME VISIT?

The natural human inclination to be hospitable, proper, and correct should be challenged as necessary. Respondents should be discouraged from doing anything to prepare for the site visit. For example, if the purpose of the visit is to observe home cleaning patterns, respondents should be actively discouraged from engaging in the normal act of cleaning their homes before guests come over. Also, to maintain the integrity of the site and assure validity, respondents should be told not to buy any products they do not generally use and to wear the clothing they normally wear while engaging in the tasks to be studied rather than "dressing up" for guests.

In cultures where hospitality norms are strong, it may be unavoidable to allow the respondent to share a beverage or snack, as long as these are not the research focus. On the other hand, respondents should normally be discouraged from providing meals or other considerations to the visiting team.

WILL ANYONE BE SELLING ME SOMETHING? INSTRUCTING ME?

Respondents often cynically believe that the purpose of the site visit is commercial: to demonstrate new products or techniques with the ultimate aim of selling them to the householder. This innocent but understandable belief should be absolutely discounted. A brief point about the objectives of market research sometimes needs to be reinforced here, that the purpose is to learn from customers and to gain insights into needs and potential improvements for the general marketplace, not to sell products directly.

Unethical marketers sometimes engage in selling under the guise of research (sometimes called "sugging" by industry insiders). This practice should be exposed and condemned whenever found because it contaminates the goodwill that average consumers bring to the research process.

Questions About Privacy

WHAT ABOUT CONFIDENTIALITY?

Respondents are often reluctant to participate out of concern that their names will end up on a marketing list or database. To counter this, we must promise them the highest possible level of confidentiality for the observations and any information provided in interviews. We must assure respondents that names, identities, and areas of residence will not appear in reports based on the research.

WHO WILL BE SEEING THE TAPES AND REPORT?

Respondents should be assured that the study is only for clients' marketing information purposes and not for public broadcast or for use in advertising. In general, only clients and research consultants are privileged to see copies of any notes, photos, documents, or reports that come out of the study. If a broader usage or dissemination is planned for any of the research products, ethical guidelines require that respondents should be informed of this; they should be allowed to grant consent separately and receive additional compensation.

Questions About Recruitment

HOW DID I GET INVITED TO PARTICIPATE?

Respondents are frequently curious about how they were selected or what aspect of their profile qualified them for participation. A frank description of the range of respondents participating in the study, for example, "different types of households, including those with and without children, older and younger people," is sufficient to address the issue.

WHO ELSE IS PARTICIPATING?

Respondents often want assurance that other participants in the study are like themselves. Specific names of other participants should not be divulged unless references have been required to complete recruitment. If another respondent's name needs to be provided, ethical obligations require that the person's consent is obtained in a noncoercive manner first.

WILL ANYTHING HAPPEN IF I DECLINE OR CONSENT TO ONLY ONE PART OF THE OBSERVATIONAL INTERVIEW?

This is a very delicate matter. Normally, if someone agrees to participate, they should make a commitment to cooperate with all aspects of the research project as long as they are informed of all relevant details. On the other hand, if respondents change their mind and do not wish to participate for any reason, they have every right to decline. Similarly, if respondents elect to terminate the visit before the research is concluded, their wishes should be respected.

HOW MUCH WILL I GET PAID?

The amount and form of payment should be settled at the time of recruitment. Respondents should be assured that at the end of the observation period, in appreciation for their time and cooperation, they will receive the cash stipend promised by the research company. However, it should be stressed that participation in the project should be novel and enjoyable—by no means done under duress. Again, respondents may need reminding that research participation gives them a chance to offer advice and opinions that reach the highest decision-making levels of major corporations.

WHAT IF I HAVE OTHER QUESTIONS?

Respondents should always be given the name and telephone number of the recruitment coordinator and encouraged to call in case additional issues and questions arise.

10

Logistics in the Field

I n this chapter, we discuss organizational strategies for getting teams together and facilitating their work in the field.

Teaming With Clients

Purchasers of ethnographic services vary in terms of the degree of involvement they expect during the data collection and interpretation process. Co-participation offers client representatives—whether drawn from research, marketing management, technical research and development, or senior management ranks—a valuable opportunity to interact with and learn from their customers and prospects. It should be encouraged.

Facilitating client co-observation should proceed with the understanding that it may not interfere with the goals of gathering data in the most reliable and unbiased manner. Effective co-observation involves sharing ethnographic perspectives and skills, organizing client involvement in a careful manner, and providing consistent direction and clear orientation to expectations.

Here are several guidelines to maximize client involvement.

Role of the client project manager. Clear lines of authority and accountability on the client side must be established. Responsibility for managing client co-observation logistics must reside with the client project manager. The client should determine who within the organization will get involved in site visits, how often, and when. The client project manager should handle internal scheduling, travel instructions, and participation in client training.

Participation of nonresearch clients. Experience repeatedly has shown us that client co-observers drawn from the ranks of marketing, brand management, technical R&D, and senior management, as well as advertising agency partners are effective and enthusiastic in working with ethnographers.

Several cautions should be respected, however, in organizing their participation:

- Orientation to market research perspectives and methods is particularly important if these executives have not previously had a deep level of involvement in project execution.
- Scheduling and logistical coordination with nonresearch co-observers can present additional complications because their responsibilities tend to be more pressured.

Client training and orientation. The client project manager should guarantee that everyone involved in co-observation receives training and orientation in ethnographic approaches and skills. This is to guarantee that everyone on the team understands his or her respective roles vis-à-vis the ethnographers and respondents. Extended training also enhances the client's value in the data collection process. We need to guarantee that client co-observers do not engage in well-intentioned but misguided interactions with respondents, such as aggressive probes, improperly phrased questions, or overt praise for using the client's product. Client observers should guard against even subtle clues that may betray their corporate identity, such as speaking to respondents while wearing jackets with company insignia.

Logistical coordination. Experience has demonstrated that the following are best practices associated with coordinating client co-observation:

- Make a list of client co-observers, noting their general availability and schedule preferences, as the fieldwork is being recruited.
- If clients have a preference for certain respondent characteristics—for example, heavy users or younger respondents—they should make these clear to the client project manager before assignments to site visits are made because changing them afterward may involve complications.
- As particular sites are recruited, they should be assigned to matching clients.
- These assignments should be verified with the co-observer and put in writing as a scheduling memo. The individual schedules should then be integrated into our final master schedule.
- After co-observers have received all their site assignments, travel arrangements should be made.
- Client co-observers should inform the client project manager about their hospitality arrangements—hotel name and room, or private accommodation, address, and telephone number—as soon as these are known.

Logistics Management

Daily logistical coordination. Create a daily master schedule that provides a listing of sites, respondent characteristics, appointment times, travel directions, and the identity of the lead ethnographer at each site. Make copies of the daily master schedule for all of the site visitors so that everyone is aware of the overall plan for the day and knows where other team members can be found at any given time slot.

Daily coordinator. One of the ethnographers should be designated each day in the field as the daily coordinator. This person has the final accountability for sharing schedule changes and dealing with issues that arise during the day. Some daily matters that might need attention include correcting schedule details, informing everyone of a time change, or arranging for a client orientation session. The daily coordinator should be contacted by all site teams at the end of their visits.

Site teams. Each day, all project participants should be aware of their own site teams. Our practice is to "mix and match;" that is, alternate team composition each day so that the strengths of everyone involved in the project may be leveraged best.

Material distribution. The daily coordinator has final responsibility for making sure that all site teams have the necessary ethnography kits and observation guides in their possession and for organizing the activities of videographers on the project.

Transportation to sites. The research agency should also take responsibility for coordinating transportation to sites. In some cases, this involves hiring cars or drivers.

Mobile phones. It is a good idea to share mobile phone numbers so that problems can be solved or arrangements discussed with the daily coordinator. The mobile phone numbers for the daily coordinator and each team may be listed on the daily schedule.

Morning or evening (de)briefing. It is usually helpful to schedule a meeting of all site teams each morning or evening to share experiences, discuss observations at sites during the day, inform everyone of schedule changes, and discuss site protocols or any other relevant matters.

Teamwork. Even though local logistical arrangements can be challenging, we find that a high degree of solidarity and team spirit develops on each project. Being off in unfamiliar places together, learning about each other as people, sharing daily discoveries, and overcoming routine problems stimulate feelings of mutual support and friendship. Ethnography is a shared, enjoyable experience—it's fun!

However, to support congeniality and teamwork all project team members should be sure to show respect and consideration to everyone else, to avoid letting their own concerns and agendas overwhelm everyone else on the team, to refrain from judging others on the team, to respect site formalities, and to maintain a positive attitude.

Site protocols. As a component of the scheduling memo distributed to site visitors, it is helpful to include a list of site protocols that define relationships and process during the visit. An important feature of site relationships is that the ethnographer takes the role of lead interviewer, and client site-visit team members act in a supporting role. It is also necessary for everyone to meet at the location several minutes before the visit is scheduled to begin and enter the site together so that the lead ethnographer can initiate the interview.

Cautions and Contingencies

To guarantee smooth operation of the ethnographic research process despite the inevitable challenges, we recommend the following:

Maximum number of site visitors. Our recommendation is that the number of visitors at a site be limited to three. In extreme circumstances, a fourth visitor may be acceptable; however, numbers greater than this tend to be disruptive and compromise validity in data collection.

No nit-picking. If client co-observers need to discuss issues with ethnographers, the appropriate moment for this is after the visit and out of earshot of the respondents. Public displays of disagreements are never warranted.

Schedule changes. Because ethnographic research is conducted in the real world, there will be inevitable cancellations and delays. If such problems occur, communication is the best remedy. Everyone on the site team and respondents should be made aware of any changes immediately.

Early departures to and from the site. We recommend that the entire team enter and depart together. Nevertheless, if someone needs to depart, we let respondents know about this at the outset, lest they feel insulted or aggrieved by an abrupt early departure.

If all of the project management procedures and site arrangements have proceeded as planned, the marketing ethnographer should now be ready to initiate fieldwork. To guide these next steps, this text will now discuss tactics and procedures for conducting site visits.

PART III

Conducting Site Visits

11

Site Visit Overview

This section reviews the issues involved in conducting site visits. Numerous challenges must be met to obtain high-quality data. Researchers are required to enter the field with the proper frame of mind and be prepared to manage sometimes unpredictable situations. Our intention is to establish a consistent framework of ground rules and strategies for achieving the highest level of researcher confidence and professionalism.

Challenges of Ethnography

Marketing ethnography is part of a family of overlapping qualitative research approaches and methods that, depending on the discipline, may be called on-site or in-home studies, observational research, hermeneutics, ethnomethodology, symbolic interactionism, participant observation, and phenomenological research. There are subtle differences between these approaches; however, extensive detail on these distinctions is beyond the purpose of this text.

Participant observation normally refers to the technique of going to live within another culture for an extended period of time, taking a community role, and eventually gaining an insider's perspective on the life ways of the group being studied. *Observational research*, in contrast, is restricted to direct observation in a manner more detached than participant observation. Researchers do not try to become community members; their exteriority is assumed and accepted. Direct observers strive to be as neutral and unobtrusive as possible to reduce the potential biasing impact they might have on respondents. Nevertheless, researchers are watching behavior rather than taking part in another culture.

Marketing ethnography makes extensive use of theories and ideas cultivated by the social scientific schools known as symbolic interactionism and phenomenology. Symbolic interactionism refers to a set of ideas about social behavior that emphasize centrality of the *definition of the situation* as the basis of social reality. Phenomenology is an important approach because it is concerned with the individual's inner experiences and how these are shaped by various assumptions and perceptions. Because they emphasize personal perspective and interpretation, symbolic interactionist and phenomenological concepts help to achieve an understanding of subjective experience, promote insights into people's motivations and actions, and reduce the clutter of taken-for-granted assumptions and conventional wisdom.[1]

As a market research approach, ethnography is distinct from other currently applied qualitative and quantitative research techniques because it minimizes the use of focus group studios, laboratories, telephones, or any other artificial barriers that mediate the relationship between the researcher and respondent. This bare-knuckled confrontation with the consumer entails solving a host of problems in pursuit of valid, reliable, and useful information. The issues are similar to those encountered by ethnographers throughout history:

- Recruiting representative and reliable informants
- Gaining access to the locations where products are purchased, consumed, and used
- Respecting the rights and privacy of research subjects
- Cultivating rapport with cooperating participants in a way that maximizes honest disclosure but prevents exploitation and manipulation
- Making observations in a fair and dispassionate manner
- Recording data without bias
- Respecting the integrity of the site—not changing what you are watching

Ethnography involves a combination of structured and improvisational data collection techniques at the site. The researcher may use a combination of both active and passive data-collection techniques.

Anything in and about the setting—not just responses to questions—can be considered relevant data, including many types of information that are not collected in other forms of market research:

- Handwritten fieldnotes that describe behavioral observations
- Tape recordings of conversations among people at the site or in-depth interviews conducted by the ethnographer
- Video recordings of consumers using products
- Personal documents collected at the site, such as a favorite recipe for a breakfast treat or a special home-cleaning remedy

- Product samples
- Photographs made to document observations
- Physical traces; for example, soiling left behind after an item is washed or floor markings on heavily used areas of the home

Goals and Ideals of Ethnographic Observation

Ethnography as a form of qualitative research is both a science and an art. It combines disciplined and structured investigation to pursue objectives with intuition and creative exploratory tools. It depends on practitioners who are skilled at searching for deeper truths and who have the interpersonal skills necessary to establish confidence and intimacy with people quickly.

The goals and ideals that structure an ethnographic study include the following:

A search for in-depth understanding of the consumer. Ethnographers go beyond surface answers and shallow observations to probe for deeper meanings and truths. Simple descriptive information is certainly important, but our objective is to go beyond that to delve for underlying meanings. Decoding behavior so that it yields insights that can teach clients how to satisfy consumer wishes more completely or to communicate with them in a more effective manner is our primary objective.

Seeing things from the consumer's point of view. Ethnographers practice empathy and work to suspend their own prejudices and predilections when they are exploring human behavior. By gaining the consumer's perspective, they become empowered as the consumer's advocate when new products are developed and communication campaigns are put in motion.

Being open to different points of view—keeping an open mind. Ethnographers should invite alternative perspectives that challenge their own ideas. They should enter the field with as few preconceptions as possible.

Exploring contexts and conditions. Ethnographers seek understanding and clarity. This may involve going beyond the product or category under study and drawing on comparisons to other products used in same environment; for example, learning about coffee usage may benefit from an understanding of evolving beverage preferences or breakfast habits in general. Ethnography looks for the why's, when's, and where's and also for the potential for flexibility and change in consumer choices. This search for context may involve the introduction of information beyond simple product usage. The ways in which consumers use paper towels in the home may relate to their feelings about cleanliness, the spread of germs, environmental waste, and other issues aside from those that inhere in product formulations.

Searching for the feelings and emotions behind people's behavior. People choose and react to products out of both rational and irrational needs. Ethnographers should probe for the emotions behind expressed attitudes by examining body language or looking for revealed meaning behind language. The perspectives of semiotics are useful in interpreting what verbal or physical expressions might really mean.

Describing attitudes and behavior with as much relevant detail as possible. This requires looking at the entire process in consumer behavior and motivations. Thus, for example, the act of doing the laundry involves more than just putting clothes into the washing machine. The ways in which items are sorted, pretreated, protected from the washing process, and so on all provide clues to underlying expectations and beliefs about laundry. Findings about the whole process offer clues to consumer expectations and standards for satisfaction that can generate ideas for new products.

Not assuming you know everything about a category. Ethnographers should approach every study as an opportunity to learn about new ideas, perspectives, and methods. They should always question assumptions and taken-for-granted truths about any brand or category.

Methodological flexibility. The specific range of tools and approaches used by ethnographers must be adapted depending on the product category of interest and consumer demographics.

Note

1. For further detail about theoretical perspectives behind ethnography and qualitative research, see Schutz (1970), Taylor and Bogdan (1984), and Denzin and Lincoln (1994).

12

Ethnographic Foundations

E thnographic market research is carried out by watching and talking
with consumers in a careful and structured way at stores, offices, the
street, homes, or anywhere else that people conduct their daily lives.

Ethnographic research strategies are most appropriate when some of
the following objectives are desired as the study's information outcomes:

- To study high-intensity interactions, such as a sales encounter or household
  decision making
- To conduct precise analyses of behavioral processes; for example, tooth
  brushing patterns or home-cleaning behaviors
- To study situations where the respondent's memory or reflection would
  not be adequate

The behaviors of interest to marketing ethnographers normally are
relevant to the interests of a sponsoring client and must be observable and
likely to occur within a reasonable time frame.

Interaction With Respondents

The degree of interaction with research subjects in ethnographic research
studies will vary along a spectrum of intensity. The two ends of the spectrum are referred to as *pure observation* and *participant observation.*

- *Pure observation:* involves very little or no contact between the
researcher and the subject; for example, watching how teenagers brush
their teeth, how passengers behave in an airport terminal or how shoppers
interact with a point-of-purchase display at their favorite supermarket.

- *Participant observation:* involves interaction between the observer and the subject. Sometimes, the observer's role as a researcher is acknowledged; at other times, it is not revealed. The traditional anthropological and sociological approach to participant observation involves having the researcher assume a community role over an extended period of time and make very general observations. In contrast, within market research the time frame is necessarily constricted, and the focus of the interaction can be very specific.

Pure observation research can be conducted in a variety of settings, including laboratories and research facilities, as would occur in a usability study or any other everyday "real world" setting. Participant observation studies, however, are usually conducted where people live their daily lives: in homes, offices, retail stores, and so on.

The role of the respondent in a marketing ethnography can be quite distinct from the manner in which respondents are managed in other forms of research. This approach seeks both behavioral and attitudinal information; that is, we both watch respondents as they enact some everyday behavior, and we also ask questions or discuss things in a manner that encourages respondents to describe the meanings and explanations behind what they are doing. Thus, the level of intimacy required is particularly critical. Researchers are required to consider the respondent as a whole person rather than just someone answering a set of questions. The respondent is the expert in this relationship, someone with a rich range of life experience whom we are trying to understand. Researchers learn a great deal about respondents, more than just which product they use to clean the kitchen counter.

Ethnographer Lisa Hardy reports a recent example:

> While interviewing a family about a vacation spot, I ended up learning that they were a close-knit Filipino household. The father had recently left them, and they missed having him with them. I viewed this information as more than just market data. I had to respect and care for the personal information they had given me about themselves. This should not be merely a deductive data-gathering session but also a chance to meet people and learn about their lives with specific attention to details regarding the subject of the study, like cleaning products or vacation spots.

The other distinction in ethnographies is that the focus is on the site and context. Consequently, even though a single household member has been recruited as the principal respondent, we should pay attention to everyone at the site when we are there; for example, members of the family, guests at a party, or fellow employees. Some of the most telling insights in a study can come from the child who challenges her mom about something she just claimed her kids prefer to eat for dinner.

In interactions with respondents, we must be concerned about a variety of issues that may damage comfort, openness, and honesty. We do not want them to think we have an agenda or a set of expectations. We do not want them to feel judged, nor do we want to heighten their suspicions and sensitivities. We do not want them to pretend or perform for the camera.

Guidelines for Interacting With Respondents

Ethnographers must act carefully and sensitively when they ask questions, note behavior, or follow up with probes with consumers about observed behaviors. Some cautions that are helpful in structuring the interaction include the following:

• Do not call attention to a behavior or practice that makes the respondent feel self-conscious; for example, "You just skipped that part of the program." Try not to probe at all until a behavioral routine is reaching completion.

• Minimize asking why a respondent is doing or not doing something in a particular way; for example, "Why didn't you clean in back of the TV set?" In general, refrain from making the respondent react defensively. With patience and keen observation, you will eventually discover if that area was avoided because the respondent believed that it was dangerous, because no current product was adequate, because he didn't care about that out-of-sight area, or other reasons. The immediate challenge is likely to provoke a defensive reaction, regardless of the true reason for the behavior.

• Avoid asking respondents directly to explain or to describe what they are doing step-by-step. This encourages self-consciousness and performance. Watch them carefully instead.

• Probe behavior gently and indirectly by asking respondents to describe their goals or intentions; for example, "Please describe what you are trying to accomplish" or "Please tell me how you expect this to go." Another way to probe is ask respondents to describe "What is going through your mind?"

• We have to respect the rights, property, and privacy of our participants. We must avoid interfering with the respondent's other responsibilities and relationships. For example, if a friend normally comes by to visit while dinner is being prepared, it is to our benefit to preserve that pattern of interaction. We must also be patient and tolerant if a nonresearch responsibility (e.g., a telephone call from a family member) suddenly breaks the respondent's attention.

- Participants must be thoroughly briefed about how the research will be implemented. Enough background information should be provided without informing respondents to such a degree that they lose spontaneity during the visits. Try to avoid surprises that are likely to confuse or disorient respondents.

- We should also try to minimize our own impact on the environment being studied so that we get to observe as much about its natural state as possible. This means not helping participants with tasks and not providing advice or otherwise influencing the way that the respondent naturally behaves. For example, if the respondent has been asked to prepare a meal, it is incorrect to accept and eat that meal—no matter how tasty it may appear—because the researcher's satisfaction, rather than respondent behavior, becomes the focus of the interaction. Similarly, if the respondent must carry unwieldy supplies from one location to another during the course of product usage, it is inappropriate for any site visitor to help.

- Be patient and tolerant about the course of activities during a site visit. Let the respondent set the pace; the ethnographer should not rush an activity or try to stop something already in motion.

- Because a high level of intimacy normally develops between ethnographer and respondent, matters that are entirely extraneous to the subject under investigation will come up for discussion: the news of the day, family composition, social activities, and personal interests. It is only natural for visiting researchers to share details about their own children or a recent vacation destination. Innocuous small talk supports rapport building especially when people find they share some commonality. Nevertheless, researchers should be careful about discussing their own opinions about professional matters or the category under investigation because these would also be out of role.

- Respondents sometimes encourage ethnographers to be more informal than would be optimal for the researcher role they need to play. Site visitors are sometimes offered a cocktail or a "social drug" for sharing with the host. This is usually a positive indication that a high level of trust and rapport has been established. As a general policy, however, ethnographers should not indulge in intoxicants at a site visit and should demur in a manner that does not indicate any judgment of the respondent's choices.

- Even though the observation guide will be used as a map or a blueprint to the process or behaviors we are exploring, it is not a strict questionnaire or program of events. We try to follow the guide as much as possible; nevertheless, we should be ready to stray from the guide as needed to follow, engage, or understand a respondent.

• The number of interviewer/observers should be restricted to no more than two or three people so that they don't become intrusive in the household.

• Respondents often incorrectly position ethnography visitors in the role of authorities and specialists on the category being studied. It is only natural for respondents to ask us to evaluate their behavior or make suggestions for solving vexing problems they have experienced. We have to decline graciously because playing the authority will diminish the respondent's sense of autonomy and aptitude. A good way to deflect a request for an evaluation is to make a noncommittal remark about the respondent's effort without commenting on results. For example:

Respondent: Doesn't this product put a great shine on my stove top?

Ethnographer: It certainly seems like you were trying to shine it.

If the respondent is given space to feel like the host and expert and the ethnographer remains modest and behaves as a privileged guest, the ethnographic encounter will prove to be enriching and satisfying for both parties.

Ethical Responsibilities

In conducting research at consumers' homes or places of business, several rules must be followed to preserve everyone's personal probity and to maintain proper research ethics.[1] The purpose of these principles primarily is to respect and defend the dignity, autonomy, and integrity of citizens who cooperate in the research enterprise. Moreover, ethical principles are necessary to sustain our ability to conduct research in an atmosphere of freedom and professionalism. In addition to meeting responsibilities toward research participants, ethnographers must also reflect a sense of accountability to the discipline and profession. The ethnographic enterprise can be sustained and maintain longevity only if its practitioners practice scrupulous ethics.[2] Our responsibility to participants includes these components.

Gain in advance the informed consent of individuals and environments being studied. The researcher must provide sufficient background about the study so that the respondent has an idea of its uses and who will have access to the collected material. Most market research studies, pointedly, are conducted in a context of client confidentiality, restricted access to data, and a competitive marketplace consistent with mature capitalism. If the researcher may not disclose the sponsoring client's identity for these reasons, the respondent should be made aware of that fact and be comfortable with its implications. If there will be any public use of the information—for example, in public service messages or in advertising—the respondent should provide separate consent for public uses.

Protect the confidentiality of information uncovered at the site. The ethnographer and client should make certain that details about the respondent's identity, personal behavior, and attitudes are not used for purposes other than those agreed on in advance. Data collected at the site should not be used for sales or marketing to the individuals being studied.

Similarly, if private information is discovered about the individual that goes beyond the purposes of the study and could be used in a desultory fashion at some later date, this should be eliminated from the record. For example, if a respondent is observed engaging in some illegal behavior at home that does not endanger anyone visiting the site—perhaps smoking a marijuana joint at a social event—this should not be reported on record.

In general, the data presentation should be aggregated; that is, respondents should be represented as members of a category rather than as individuals unless steps are taken to protect their privacy and autonomy if their identity is revealed.

If there will be any linkages between ethnographic data and other sources of information, such as motor vehicle records or supermarket purchase history, these external data collection efforts should be disclosed to participants in advance. A study of male sexual behavior in public restrooms conducted in the 1970s, Laud Humphreys' (1975) *Tearoom Trade* was widely condemned on ethical grounds because the researcher followed up observations of public sex by tracking the participants' home addresses and conducting follow-up interviews while concealing the grounds on which the respondents were selected. Although this study produced breakthrough findings on the characteristics of men engaged in public homosexual acts and demystified the attributes of this supposedly deviant subculture, it was conducted on the basis of questionable ethical premises.

RESPONSIBILITIES TO RESPONDENTS

Do no harm. The researcher must guarantee that on-site and outside activities and procedures in relation to respondents will not harm them physically, materially, or emotionally. At no point should a respondent be asked to do something dangerous. The need to practice this injunction may arise in unusual circumstances: During a site visit on home cleaning methods, a respondent was observed mixing ammonia and chlorine bleach—something most high school chemistry students learn produces a lethal gas. Even though one of the ethnographer's main injunctions is not to alter any practices observed at the site, in this case, the visitors held that ethical obligations to the respondent required us to warn her that this mixture was dangerous and should be avoided. As the respondent recovered from the dizzying effects of inhaling the fumes, she thanked us profusely for the advice.

Avoid discriminatory practices in respondent selection. Some research topics may require a focus on consumers who are identified with particular age, gender, ethnic, linguistic, racial, or religious categories. For example, in developing a communications program targeted to recent Latino immigrants, a cleaning products manufacturer may find it helpful to understand the cleanliness standards, brand memories, and product preferences of this group. Nevertheless, unless the action is clearly justified by research objectives, researchers should not arbitrarily exclude participants based on their identity status.

Respect respondent rights. Respondents have the right to refuse to answer any particular question and may terminate the site visit at will. They have the right to handle family matters in private, if necessary, or to invite someone to be present at the site visit simply to elevate their comfort level. The researcher must not manipulate personal authority or the offer of the respondent incentive to coerce behavior of any type.

Do no professional damage. The activities of marketing ethnographers should be structured so as to protect the interests and future work of those engaged in professional ethnography. Any activity and public disclosure that can jeopardize the ongoing work of others in the field and defame the profession should be avoided.

RESPONSIBILITIES TO CLIENTS

In addition to ethical responsibilities with respect to the profession and participants in a study, the ethnographer has strict responsibilities toward the sponsoring client.

Honest personal representation. Researchers may not misrepresent their credentials, qualifications, experience, and skill sets to obtain employment or a research contract. They should be truthful about the limitations of ethnographic methods and their own skills and experience. For example, they should not claim to have conducted research for a competitive client if they did not actually do so or obscure the fact of having worked for a competitor if they have.

Respect client confidentiality. Regardless of whether they have actually signed nondisclosure agreements, which makes this responsibility legally as well as ethically binding, researchers should not reveal proprietary research findings without prior approval. Some clients, for competitive reasons, prefer not to make public the methods they use in studying consumers; some even go so far as to abhor public announcement that they conduct market research.

Scrupulous record keeping. Consultants have both an ethical and practical obligation to maintain exacting records related to their interaction with respondents. Thus, if details are in question, the client can refer to the available data to confirm or challenge the matter of interest.

CLIENTS' ETHICAL RESPONSIBILITIES

As sponsors of ethnographic research, clients incur ethical responsibilities toward practitioners and the general public.

Taking ethical responsibility. Sponsoring clients should make certain that the work they commission does not neglect or subvert the ethical responsibilities that their employees and consultants are trying to maintain.

Permitting the highest level of disclosure. Research sponsors should allow the highest level of disclosure possible within their competitive business culture. Anything that can be disclosed to prospective participants or the general public—for example, auspices, study purposes, use of results—should be disclosed. Users of research should allow for public dissemination of data and findings, particularly if they are to be used in the education of ethnographers, after the confidentiality needs associated with data protection have expired.

Dispassionate stance. The research sponsor should enter the field in a frame of mind that is fair and dispassionate. The client should have no hidden agenda or attempt to guide findings so that they confirm previously held expectations. Any hypotheses or hunches going into the study should be allowed to fail on the presentation of contrary evidence.

Disclosure and orientation of practitioners. The practice of marketing ethnography proceeds best when clients treat practitioners like true partners. This includes providing sufficient orientation to the product category under study, offering the results of previous confidential research for review, and not misleading or withholding relevant information from the research supplier.

Ethical dealings with practitioners. Ethnography practitioners are entitled to fair and reasonable compensation. Research sponsors should not use their power advantage due to control over financial resources to coerce improper, unreasonable, or discourteous behavior toward participants. Clients should compensate practitioners within contracted limits and abide by contracted terms.

The Qualitative Researcher's Frame of Mind

Qualitative researchers are not detached from the process of data collection. Their faculties and insights are essential to selecting the behaviors or respondent statements that should be noted in the record. They are a critical resource that guarantees that valid and reliable information is being collected. Some cynical postmodern thinkers argue that ethnography may be nothing more than a fiction created by researchers, but we believe that this criticism goes too far and minimizes the commitment and concern exercised by the individual investigator.

Conducting qualitative research is an important responsibility that requires a unique frame of mind. It also demands that researchers project several personal qualities to facilitate respondent acceptance, to sustain rapport, and to collect valid data. Listed below are several qualities that the ethnographer should internalize:

Objectivity. Researchers should be aware of and set aside their own beliefs, attitudes, expectations, and prejudices. This form of reflexivity is not easy because most of the time one's own mind-set is invisible; it is only the contrast with another pattern of thought that your own is revealed. A personal example: I never thought very much about what I did during my morning shower until I carefully watched others (see Rydholm, 2002). It was always my habit to shampoo my hair after I washed and rinsed my body. My taken-for-granted behavior did not seem to make much sense after I watched others shampoo their hair first. Keeping the lather on while the rest of the body was being washed seemed a more effective way of using the product. It changed my life.

Being direct and specific. Even tough questions should be asked directly and without equivocation. Behavioral probing sometimes gets intimate and personal; however, without delving into these sensitive regions, the full range of consumer feelings cannot be explored. In the laundry category, for example, soils can come from a range of increasingly touchy sources, from dust to personal waste products. Thus, one should be confident, compassionate, and direct when asking things like, "What techniques do you use to remove blood stains from bed sheets?"

Nonjudgmental attitude. The observer should stay emotionally neutral in reacting to respondent behavior. Judgmental reinforcements, like "that's good," should be avoided if they refer to a practice being observed. It is not a bad thing to encourage people or to let them know their input is valuable by telling them they are doing a good job; however, the ethnographer should avoid making such comments about specific products or outcomes because they place the researcher's standards above those of the consumer. Be careful of words and phrases that encourage defensiveness, such as, "Why didn't you do that?" or "How could you have done that better?"

Good listening skills. Researchers should establish and maintain strong rapport. They should avoid talking more than necessary and help respondents speak and reveal themselves. Responses should not be channeled to support the expectations of the researcher or the client.

Sensitivity to body language. Researchers should be acutely aware of their own as well as the respondents' body language. Maintaining eye contact with participants, maintaining an open and relaxed posture; and leaning toward respondents while speaking are examples of helpful body language. Researchers should go beyond respondents' verbal expressions and observe the level of fatigue they are experiencing and how their demeanor might suggest frustration or delight in the activities that are being examined. A later section provides more helpful hints about reading body language.

Friendliness. Observers should be lighthearted and nonthreatening. They should be relaxed and easy with smiles and friendly gestures. Being stiff, demanding, or formal can inhibit respondent disclosures.

Professionalism. Researchers should maintain a degree of professional distance from respondents. They should avoid expressing their own opinions, making suggestions, or acting like a participant. Ethnographers should make sure respondents understand the observer's role and responsibilities— that they may appear to be a congenial household guest but are actually there for serious scientific and commercial purposes.

Reciprocity. Good researchers have giving personalities. They try to make research a good experience for the participants. It is OK to thank the respondent at frequent intervals for making time and private space available. Nice words about the family pets, interior design, or politeness of the children, for example—if they are authentically felt—are always appreciated.

Respect. Good researchers show respect not only for the feelings and opinions of participants but for all the information that is being shared—including the fact that respondents are whole people involved in families, organizations, and communities, who are just allowing a small part of themselves to be revealed to the researcher.

Flexibility. Good researchers can adjust themselves to different personalities and respondent types. They are not rigid or rushed about time schedules or other expectations. They can change the course of an interview quickly if respondents' attitudes demand such a change.

Creativity. Good researchers embrace a creative outlook. They are prepared to see familiar activities in new ways, draw new implications, envision new futures. Ethnographers do not look at their work as routine and undifferentiated. Each encounter is an opportunity to go beyond previous experience.

Notes

1. Quite a few of the professional associations that have ethnographers as members maintain active codes of ethics. These may be consulted at the following Web sites: American Anthropological Association (www.aaanet.org/committees/ ethics/ethcode.htm), Society for Applied Anthropology (www.sfaa.net/sfaaethic .html), National Association for the Practice of Anthropology (www.practicin ganthropology.org/about/?section=ethical_guidelines), American Sociological Association (www.asanet.org/members/ecoderev.html), and Qualitative Research Consultants Association (www.qrca.org/ethics.asp).

2. For a thorough review of issues related to the ethical conduct of ethnography, see Murphy and Dingwall (2001).

13

Ways of Looking

E thnography involves a combination of induction and intuition, absorbing
the details of everyday behavior as comprehensively as possible while
applying imagination and educated insights to explain and prognosticate
about the implications of what is observed. Obviously, to do ethnography
well, researchers should begin with a critical examination of their own
ability to view behavior—indeed, the entire thing we call the "real world"—
in a dispassionate and thoughtful manner.

Observation is the ultimate subjective experience: It is shaped by the
observer's own cognitive limitations, unacknowledged prejudices, and preconceived categorization of reality. Nevertheless, to be effective, ethnographers
have to grapple with their own potential biases. Without bracketing their
own inner experience, they have no chance of thoroughly understanding others from the others' points of view. The *epoché*, as the process of
setting aside your own perspectives has been called, is an essential process
on the way toward understanding the experience of everyday life from the
perspective of others. Recent humanist and feminist researchers (e.g., see
Plummer, 1983; Stanley & Wise, 1993) go even further by insisting that in
the absence of any thorough ability to set aside their own point of view,
researchers ought to expose how interpretations and meanings have been
placed on findings. They hold that researchers should acknowledge being
central to the frame of the research as interested and subjective actors rather
than as detached and impartial observers (Lester, 1999).

Looking and the Phenomenology of Perception

What do we do when we look at everyday behavior? It is not a simple task.
We may count, name, or categorize what we see. We may classify or provide
some order, perhaps a ranking into some meaningful spectrum or range,

say, familiar versus unfamiliar or people versus inanimate objects. We may order things by some form of rational calculation—things closer or farther—or we may rank things by some subconscious or emotional meaning—things I like versus things I detest.

We may practice selective attention or inattention. We may embed some of the things we perceive into other categories or classify them in isolation. For example, we may think about having enough money in our pocket for the day and not care how much or what units are included. However, if we need to produce a bill or coin to pay for a soft drink from a dispenser or for admission to public transport, suddenly the particular composition of our pocket achieves heightened relevance. We may care very little about precise numbers until some tipping point is reached. For example, it makes little difference if there are 10 or 30 flies in a room; what matters is whether the numbers represent a minor annoyance or a serious infestation.

The process of culture acquisition, the manner in which people fashion categories of experience, and the psychology of expectations represent three broad complications for the collection of social facts about consumers. These factors build a sense of routine and normality in everyday life that must be continuously confronted if we are going to become astute observers and chroniclers of the real world.

Culture. Culture represents the baseline of our experience as human beings living in society. It is a broad concept encompassing the individual world-views, social rules, and interpersonal dynamics characterizing a group of people set in a particular time and place. Culture works through religious beliefs, language, social institutions, and other group dynamics to create a pattern, a taken-for-granted set of ideas and instincts that delimit and define people in their social settings. Although cultures are highly mutable, they have a conservative tendency and can sometimes be changed only by circumstances of military conquest, rapid technological change, or the militancy associated with social movements. People tend to defend their cultures and view alternatives as different or even wrong. Dietary customs, for example, will dictate whether someone experiences a particular food, such as a ham sandwich, as tasty or disgusting.

As actors in multicultural societies, ethnographers must understand the role that cultures play in shaping their own perceptual and evaluative consciousness. It is impossible to transcend culture, but it is necessary to reflect on its impact when encountering respondents. How do ethnographers feel when they observe an unfamiliar family practice in the home, perhaps witnessing a moment of prayer or watching the way family members interact with the family pet? Regardless, ethnographers need to set aside their own culturally based biases and seek to represent these practices through the lens of the respondents' own emotions and perceptions.

Categories. Culture has a strong impact on the way we slice up reality: the categories that we use to define everyday experience and aspirations. The human propensity for categorization is intrinsically linked to our capacity for language and creates a structure for organizing perception. Thus, perception cannot be regarded as objective without reference to the principles that shape what we see and experience.

Marketers have a way of organizing reality that often is only loosely connected to consumers' mutually shared language and categories. For example, they may talk about "brown goods" versus "white goods" in the alcoholic beverage category, which has little meaning to consumers, for whom that classification is unnecessarily broad and not consistent with their tastes for individual spirits such as scotch or vodka. If a client asks us to discover consumer attitudes toward white versus brown goods, it may be a very difficult issue to address because consumers do not organize their tastes through these terms.

Ethnographers have an obligation to understand consumer perceptions in their own terms first and to reconcile the differences between what consumers experience and the categories that marketers use only after the data are collected and thoroughly analyzed. Ethnographers need to be aware constantly of consumer language; consumer terms for the benefits, processes, and outcomes of product usage must always have priority in the marketer's vocabulary.

Expectations. Living their lives in routine ways, people expect a high degree of consistency and repetitiveness in daily experience. Habits, rituals, and customs reinforce this recurring cycle and delimit the choices and options involved in everyday lives. Washday may be Tuesday and Saturday; the weekly bath may take place on Friday; liver and onions are served Monday—the life of most people is regular in ways both large and small. In some cases, these regularities are widely shared; in others, they constitute individual idiosyncrasies. In either case, the regularities of our existence create a set of expectations for others' behavior.

Ethnographers should respect this regularity process in others but should avoid expectations that could make respondents feel awkward and unusual. Anticipating that others behave normatively and do things in the same ways that we do can be blinding. Minimizing expectations based on the researcher's own behavioral patterns is an important way to guarantee objectivity and acceptance of individual differences.

Ethnography and Gender

Gender represents a key framework for differentiating people within societies by virtue of their sexual characteristics, orientations, and gender-associated roles. Its influence represents an intersection of biological and sociocultural factors mediated on the personal level through social interaction within a culture.

Gender can be the basis of identity—not just the polarities representing male and female but all of the multiple options and possibilities in between. Gender can provide the source of self-representation; it is a form of discourse and a component of the differentiated power that pervades societies and their component arrangements. Gender-based structures are normally abstracted, typified, and stereotyped; many groups practice strict partitioning of males and females through associated forms of dress and address. Even in societies that do not go quite so far, gender can provide the basis of ideas about appropriateness in comportment and manner and for notions about inherent capabilities, interests, and drives.

Ethnographers constantly confront gender in their work, and it must stand as a basis for reflexivity (see Meyerhoff & Ruby, 1982; Skeggs, 2001). We live in society and cannot automatically assume a position above or separated from the gender-based expectations and disabilities that are routine in social interaction. In practice, gender may determine what patterns of interaction prevail in a situation and may supersede the negotiated roles that have been established through the ethnographic encounter. Some of the complications and questions may be set in motion by the separation of men's and women's space in the household. For example, it is useful to ask, as the study is initiated, whether a female ethnographer can go behind the scenes to watch, understand, and accurately record what men do in their garages and workrooms. Alternatively, gender-based role performance may be the source of other complications; for example, will women reveal all the details of their facial care routine, including their concerns and worries about beauty and self-presentation, to a male ethnographer?

Gender-based issues often pervade the selection of research firms by clients. Some users favor a female project manager over a male when the topic relates to personal care or children's behavior. Others may demand a male when the subject under examination involves things that need fixing.

Gender is an issue that pervades the interaction of respondent and ethnographer on site. Often, what is disclosed, taken for granted, or obscured is related to gender-based ideas. This can sometimes be played to the interviewer's advantage. By appearing naïve as gender-based knowledge is negotiated, the ethnographer can coax out unrevealed facets of a respondent's feelings; for example, an outsider's perspective can be delivered by a female respondent, who expects that a male ethnographer knows nothing about infant care or make-up. In a study completed by QualiData for an automotive supplies manufacturer, female ethnographers were able to gain entry to the world of car customizers, a largely male world, by playing in part the culturally and situationally approved role of the admiring female.

The gender implications of ethnographic practice obviously cannot be dismissed as irrelevant; they need to measured, understood, and managed throughout each encounter and must receive some recognition in the analysis.

Race, Status, and Class

Gender is not the only feature of the human condition that merits consideration as site visits are conducted. Racial characteristics, social status, and social class may also confound the manner of self-presentation, the degree of disclosure, and the interaction between researcher and respondent. The fact that members of different social classes frequently mischaracterize and misunderstand each other ought to give the ethnographer an extra reason for being sensitive and thoughtful.

Social class implications should also permeate the analysis if there are distinctions in the ways different social classes think about products. When QualiData has conducted studies in the insect control category, for example, the class issue has risen to some prominence. Insect infestations are a great social leveler; ants and roaches pay little regard to a victim's wealth or color. Nevertheless, people at the low end of the social ladder may see an infestation as evidence of some moral failing, whereas members of the middle class may dismiss an infestation's moral dimension entirely and consider the problem as a consequence of not having the right products at hand.

Visual Data

Unlike most forms of survey and interview methodology, ethnography collects more than people's words and utterances as its basic source of data. The contexts and behaviors that we observe are sometimes recorded as fieldnotes, written documents created by the researcher. Most often, they are also documented using image-capture technology such as film, video, and still photography. Recording images in an ethnographic context turns pictures and tapes into visual data worthy of analysis in their own right.

Recording and making sense of visual data are not uncomplicated tasks. Captured images may reflect our own biases, predilections, the ease or difficulty of access, and the stance associated with the person taking the pictures. Images normally reflect society's structures of self-presentation and representation, shared forms of perception, and established conventions about what is worthy of being recorded (Bourdieu, 1990). Recording technology gravitates to that which is easy to film or photograph, which may sometimes be at variance with what is "real." Similarly, the presence of recording devices may sometimes call forth an idealized behavioral performance. For example, women doing the laundry may pay extra attention to stains when they are under the scrutiny of the camera.

There is nothing inherently *ethnographic* about any representation of reality; it achieves that designation through usage and interpretation in an ethnographic context. Thus, there is no methodological advantage or disadvantage associated with what we may think of as amateur, tourist, professional, or artistic photography. Who takes the picture does not matter as long as it gets used as documentation for a certain kind of representation of reality. The quality of the recorded images is at issue only if they will have to be used for presentation or communication purposes. We cannot assert that visual data necessarily have priority over verbal data or a higher claim to truth than taking written notes, nor can we claim that the photographic record alone is sufficient in producing ethnographic knowledge (Pink, 2001, p. 17).

Some but not all of the limitations associated with visual ethnographic data can be overcome by turning the respondent into the photographer. It is relatively easy now to leave digital cameras or video recorders with respondents for some designated period of time to allow them to create representations of their own lives in their own terms. This approach has been used successfully in studies of teenage consumers, among whom access by adult ethnographers is difficult and sensitive. Having the teenager or any other respondent create the documentary record has the additional advantage of allowing us to analyze the process of selection and the domains of relevance that might be difficult to capture under any other circumstances.

Regardless of who is doing the filming, a context of trust and rapport is necessary for the production of good visual data. For ethnographers using a participatory approach, a solid explanation of why a visual record is necessary must accompany the respondent's introduction to the site visit.

Researchers conducting covert image capture in public spaces also need to appreciate the limitations and biases as well as the advantages of this approach. The area of coverage and the zone of image capture must be relevant to the study's objectives. In a retail ethnography that QualiData recently conducted on hand-held electronic devices, we needed to position our cameras so they could capture salesperson interactions across a broad range of categories. Our analysis confirmed that different devices were in competition for the sales force's attention. Less costly products were at a disadvantage because sales associates were more motivated and knowledgeable about pricier categories.

Video and photographic documentation are becoming an essential form of note taking, diary keeping, and data archiving. They are important resources for data transmission, information sharing and presentation. As a result of computer-based electronic communication and efficient presentation software, the impact of visual ethnographic data will grow.

Observation and Measurement

Ethnographic studies are generally devoted to cultural discovery, grounded theory, and rich description rather than to substantiating social scientific theories through systematic measurement. Most ethnography participants are not randomly chosen; on the contrary, their selection must be theoretically purposive and related to the specific demands of the study. In other words, we select respondents on the presumption of their willingness to cooperate as informants and because they are broadly drawn from consumer segments and targeted markets of interest to the client. Thus, a study of infant care may look specifically for mothers who are having their first baby; a study of home cleaning may require respondents who have recently built or renovated their homes.

In some studies, however, systematic measurement may be necessary to achieve study objectives. For example, it may be helpful to know the differences between men and women's behavior in a retail space devoted to breakfast cereal or the average elapsed time for concluding a household cleaning activity. In this case, it is necessary to design meaningful, fair, and objective scales and classification systems and to guarantee that their application is consistent and reliable.

Because ethnography is generally applied for qualitative insights, the use of probabilistic and mathematical models to describe and analyze findings or address questions of reliability and validity is normally inappropriate. Nevertheless, if quantitative assertions will be made, they need to be grounded in generally accepted standards of proof. Chief among these standards is the need for a sufficiently large and meaningfully selected sample. Unless samples are sufficiently robust and randomly selected relative to the assertions made, conclusions may be regarded only as hypothetical and awaiting further confirmation from further research.

14

What Ethnography Seeks

E thnography represents a synthesis of several social science disciplines, and its practitioners should be good students of human behavior. They should have considerable insight into the nature of social institutions and the basis of social stasis and change. The structure of people's self-image, self-presentation, and interpersonal communication—in other words, how people express themselves and interact with others—should be part of the ethnographer's vocabulary. Ethnographers should be conversant with perspectives drawn from psychology, sociology, anthropology, linguistics, and economics.

A highly developed reflexivity also needs to guide ethnographic practice. To observe others, practitioners need to understand the basis of their own ideas and perspectives, preferences and biases. Total objectivity is impossible. Ethnographic findings are just another form of socially constructed reality. They have no inherent right to claim superiority over any other form of wisdom. A degree of subjectivity needs to be embraced in the creation of ethnographic findings; perfect harmony between the perceptions of multiple observers is rare. The value of ethnographic knowledge emerges through the pragmatic guidelines of clarity, sensibility, and usefulness rather than through some inherent insight into truth.

The social scientific literature provides qualitative research with several ways of describing and understanding behavioral patterns. It offers a vocabulary and framework for seeking insights into consumers' inner experience and public activities. This chapter draws on this literature to provide a series of concepts that may help researchers achieve focus in conducting research.

Understanding Culture

We have already argued that the ethnographic approach is a useful way to assess the impact of culture on product purchase and usage. Culture is important as both a heuristic principle for describing and classifying behaviors and as an analytic concept that begins to explain how people's choices result from the interpersonal influences and symbolic universe that circumscribe everyday life.

Culture operates on both the material and nonmaterial levels of human experience. It serves as the foundation for the *behaviors, meanings,* and *tools* of all human collectivities. By cultural tools, we mean all of the physical components of a group's life ways, its technology and materials, as well as the fundamental rules, codes, and techniques for accomplishing daily affairs. Cultural behaviors are the totality of activities associated with membership in a group, whether or not they are practical, goal-oriented, sensate, or mystical. Cultural meanings refer to the sense-making process: how we intellectually or emotionally understand the purposes, implications, and associations that underlie all of our behaviors and the tools we use in everyday life.

Some additional explanation will help clarify the definitions of these terms and others that are useful in analyzing culture.

Cultural Behaviors

The concept of cultural behavior can include any human action outside of biologically imposed conditions (such as sleep and digestion). Behaviors can be conscious and purposeful or subconscious and non-goal directed. Here are several ways of classifying behaviors.

Rituals. These are patterned behaviors, usually performed without thought, that are repeated by force of habit or belief. Examples of rituals we may observe in the course of ethnographic practice may include the order of dishes in a meal or one's own particular pattern of personal care and grooming in the morning. An Italian meal, for instance, may be initiated with a hot or cold appetizer, the antipasto designed to stimulate hunger and digestion. Next, a pasta course may be served or, depending on regional preferences, perhaps a dish of risotto, polenta, or gnocchi. That is followed by a meat or a fish dish, then, a vegetable or salad. The meal often closes with sweets, cakes, or biscuits accompanied by coffee and strong drink, perhaps a bracing tumbler of grappa or brandy. The order of an Italian meal represents a strong cultural ritual enacted with an inflexible attention to order and staging comparable to the celebration of the Mass.

Roles. Through these behaviors, we enact a relationship to other members of a group. Being a boss and being a father are examples of roles. Statuses refer to behaviors that dramatize differential power or prestige in a social setting. Thus, being a father implies not just having particular role-related responsibilities, such as nurturance of children. The father role also possesses inherent authority and decision-making potential, based in cultural and situational factors, which are able to induce conformity among people playing dependent roles, such as minor children.

Particular brands are often purchased to reinforce the roles played by consumers or their status in a group. A luxury brand icon on an automobile or premium cigarette brands may be selected to demonstrate a certain level of authority and power. The buyer is not just buying smokes to satisfy a craving. In his mind, he also may be trying to present himself as chic or sophisticated, or naughtily boyish depending on which brand sits in his shirt pocket.

Ethnographic findings can often demonstrate opportunities for role-related new products. In a study conducted for a major manufacturer of paper goods, we were able to demonstrate a need, primarily among men, for an alternative paper towel—a product generally used by men and women in the kitchen or bathroom—suited for the distinctive demands of the garage and workroom. The client met this opportunity by developing a paper towel with greater weight and tensile strength, colored in a muted blue denim instead of a floral print, and available in locations such as home improvement stores and automotive outlets where these household and car do-it-yourself fanatics shopped.

Practical activities and goal-oriented behaviors. These include work, shopping, cooking, cleaning, or anything else that is directed toward accomplishing actions necessary in everyday life. Carrying out these daily tasks normally involves a range of habits, routines, skills, and styles that have been learned or otherwise channeled through social influence.

Creating taxonomies or rich description of practical activities—how people actually go about using the brands that surround daily life—is the focus of most marketing ethnographies. As marketers, however, we do not stop with this description but seek insights that strengthen the ties between the consumer and the brand. Understanding how an essential routine is accomplished by a commercial business is not just interesting in itself; it can lead to the development of software programs to facilitate those tasks electronically.

Several years ago during the "all-paper" era, for example, QualiData was asked to observe how insurance claims were processed with an eye toward imagining how these activities could be reconstructed to fit the emerging electronic environment. The conclusions of our ethnographic study led us to recommend ways of speeding up the process by facilitating such features as e-mailing applications and assembling complete files, including forms, testimony, photographs, and so on, using file transfers via computers.

Performances. These patterned behaviors are staged for the benefit of an observer. Baking cookies for the family, for example, may be a response to the homemaker's desire to perform the role of "good parent." Everyone dramatizes their accomplishments with some regularity by presenting desserts with some flourish; in another example, the garage mechanic may deliver your newly repaired vehicle and rev the engine for effect. How consumers naturally stage moments of accomplishment provides clues that help marketers communicate about products in relevant ways.

From the ethnographer's perspective, however, role performances can have both helpful and harmful aspects. As a practical matter, we want to observe actual performance of household, public, and work-related roles to get an understanding of the inherent issues and opportunities offered to marketers whose products connect to those roles. Nevertheless, as Goffman (1959) has pointed out, role performance can have its insincere, cynical, and manipulative components. The careful observer should make sure that the respondent is not doing things just to make the observer happy or to conform to some set of presumed expectations. In some cases, respondents may exaggerate their physical movements or utterances while completing a task under the assumption that it will look better on the final video recording. These obvious instances of counterfeit role performance should be discouraged with mild but firm criticism.

Play, games, and diversions. Although these activities are believed to induce personal relaxation or bonding between individuals, they may also serve functions with greater meaning. They also can provide the basis for various social relationships and either reinforce or negate status differences between individuals. For example, when the boss invites a junior employee to join in a golf outing, he or she is encouraging team commitment and inviting the employee to join an inner circle.

Ethnographers should be aware that most social exchange is not conducted in deadpan seriousness, regardless of how much importance is attached to the expected outcome or interaction's function. We have observed parents teaching their children how to use personal care products or home cleaning supplies through game playing rather than through direct instruction. Brand image and choice influence are communicated between users through play and teasing.

Cultural Meanings

Meanings are the ideas, emotions, or beliefs that we attach to an object, a behavior, or another idea. Researchers make sense of behaviors by trying to understand the meanings behind them. The purpose or function of a behavior is not always self-evident. Ethnographers typically have to probe the respondent and deeply understand the context if they wish to gain insights into the underlying meanings attached to observed behaviors. The language of cultural patterns that hold or convey meaning includes these concepts.

Symbols. These are things that stand for something else, including simple shapes or marks, such as the cross, which stands for Christianity, the crucifixion, Christ's suffering, salvation, or other religious ideas. Alternatively, symbols can be much less ethereal, such as a corporate logo. Symbols connect an idea or thing to some underlying system of meaning. Thus, for example, a Coca-Cola logo can stand for youth, energy, refreshment, or tradition. Consumers typically react to brands and product categories on the symbolic level as well as through functional considerations. A Honda can get a shopper between home and the supermarket as effectively as a BMW, but their differences lie in the BMW's perceived value, enhanced pride of ownership, and status demonstration, which far exceed the purpose of any driving occasion.

Signs. These markings point to something in the environment. A highway sign, for example, directs you to your exit. The McDonald's arches point consumers to a place where they can enjoy a consistent and predictable family meal and share each other's company. Consumer households, public areas, and work environments are filled with signs that orient people and structure their behavior within the setting. An observational study of an airport terminal that we conducted, for example, showed that ineffective signage produced disorientation and crowding in selected areas as passengers sought direction to complete their ticketing and check-in procedures.

Language, jargon, and slang. Words are tools of communication that have meanings beyond their basic communication value. They serve as code words to distinguish "in" groups from the "outs;" words provide a cipher or code to communicate meanings within closed groups such as business organizations and religious or ethnic subcultures. Language can subtly condemn, insult, and defame without resorting to profanity. A clear example of this is sexist language, such as, referring to an adult woman as a girl. Language differences help to define membership in various class, regional, and national origin groups.

Using the right words to communicate about a product is an important consideration for gaining positive consumer response. That is one reason why marketing ethnographers are acutely sensitive to the exact language used by respondents. Words sometimes represent ideals and aspirations rather than actual conditions. Randall Rothenberg (2003) describes corporate vernacular as "an ambition in the act of fulfillment" (p. A25). Thus, he defends the use of business jargon such as *strategy-based transformation* as a way of defining a destination rather than a description of institutional structure.

Marketing ethnographies provide opportunities to study language in its natural context by listening in to what consumers say to each other in addition to what they say in response to a question posed by a researcher. We can learn a great deal about beer brands or mobile phones by studying the ways that young consumers talk about these subjects during a night out with friends.

Beliefs and values. These are meaning filters or standards of truth for everyday life. They provide legitimacy to personal behavior and help you tell right from wrong. Broad patterns of values—for example, the refusal to eat meat or a concern about the environment—can be the basis for consumer behavior across a range of categories.

The degree to which actual consumer behaviors are consistent with beliefs and values is open to question. Sometimes, contradictory values are in play, and shoppers operate on several levels when applying them to brand decisions. In studies of home cleaning, for example, we often encounter consumers who verbalize a preference for environmentally sensitive brands. They definitely have purchased "green" cleaning products, but when we conduct a closet inventory, these brands appear relegated to the archival space in the back of the closet. In practice, however, they use the most popular and effective cleaning agents. What is happening here? This is a conflict of values, generally, between environmental sensitivity, which leads the shopper to buy an environmentally positioned product, and the demand for unassailable hygiene, which impels them to clean with whatever offers the most gleaming and bacteria-reducing results.

Attitudes and opinions. These expressions of a point of view toward people, things, and events can range from positive to neutral to negative. They can be intensely upheld or maintained with minimal salience. Attitudes and opinions are occasionally rooted in deeply held principles and values, but, more likely, they are situational and less character-based. A preference for Coke versus Pepsi does not arise out of fundamental beliefs about life's purpose but, rather, experiences with peers and family members or, perhaps, identification with a character that inhabited the communications of one brand or the other.

As ethnographers, we sometimes find that opinions are expressed after the fact, when respondents are invited to explain an observed behavior and are groping for a rationale. Beliefs thereby constitute a vocabulary of motives that make consumer actions appear logical and defensible. We need not reject these as inaccurate. The means through which consumers make sense of their marketplace actions are as important to us as their actual behaviors.

Interpretation. Through interpretation, we make sense of things that are communicated to us. Two people may see the same advertisement or read the same novel but interpret them differently. Interpretation is an essential component of the marketing communication process; it's what consumers *hear* when marketers talk.

Emotions and feelings. These inner conscious and unconscious experiences normally occur reflexively; sometimes, we actively attach them to people, behaviors, or ideas. In a marketing context, emotions are consumers' inner response to the external world. Listening to a commercial might make us angry or curious; admiring a neighbor's new car might make us envious or puzzled; tasting a new yogurt flavor might make us feel disgusted or charmed.

The degree to which emotional attribution and aspiration contribute to consumer choice is very high. Consequently, a rich ethnographic reflection of consumer emotions as they engage in everyday routines offers insights into potential influencers and interventions that may change current purchase patterns.

Relationships. Socially constructed ties between things or individuals—for example, being part of a family, nation, or club—have a tremendous impact on our daily life, our work habits, and our beliefs. Many brands are used to tie people into larger communities. Harley Davidson owners, for example, think of themselves as part of a larger community of somewhat rebellious, adventure-seeking individuals. These linkages may then produce associated patterns of brand usage, possibly for Camel cigarettes and Jack Daniels whiskey, which have similar brand images.

Cultural Tools

Tools are culturally produced devices—both objects and ideas—that expand human powers. Tools can help us live life more comfortably or securely; they can help us perform our work, defend ourselves, and organize our social ties. To a considerable degree, the practice of marketing ethnography is directed toward evaluating the marketplace tools that are available to consumers and, potentially, creating new tools that expand consumer satisfaction, stimulate productive efficiencies, and boost client profitability. In a broad ethnographic context, tools may take a variety of forms.

Physical space. The environment, including our homes, workplaces, shopping locations, and cities, is the most basic tool. The ways in which we structure the space in which we perform our daily tasks create opportunities and limitations. Whyte (1980) has demonstrated how the structure of urban spaces can stimulate feelings of safety and relaxation. Underhill (2000) has proven that arrangements of retail space can stimulate sales performance. In other words, merchandising a product so that its shelf presence is easily apprehended by its targeted customers will make them more likely to buy the item.

Technology—low to high. The conventional meaning of tool is anything that expands human powers, from paper clips to supercomputers. We have previously discussed how usability studies, as a branch of ethnographic practice, are focused on the relationship between users and advanced technological tools. Computer software or telecommunications devices can make themselves easier to use and more satisfying if they conform to consumers' mental images of how they are supposed to work.

Advances in chemistry have also provided technological options, which have not always been easy for consumers to understand. Surfactants are able to clean soils from textiles in a manner similar to chlorine bleach except they do not damage the fabric's color. It was initially very difficult for shoppers to understand the concept of "color-safe" bleach. Experience and promotion eventually got consumers to differentiate between the two alternative products and gave them a reason to buy two bleaching products, one for their whites and another for their colored garments.

Rules. These provide a systematic framework for the operation of social organizations and processes: nation states, professions, commercial enterprises, and families. They guarantee that everyday life proceeds with some degree of predictability and security. Rules can be both formal—written, codified, and elaborated as Robert's Rules of Order—or they can be informal—a set of understandings that guide everyday behavior such as the rules for queuing for the commuter bus. A simple company policy statement, the rules of baseball, and the U.S. Constitution are examples of rules that help us carry on our lives.

An important component of ethnographic practice is decoding the rules that are operating in the settings under study. In many cases, particularly where informal rules are active, consumers may not be aware that they are following any set of patterned behaviors until the basis of their actions is questioned. In studying home barbecue grilling, for example, we found that knowledgeable consumers generally followed a highly prescriptive set of rules for the steps in tasks such as how meats should be prepared and how charcoal fires should be started and maintained. Less-successful chefs were less aware of the rules and, consequently, were susceptible to switching to gas grills, a competing technology, because of the larger tolerance for error that gas grilling offered. The client learned that rules for successful charcoal barbecuing needed to be made more apparent and that specialized products to meet the needs of less knowledgeable cooks were a development opportunity.

Techniques. Ways of getting things done are the "how-to's" of our daily lives. Techniques work together with technologies and rules to advance human potential. The techniques that people use to complete the tasks of daily living in a culture may serve as clues to how well people are satisfied with the technologies available to them. Many consumers clean floors on their hands and knees in the belief that nothing else produces their desired state of cleanliness. The ways in which we complete everyday tasks may be creative and innovative; alternatively, they may follow conventional rules quite ritualistically. Ethnographic study proves its value to marketers when it can use findings about techniques to structure innovations and incremental improvements in product formulations and delivery.

Conclusion: Behavior and Culture

Viewing our own or others' behaviors, meanings, and tools with objectivity is very difficult. We take so much for granted and expect that our own cultural or personal patterns are the normal ways of getting things done. However, when we conduct research in a different national or international culture or even another social class or ethnic group, we have to step outside of our own routines and expectations to see things clearly. To achieve a higher truth, ethnographers have to suspend their own values and expectations and try to understand the consumers' perspective: to walk in their shoes, so to speak.

When conducting cross-cultural research, it is easy to misinterpret the meaning behind various behaviors encountered in an unfamiliar culture. People generally have a tendency to use their own culture as the basis for apprehending and interpreting the world; nevertheless, cross-cultural researchers have to apply a higher standard of self-challenge and objectivity. Without insight into the cultural and situational context of a behavior, it is easy to misunderstand its true meaning. Thus, cross-cultural researchers need to understand behavioral patterns and meanings from the perspective of the culture being observed rather than through the eyes of their own particular culture.

15

Approaching the Site Visit

This chapter examines various strategies for preparing to conduct the key element in ethnography—the site visit.

Creative Thinking in Ethnographic Practice

When clients commission an ethnographic study, they are generally attempting to stimulate breakthrough thinking within the marketing group. Going on-site to systematically explore unfamiliar consumer territory is an effort they expect will open management's eyes to new possibilities for product development and strategic marketing. Ethnographic studies require considerable investment and employee time and commitment. Consequently, a better understanding of the creative process and how it may be integrated into practice is a useful quest.

Creative engagement in ethnography begins with the way that the study is conceptualized and organized and continues through the process of data collection and analysis. Each study requires what Edward de Bono (1970) has called *lateral thinking*, which involves looking for new pathways. Rather than merely working within accepted boundaries, lateral thinking invites an effort to begin afresh, to go even further when one feels that a conclusion has been reached. Lateral thinking is provocative; it asks for what is next, what is better. Lateral thinking is not one-directional or one-dimensional; it can go in any way that seems to fit. It looks for new ways of defining, naming, and classifying things. Instead of following the consensus, lateral thinking provokes eccentricity and uniqueness. It invites risk and does not guarantee answers.

Roger von Oech's (1983) *A Whack on the Side of the Head* describes creativity as a thought process that can be achieved after several barriers that thwart creative processes are broken. Ethnographers must be conscious of the "mental locks" that von Oech describes and take steps to overcome them while observing respondents and drawing conclusions based on the encounters.

- Clients often expect us to look for the *one right answer*. That approach may fit well with corporate agendas, but thinking that way leads us away from alternative answers and new ways of thinking. A creative ethnographer validates diversity and allows many different points of view to emerge. Sometimes, ethnographies discover a modal way that consumers achieve some benefit, but it is important also to appreciate the outliers—those that are currently outside the norm—because they are pointing to trends or alternative ways of viewing a category.

- Logic has its place when you need to plan or get organized. When you're trying to be creative, *excessive logic can be a hindrance*. Good researchers are ready to use and invite the use of abstractions, metaphors, and ambiguity. Being on site and interacting with consumers force us to let go of our preconceived ideas. We need to understand what they are really doing rather than expect them to follow any specific agenda.

- *Following rules too rigidly* can lead to dead ends. In conducting research, we need to be disciplined and systematic, but we also need to be improvisational: to shift our lines of questions or move on to another subject faster than anticipated. In addition, in interpreting and making sense of the data, good researchers must be ready to innovate and break rules if the situation requires this kind of flexibility.

- Valuable ideas may not seem practical at the outset; they only become so after considerably more ingenuity and effort. Good researchers *don't judge everything by the standard of practicality* because that can be a trap that locks everyone into a single pattern of thinking. Creative thinking requires going into a "what-if" mode and drifting imaginatively. Good clients invite this kind of creative complexity and avoid restricting their consultants while they are still thinking deeply about an issue.

- Researchers have learned to *avoid ambiguity* because, most of the time, we need to be precise to communicate clearly. Ethnographers searching for new ideas, however, encourage a strong dose of ambiguity because that better reflects the situation in the real world.

- Researchers who *fear errors and mistakes* will seek out only safe solutions rather than breakthrough innovations. Creative marketers learn from trial and error. If failure is never an option, then innovativeness cannot thrive.

- Good researchers *encourage play and fun* when the situation calls for innovation. A spirit of lightheartedness will free participants' minds for creativity. Encouraging respondents to appreciate the playful aspects of participating in the ethnographic process will reduce their innate caution and defensiveness.

- *Specialization* is a fact of life, but it can also make our thinking banal and rigid. Good researchers are not afraid to learn from people who approach problems from alternative perspectives. Ethnography has the advantage of potentially inviting thinking from the social sciences, but it can go even farther. How can ideas from music or physics educate what you are watching in consumers' homes?

- *Conformity,* also known as *groupthink* or "the way things are done around here," has a deadening impact on creativity. Good researchers are able to reduce conformity to group pressures and have the courage to stand out.

- If researchers *don't think they are creative,* it becomes a self-fulfilling prophecy. Good observers are inspirational and reassuring.

The Stages of a Site Visit

Site visits go through a relatively predictable sequence of stages. Respecting this cycle helps ensure favorable interaction with respondents, which, in turn, leads to collecting richer data. These stages cannot be rushed; adequate time and attention must be devoted to each step in the process. It pays to overestimate the amount of time necessary for making behavioral observations, if only to guarantee that enough time will be set aside for such preliminary responsibilities as establishing rapport and providing respondents with adequate explanations of the techniques and expectations the ethnographer will be implementing.

In composing the observation guide, ethnographers should adhere to the structure of site visit stages described in this section. We have previously (Mariampolski, 2001, p. 199) described the stages of an ethnographic interview as comparable to the stages of any group experience. The metaphor of the life cycle can be used to describe the development that occurs as the site visit proceeds: infancy, childhood and adolescence, young adulthood, mature adulthood, old age.

Stage 1: The introductory stage (infancy). The primary issue at the outset of a site visit is for the researchers to greet respondents, introduce all the visitors, explain the roles they will be taking, and help respondents get oriented to this novel situation. It is unlikely that people who have been recruited for participation have previously experienced this type of intervention in their daily lives. This is the time to explain the purpose and the ground rules of the research and to allow the visitors and the respondents to get comfortable with each other. If any paperwork is involved—for example, if consent forms have not been signed prior to arrival—now is the time to make certain that this formality is completed.

Stage 2: The role-taking and rapport-building stage (childhood and adolescence): In this stage, the researchers' main tasks are to establish rapport, to set an appropriate tone, and to gain the confidence of participants. At this point, respondents are expected to begin speaking about themselves and their experiences with the brands and categories under study.

Observers may initiate this phase of the visit by having respondents discuss some neutral topic, such as their family composition, physical structure of their home (how old, what materials), occupations, civic activities, interests, and neighborhood, rather than issues directly relevant to the subject under study. It is also a good time to have observers reveal a little about themselves: hometown, common interests, sports, and similar topics to build rapport.

Stage 3: The general questions stage (young adulthood): In this part of the research process, a constructive pace is being established, as the site visit shifts to the main event. Observers may ask general questions and seek statements of fact; for example, about usage experience, brand awareness, or general attitudes toward the category. This is also a good time to conduct an inventory of equipment and products used in whatever household process is being observed; for example, if Italian cooking habits are under investigation, the ethnographer may want to examine food storage areas, the wine cabinet, spice rack, the cookbook shelf, fresh ingredients in the refrigerator, special utensils, tabletop accessories and dishes, and anything that comes to mind when cooking Italian food.

Stage 4: The specific questions and activities stage (mature adulthood): After gaining a basic understanding of factual issues and the participants' perspectives, it is time for direct observations of consumer behavior. The ethnographer should be ready also for riskier questions. At this point, for example, we can probe and challenge for deeper feelings and emotions, ask more pointed and specific questions, ask respondents to explain what they are doing in greater detail, delve into sensitive issues, and ask creative and "what if" questions. This section of the site visit is the longest.

Stage 5: Closing (old age): This is the wind-down stage. It is the research team's last chance to gain factual information, feelings, and projections from respondents. Many observers use this time to review and summarize attitudes and feelings that have been shared and validate their own perceptions and hunches, as they have emerged during the session. The visitor's job is also to anticipate the end of the experience, to make the respondents feel good about their contributions, and to break off the relationship in a positive and constructive manner.

Researchers who fail to respect these stages risk alienating their subjects and damaging research validity. Delving into emotions, for example, before a constructive pace and high level of rapport have been established can risk threatening respondents and making them less likely to disclose these personal details.

Creating and Using Observation Guides

The basic tool for conducting observational research is the *observation guide.* The guide is a statement of intent about how the visits will proceed in terms of behaviors to be observed, topics to be covered, the approximate amount of time to be spent on each area, and the sequence of questions or probes that might be introduced.

Constructing an effective observation guide and understanding how to use this tool is an essential step in the research process. The guide is a map of anticipated behaviors that will be systematically observed across a range of respondents during the research project. Consequently, it is very important to have the client and researcher agree on its structure and to use this tool as the basis for training the entire team.

Recommendations for creating and using observation guides are provided in this chapter.

• *The guide should be comprehensive and stand on its own.* It includes both areas that are to be watched, such as the process of brushing teeth, as well as discussion points and probes that may be inserted at specific times, such as questions about the importance of dental hygiene.

• *The guide is an educated guess about how the encounter may proceed.* The guide tries to break down each behavior that will be observed into all of its logical components. Nevertheless, it is hypothetical in this respect, not perfect or complete nor based as yet on observation, unless previous studies have been completed. Ethnographers should expect and allow for unanticipated behavioral patterns. The primary point of reference should be the respondents and how they go about their tasks, not the expectations of research or marketing personnel.

In other words, the guide cannot anticipate the natural order in which respondents will perform a task, nor can it foresee the range of solutions that consumers will adopt to complete daily routines. Ethnographic observers allow respondents to do things in their own way; record these behaviors, meanings, and tools faithfully; and do not challenge the respondents or confront their particular logic.

• Make sure that the behaviors to be observed can be watched without too much researcher intrusiveness. Excessive encroachment makes participants self-conscious and less spontaneous about their behavior.

• The research should begin with exploratory and factual questions and become more focused and opinion-seeking later in the session. Early questions should avoid sensitive issues or excessive probing, which should be saved until a degree of rapport has been established.

• An observation guide is a topic outline, not a questionnaire. It includes the issues that are to be addressed, not necessarily the questions the ethnographers ought to ask. Observers must have the flexibility to raise issues in a manner appropriate for the respondents and situation. A great deal of freedom and improvisational skills are necessary to follow the respondent's natural flow of behavior and to ask questions at appropriate moments.

• Questions should be open-ended rather than requiring a yes/no response. They should stimulate thinking, discussion, and exploration rather than just demand fixed reactions to the question. In this respect, ethnographic discourse may have more similarity to therapeutic discourse than to natural conversation.

• Follow the respondents. In a statistical survey, it is important and necessary for all the questions to be asked in the same way at the same point in the interview. Otherwise, subtle biases of question order and structure may bias the results. This is not the case with the observation guides used in ethnographic studies. The researchers are expected to follow the respondents' behaviors, interests, and sentiments. The researcher should never tell the respondent that "now is the time" to complete any particular task. Instead, they should be attentive to respondent cues and frames of reference. Being overly structured in an ethnographic encounter may, in fact, bias results because acquiescent respondents may pick up cues to researcher expectations and alter their standard practices in a mistaken effort to conform.

- Be flexible. Observers are allowed to digress when necessary as long as they are following the natural structure of consumer behavior, and it is consistent with research objectives.

- Be spontaneous and personable with the respondent. Do not act like an interviewer. Ethnographers should not read from the observation guide while asking questions. They should have committed its overall contents to memory before the visit begins. The observation guide should be consulted primarily to make sure that no important, substantive area is skipped.

- Prepare for surprises. Do not expect behavior in the real world to follow the observation guide. Respondents will enact behaviors in their own unique ways. Our objective is to document behavior and related tools and to identify how consumers construct meanings around their unique practices.

- Research managers should not insist on too much detail in the observation guide. Ethnographers should use color markers to highlight key topics on the observation guide and key words that will jog memory during the visit and allow them to maintain an active and interested interaction with respondents without constantly referring to guide topics and probes.

- Be comprehensive in outlining the process. Sometimes details involved in preparation and storage are as important to the overall results as focusing on the process of product usage. The seemingly extraneous factors may offer significant opportunities for innovation. For example, if the ethnographer were watching men's shaving behavior, attention to the entire process might include:

  - Razor storage
  - Shaver storage
  - Soap storage
  - Conditioner storage
  - Shaving product (gel, foam, cream) storage
  - Preparation of razor, shaver
  - Preparation of soap, conditioner, shaving product
  - Preparation of face and other areas being shaved

- Application of products on face
- Method of shaving
- Length of time devoted to shaving
- Ease of access to all parts of face being shaved; for example, under chin
- Rinsing
- Washing
- Cleaning utensils
- Returning utensils to storage
- Returning soap, conditioner, shaving product to storage
- Examination/correction of results
- Finishing

This list of behaviors approximates the behavioral aspects likely to be included in the observation guide on this topic.

16

Collecting Data

In any ethnography, data analysis begins at the same time as data collection and continues after everyone is out of the field. Observers should look and listen for patterns while respondents are carrying out their tasks and speaking. Rich, descriptive detail will emerge as consumers go about their daily tasks. In addition, probing with validation questions is used to elaborate contextual observations and to provide evidence for conclusions drawn about consumer attitudes and practices.

Members of the research team should be careful about drawing conclusions and developing analyses that are too hurried. Do not generalize after a single observation. Good qualitative analysis depends on some degree of reflection and detailed examination of the documentary evidence. Furthermore, team research requires consideration of the views of other observers. Quick analysis tends to be impressionistic, rather than systematic, and lacks the richness and nuances that are hallmarks of high-quality qualitative analysis.

Qualitative Data

Data that may be available for analysis as the completed site visits of a project accumulate can include all or some of the following materials:

- Audiotapes of the discussion
- Videotapes
- Interview notes
- Observation notes
- Still photographs
- Measurements
- Documents and physical traces
- Ideas that emerge from the debriefing

Qualitative data at the start appear unordered, and their analysis represents a stream of consciousness rather than systematic scrutiny of evidence. A thorough analytic process is needed to make sense of the disparate information. All of the evidence collected should be used dispassionately in conducting this analysis; otherwise, subtle biases may cloud the conclusions.

Everything collected on site is a potential source of data—including observations of gestures, voice intonations, and mannerisms—if it can be meaningfully integrated into the researcher's conclusions and recommendations.

Mapping

Plotting the dimensions and traffic patterns of an environment is a helpful way to organize observations. Attention to the social ecology of the home, a workplace, or a public space provides a frame of reference in which behavior takes place.

In retail environments, the spatial organization of selling space has a great deal of influence on ease of use and the likelihood of sales being completed. Putting promotional and fast-moving items on the front of shelves is not done by chance. This is where these items are more likely to be seen and provide an impetus for impulse purchase.

Carefully drawn maps that show how behaviors take place are valuable both for analysis and for heuristic purposes in reports and presentations.

Product Inventory

A product or category inventory is an important early step in conducting an ethnographic site visit. The locations where items are kept for easy dispensing, storage, emergency use, and so on betray a great deal about people's feelings and expectations for the product. For example, in a study QualiData conducted for a major manufacturer of paper goods, we found that whereas there were numerous dispensing options for paper towels in the kitchen, these grew scarce in the bathroom, garage, and other locations where paper towels had additional potential uses. As a result, consumers were drifting to pop-up "wet wipes" and other categories with easy dispensing solutions in locations outside the kitchen. This finding suggested an opportunity for the client, who wanted to widen the potential usage of the company's paper towels, to provide new dispensing solutions.

In the current retailing environment, we have noticed that dry goods and nonperishables purchased in volume from the so-called warehouse stores are taking up increasing amounts of the home's storage space. This has become highly problematic for urban consumers with relatively less discretionary space than suburban shoppers.

Within the storage space, we have observed a hierarchy of product locations, with favored brands being more accessible whereas products that are less enticing are kept in the back of the storage space. Often, shoppers are induced to purchase products they really do not like, or they reserve particular items for rare rather than regular usage. For example, we have noticed that many consumers purchase products from relatives or work associates through various relationship marketing schemes but really do not like these brands because they are found to be less effective or require dilution. As a result, consumers keep these brands in reduced access storage—in case they are asked to repurchase—but never actually use these products.

Conducting the product inventory provides an occasion to discuss products in detail, allowing consumers to categorize the brands in their possession and to discuss related expectations. In the example that follows, the ethnographer is able to elicit numerous particulars about how the brand is used and how it relates to experience with competitive brands.

Ethnographer: I'm interested in what you have here. Let's start with the SOS Juniors.

Respondent: Uh hum.

Ethnographer: What do you use those for?

Respondent: Oh, what don't you use them for? (She picks up the box and looks at it.) They're another thing that's great, multi-purpose, all over the place. I use them for some pots and pans when they're scorched. I use them to clean my ovens. I use them on my floor. Um, I use them on the toilet, on the inside. That's basically it on those.

Ethnographer: Do you always buy the SOS?

Respondent: It's usually SOS or Brillo. I'm not really . . . I always buy one of the two.

Ethnographer: Are they different?

Respondent: No. One's pink, one's blue. One's square, one's not. This is the first time I've bought the little SOS Juniors, and I kind of like this concept because [it's] for one person. You know, whenever I have it up here, I don't use it that often, and I don't want them to get rusty. When I had those big ones, they would get rusty and break apart. (She takes one out of the box and holds it up and shows where she would place it on the kitchen sink.)

Ethnographer: So you like this one?

Respondent: So I like this, yeah, because otherwise it sits up there and it rusts. And so the small one is good.

Ethnographer: You're nearly done with that box there!

Respondent: Yes, it's my last one. I need more! Yeah. (She puts them back.) See, I followed your letter! I did not go out and buy any new cleaning products! (She refers to the respondent information letter she received asking her not to make any special preparations for the home visit.)

Ethnographer: Great! And you have plastic gloves.

Respondent: Always.

Ethnographer: Always?

Respondent: Always. I have a pair downstairs and a pair upstairs. Gloves, always. I use them for everything. (She picks them up and puts them on to demonstrate.)

Ethnographer: What are you trying to achieve when you use plastic gloves?

Respondent: A multitude of purposes. Sometimes when I use things that have bleach or sticky fluids, I don't want my hands to smell that way, especially when I scour out the sink because you can't get the smell of the cleanser out of my hands. I also like them because I have really crappy nails and so it protects that, and when I'm washing dishes it doesn't dry out my hands or anything.

Ethnographer: OK. And Ajax?

Respondent: (She puts away the gloves and picks up the Ajax.) Ajax. Scour my sink. Sometimes I use it on the floor. You know whatever mood strikes. Sometimes I grab the Ajax, sometimes the Brillo pad for something that's splattered on the wall that I can't get off.

Ethnographer: Is there any situation in which you would prefer the Ajax over something like the SOS pad?

Respondent: Um, I don't use cleanser on my pots and pans. I know some people do. I wouldn't do that. I don't know. I might use the cleanser on the toilet first because I don't want to scratch it.

Ethnographer: What's this behind here (indicating a bottle which she picks up and looks at)? I'm curious, I have never seen this.

Respondent: Really?

Ethnographer: It specifically says for any wooden surfaces.

Respondent: Um. Yeah, I use it for all my wooden handled things . . .

Ethnographer: How did you find out about this product?

Respondent: My sister used it and liked it. She told me about it and recommended that I try it.

Diaries

In contemporary research practice, it has become quite common to use diaries as a way of seeing consumer behavior outside of the context of the site visit. There are quite a few advantages to this practice: It provides a longitudinal aspect to the site visit; it provides insights into the larger usage cycle; it gives clues to both planned and unplanned uses of products.

Diaries can be kept in traditional written form, or they may be enhanced with a visual record through the use of still photography, video, and collection of materials. They may be kept as private Web logs that combine text and images. Diaries can record the activities of peers, household members, and others. They may demonstrate actions as well as provide a record of feelings and attitudes during product usage. It is fallacious to assume, however, that video or photographic diaries kept by consumers to record other people in their own environment are inherently superior to the record produced by a trained ethnographer. Consumers bring their own biases and selectivity factors to the mix, and it is wrong to believe that they produce a more comprehensive record.

If some degree of interaction among respondents is considered desirable following the site visits, diaries may be kept on an online bulletin board or similar service. This approach may help to understand patterns of behavioral change and adaptation following the site visits.

When diaries are used, they should be carefully structured so that the respondent is guided to include all relevant contextual details. For example, in a study QualiData conducted on the use of glucose monitors among people with diabetes, respondents kept a diary for a week prior to a daylong site visit. Diary instructions prompted them to record the time and place of monitoring, what products were used, what they were feeling, and whether any product failure occurred.

Note Taking

Here are several tips for note taking while visiting a site.

- A small wire-bound (spiral or secretarial) notebook is the easiest to manage during a site visit.

- Excessive note taking during a discussion can be a problem. Do not try to get a full transcript of the discussion during a site visit. Taking notes is potentially distracting; that is, it can keep the observer from paying full attention to behavioral details. Outlining is a good way to take notes because additional information can be filled in from firsthand recollection during lulls or after the visits have been completed. If a video- or audiotape is being made, detailed notes during a site visit are particularly unnecessary.

- In making observations, take notes by making lists and descriptions of behavioral sequences and processes.

- It is sometimes difficult to listen to the respondent speak and make observations of behavior simultaneously. It helps to assign different team members to distinct responsibilities, so that at least one observer pays attention only to behavior.

- In taking notes, use key words and marks, diagrams, and sketches. Every sentiment cannot be recorded in the notes; you should write economically and quickly.

- Observers should avoid looking at notes when respondents are addressing them because it breaks rapport.

- Notes should be made for observations that will assist in the analysis; for example, notes about body language or gestures when a particular topic is being discussed or a particular behavior is being enacted.

- Use signs and markers to distinguish between different types of notes. An arrow can indicate your own observation, a quotation mark for a direct quote, "R" for something a respondent said, "B" for an observation of gesture or body language.

- Use diagrams to describe processes or sequences.

- Record what you don't understand and come back to it later. Everything will not make sense to you immediately. Sometimes, a *brief* period of reflection and review helps you make sense of things.

- Share your notes and observations with the other on-site visitors, but expect that there may sometimes be disagreements based on your different perspectives. Suspend your own judgments until you have had a chance to review others' observations.

Audio and Video Recordings

Audio and video recordings are key sources of ethnographic data. A good set of videos, in particular, will help the researcher analyze body language, which is difficult with only audio. The video record is also helpful for those who did not participate in the site visit and want to gain richer impressions of research results.

- Make sure tapes and other media are labeled with the date, location, brief project name, respondent first name or nickname, and principal distinguishing characteristics of the site for easy reference afterward.

- Review tapes carefully after the visits to see if they confirm your hunches and hypotheses. To work with the recorded interviews, it is sometimes helpful to have tapes converted to a written form if client preferences and budget allow that. There are two ways of converting the tapes:
  - Transcripts: Detailed and exacting translation of the oral record. These become necessary if the discussion is highly nuanced or technical or if many verbatim responses will be reported.
  - Fieldnotes: Briefer and less specific depictions of the oral record. They may contain summaries of the drift of a conversation and only the most critical quotations.

Structured Activities

During the course of a site visit, it is sometimes helpful to ask the respondent to engage in an unaccustomed activity. The reasons for structuring this into the research may vary:

- To watch respondents use an unfamiliar product or brand. This may, in fact be the primary objective of the study.
- To see how the respondent reacts to an unfamiliar routine. Usually, this is to test whether a new way of performing the routine—for example, an alternative device for measuring blood glucose—can fit comfortably into the respondent's lifestyle.
- To guarantee that observations can be made of specific brand, categories, and so on in the field. If an accustomed brand or routine is being evaluated, the researcher needs to point out that this activity is a test and is recognized as a deviation from conventional behavior.

Special Issues in Usability Research

Usability research is conducted to understand the user interface: the manner of interaction between people and technology. Originating in the military as human factors research, the approach seeks to assess how easily users manage their prospective technological tools and how much satisfaction that engagement produces (Fox & Fisher, 2002; Nielsen, 2000). It is normally applied to such technologies as Web sites and computer software; however, QualiData has also conducted usability studies in connection with such varied categories as ATM dialogs, automobile dashboard technologies, and cell phone functionality.

Although not always strictly ethnographic in its application, usability research requires careful attention to principles of effective observation identical to ethnography to guarantee systematic and objective results. Several special issues are introduced when conducting usability studies, and they merit some review here.

Whose equipment? It is only natural to start by considering the location of the study: either within special usability laboratories sponsored by technology companies or various research facilities, as opposed to the respondent's own equipment at home or at work. Research sponsors gain the advantage of consistency and uniformity when they invite respondents to try out Web sites or software in their own labs.

What factors will be analyzed? Specific user-interface metrics that may be observed include:

- Ease of learning: How quickly can users acquire skills at negotiating the technology?

- Efficiency of use: Are the steps associated with achieving a user-defined objective, such as sending and receiving instant messaging, economical and logical?
- Memorability: Can users recall how to complete tasks after some time has elapsed, or, like most of us, do they have to relearn functions?
- Error frequency and severity: When and why are mistakes made? Do the errors represent some kind of mistaken assumptions about how people naturally navigate a Web site, or is some missing information at fault?
- Subjective satisfaction: Do users like visiting the Web site? Can they quickly achieve job performance objectives using the new program?

Once factors associated with successful product implementation have been learned, they become part of the standard knowledge about a category and may be engineered into successive versions and alternative technology design.

What usability issues may be studied at Web sites? Among the issues normally assessed while conducting user-interface studies of Web sites are:

- Navigation: Does experiencing the site produce the results that users seek? Do they know where they are at every moment? Can they find what they want? Does the search mechanism produce desired results? Is there a high level of association between Web site terminology and users' terminology so that confusing jargon does not misdirect users?
- Structure of Web site: Is it organized in a logical and meaningful hierarchy?
- Layout: Is the page pleasing to the eye? Is there sufficient white space so that each page can be managed without strain? Do repeating elements have a clear relationship with changing elements? Are graphics and images aesthetically pleasing, and do they avoid downloading complications?
- Error messages: Are users empowered to take action following error messages, or do the messages produce paralysis?

What mix of objective and subjective measures need to be acquired? Completing a usability test generally requires completion of tasks that are presented to respondents as behavioral challenges. Objective measures may include time to complete tasks and error rates. Subjective analysis may depend on user comments and behavioral observations. Sometimes, the "think-aloud" technique is applied, in which respondents are encouraged to divulge what is going on in their minds continuously while completing a task.

How will data be recorded? Videorecording is often used to track respondent behavior while navigating technology. Web site evaluation is now facilitated by easy-to-use click-stream recording technology, such as ClickTracks (www.clicktracks.com) or Clicklab (www.clicklab.com), which facilitate real time recording of user-interface data.

17

Developing Rapport With Respondents

R apport with respondents is probably the most important interpersonal issue that governs the progress of the visit. The process of developing rapport starts immediately when the observer begins to interact with respondents. Rapport is a feeling of comfort, a sympathetic relationship between the researchers and respondents. It involves becoming accepted by informants to the degree that they will open up with minimal hesitation. Maintaining rapport also requires the researcher to be sensitive to time pressures and to the respondents' needs. It requires displaying sensitive and affirmative personal qualities.

Rapport is promoted if respondents gain the right information at the start of the visit:

- Review the purpose and methods of the research.
- Introduce all members of the observation team to everyone present at the site.
- Explain that, for security and confidentiality reasons, the client's name cannot be disclosed.
- Pay extra attention to children and pets if present. Establishing a high level of comfort with children and pets gives the householder freedom to relax and cooperate.
- Explain the ground rules.
- Assure respondents that their contributions are important.
- Make respondents feel confident that they may speak their minds, that there are no right or wrong answers to any questions.
- Reassure respondents that they are in charge in their own environment; no one will interfere with their routines, and they may call a break if other responsibilities demand attention.
- Reassure them that there are no hidden agendas.

Here are several recommendations for conducting the first two stages of the interview in a manner that maximizes rapport building.

The Introductory Stage

As the visitors enter the scheduled location, all team members should greet each person at the site individually. It is helpful to make eye contact with each person, shake hands or make other gestures, such as bowing, appropriate to the culture that you are entering. Speak appreciatively of the hospitality being extended, using phrases such as "Thank you for letting us visit" and "Nice to be here."

Next, members of the team should introduce themselves by name and possibly hometown. There is no need to go far beyond this. Some aspects of conventional introductions will be distinctly unhelpful; for example, naming employers and job titles may set up unusual expectations among respondents.

In American households, greetings extended toward children and pets are particularly important. Youngsters often find the ethnographic situation vague, strange, and unconventional. They may feel that their household is being invaded by strangers and will often be fearful of interacting with visitors because, at school, they are warned about speaking with strangers. QualiData has been involved in numerous site visits that, for the parents, served as pretexts for lessons about various categories of strangers.

Pets are also considered household members in many Western countries, and they have to be made comfortable before the visit starts; otherwise, barking dogs may disrupt the entire proceedings. Because pets are thought of as family members, many North American respondents may consider it rude if the visitor does not at least acknowledge their companion animals.

Some cultures require elaborate greeting rituals when a guest—particularly one from a foreign country—enters the home. Although respondents in North America are normally discouraged from preparing meals or snacks, this admonition would be impossible to maintain elsewhere because refusal to participate in hospitality rituals would be considered rude and hostile. In Turkey, for example, all households from the most wealthy to the most humble reserve special utensils and table settings for honored guests. It is important here and elsewhere to respect these local greeting customs.

DISCLOSURES AND GROUND RULES

The next part of the introduction deals with disclosures about just how the experience will be conducted; for example, the length of time or the use of cameras and lighting. Being open about these features actually enhances the level of trust participants will place in the situation. Even though most of these details will have been disclosed previously, it is useful to review them once again as the session begins.

The final part of the introduction should deal with participation ground rules. Here are several items that the visiting team should say to cooperating respondents:

- Do everything that you normally do in carrying out this set of tasks.
- Do not censor yourself or fail to do something that is part of your routine because observers are present.
- Do not feel that you have to rush to complete any task. We are patient; take all the time you need.
- Try not to feel self-conscious. We know it's difficult, but as time passes we hope you get accustomed to our presence.
- No one is here to judge you; on the contrary, we are trying to learn from you.

The introduction may conclude with a review of how important the research is to its sponsors. Respondents are reassured to know that major manufacturers are truly interested in how their customers use various products and are eager to adapt those products in response to consumer needs.

Participants should be invited to ask questions if any of the ground rules are unclear. Occasionally, a respondent may ask a pointed question during the introduction, which the visitor might not want to answer for fear of biasing the research; for example, "Which company is sponsoring these visits?" This situation needs to be handled tactfully and in a manner that does not spoil rapport.

> I can't answer that question right now for security and competitive reasons and because it might influence the way some participants in the study will answer questions.

The observing team should react positively and warmly toward every person at the site, individually, and thank them again for agreeing to participate and offer access to their personal space.

The Role-Taking and Rapport-Building Stage

The next step is to allow respondents to introduce themselves more extensively and begin speaking for the record. To reduce ego threat, researchers may engage in a bit of small talk and self-revelation, unrelated to the research, to promote the rapport-building process. For example, neutral questions may include: What is the most interesting thing about your job? What do you like to do most in your free time? or Where would you like to spend your next vacation?

In general, recording devices should be turned off until the introductory small talk has been completed. Entering the site with cameras running or paying too much attention to the equipment set-up before the introductions have taken place can be extremely disruptive and disorienting to the respondents.

The first substantive question should be asked after a transition remark, such as, "OK, we're ready to start." At that point, the cameras can begin to run, too.

When a topic is set up for discussion, it should be introduced with a phrase such as "Let's talk about . . . ," "Tell me about your attitude toward . . . ," "Describe how you . . . ," or "I'm curious about the ways that you . . ." In other words, the interviewer should use action verbs that open up the discussion. That will make it seem more like natural discourse and less like an interview.

Here is an example of building nice rapport on a personal level and then moving into specifics in a relaxed conversational way. The setting is a charcoal usage study; the context is a social occasion: a languid Sunday afternoon as old and new friends gather for a regular ritual enacted several times during the summer.

Ethnographer: You're here with your buddies?

Respondent 1:   Uh huh.

Ethnographer: I've met them. I know them by name, but how do you, how often do you guys get together? Under what circumstances?

Respondent 1:   Well, uh, Debbie and Larry are family friends of the last 16 years . . .

Ethnographer: Uh huh.

Respondent 1:   and we get together as much as we possibly can . . .

Ethnographer: Uh huh.

Respondent 1:   and Lori and Dan are new friends. This is the first time they've ever been here . . . and hopefully not the last.

Ethnographer: (laughs)

Respondent 1:   Debbie and Lori and I all work in the same school system.

Ethnographer: So you're all teachers?
                 (everyone talks at once)

Respondent 2:   Everybody's a teacher except me.

Ethnographer: Everybody's a teacher, except you. How do you fit?

Respondent 2:   Actually, I'm a counselor most of my life and now I'm a principal. I just changed jobs which is really . . . great!

Ethnographer: So you finally got the big promotion huh?

Respondent 2:   Well, maybe (laughs).

Ethnographer: (laughs)

Respondent 2:   We'll see.

Ethnographer: Oh great. So how often are you all sitting out here and barbecuing, sitting around here, drinking beer, how often do you do this?

Let us review some of the most important rules for how ethnographers can build and maintain rapport during an on-site visit:

- Explain as much as you can about the purpose of the session and its ground rules.
- Maintain eye contact.
- Be friendly in the way you greet and acknowledge people.
- Show concern for participants' comfort and privacy.
- Show unconditional positive regard in your reactions to participants' contributions.
- Tell a little about yourself, as long as it is not related to the topic of discussion.
- Demonstrate high energy and interest.

18

Motivating Respondent Cooperation

For the most part, research respondents are delighted to support the research team and the sponsoring company. They want to answer questions honestly, pay attention to the rules, try their hardest to complete tasks, and have a good time in the process. They are on the ethnography team's side and should never be considered as antagonists.

Nevertheless, several factors can either inhibit or facilitate honest and open discussion.[1] Keeping these factors in mind as the session is in process will help to maintain the flow of useful information.

Inhibitors: Turn-Offs

Many forces can inhibit free-flowing discussion or open revelation. The ethnographer should be careful to avoid the following situations.

Time pressures. Pushing things along too fast or not allowing participants to complete their tasks in the time it normally takes them can be very disruptive. Rushing through the observation guide without clear regard for the respondent will guarantee an alienated participant and poor data. The respondent ought to dictate the time allotted to completing tasks, and no amount of pressure should be exerted to speed things up. Once, when we were conducting observations of the laundry routine, a client observer who needed to get back to the office urged us to get the respondent to begin drying her clothes immediately after they were washed. It appeared wrong to us to hasten the process, and we declined despite the client's fervent disagreement. We were glad to have refused this request, however, when the respondent demonstrated a step of examining the wash for persistent stains prior to placing items into the dryer.

Ego threat. Asking participants to disclose things before they are ready or being judgmental in reacting to respondent practices are likely to induce ego threat. Furthermore, some topics are inherently threatening to respondent egos; for example, the insect control category can create literal minefields because everyone—rich and poor—is embarrassed by the presence of roaches in their homes. In cases like these, respondents need extra reassurance that anyone may experience insect control problems and that having these difficulties does not indicate that anyone is a poor housekeeper.

Etiquette. Politeness is often the enemy of effective ethnographic observation. Believing that certain behaviors must not be exhibited or attitudes should not be expressed in public stimulates self-censorship and harms the open confidence that needs to govern ethnographic studies. The main antidote here is a comfortable level of rapport. Letting respondents know that anything they say or do will be met with acceptance and understanding helps to resolve this problem.

Sometimes, the researcher needs to go even further by acknowledging and validating the existence of an etiquette barrier and encouraging respondents to try to get beyond this issue. In conducting the home showering studies for Moen, we at QualiData faced the problem of etiquette in the extreme because project specifications called for respondents to be videotaped in the nude. Fortunately, we were able to recruit volunteers who agreed at the outset to abide by this condition. We interviewed each recruit individually before the site visit to reassure everyone that this would not be a problem. Once we arrived at the site, steps were taken to guarantee that the filming would be completed with as much respect and dignity as possible.

Trauma. Having respondents describe an unpleasant experience or asking them to participate in tasks that are unpleasant can compromise openness. The best response is a relaxed confidence and unconditional positive regard as the respondent shares the events. Just listening without reaction is often the best way to keep the information flowing.

In studying diabetes patients, we frequently encountered this problem as we asked respondents to describe their own reactions to their initial diagnosis. As they relived this traumatic event, we were accepting, sympathetic, and affirmative listeners, never rejecting what was being said. These excerpts from the transcript illustrate how people sometimes share very personal feelings when they become comfortable with the interviewer and the situation. This also shows that deeply private information can be useful to carrying out the study's objectives.

Respondent: Oh it took me a year, over a year to accept it [a diagnosis of diabetes]. I ignored it and I didn't control it. I didn't learn anything about it and yeah . . .

Ethnographer: Yeah.

Respondent: Actually, at first, what I was doing most of the time—I was doing the wrong things because I did want to die.

Ethnographer: You wanted to die?

Respondent: Yeah. Most of the time I was just doing the wrong thing. I didn't care.

Here's what another respondent said, on the same topic:

Respondent: [I said] "Oh no, I don't want to take the shots," and he said, "You may not have to. There are all kinds of new developments happening with diabetes medications. You may or you may not have to take the shots."

Ethnographer: How did you feel while all that was going on?

Respondent: Really depressed.

Confusion. Lack of clarity and specificity about ground rules or the topic being discussed can also undermine the success of an ethnographic encounter. If the session proceeds without shared understandings between researcher and respondent, there will be problems with data collection. In a small number of instances, for example, we have arrived at the site expecting that the recruiter would have informed the respondent about videotaping. Despite all of our best intentions, this detail had been overlooked. Needless to say, when the cameras emerge as the encounter begins, the respondents are quite startled and express considerable dismay. It has been our practice in these cases to proceed without videotaping for the first half hour or so until rapport has been well established and then to reintroduce the option of video recording. In every case, respondents have agreed.

Motivating Respondents

As humans, we seek pleasure and avoid pain. Research participants are generally encouraged to get involved in studies because they believe in the intrinsic value of being a subject. Their consent is further reinforced by situational factors under the ethnographer's control: by feelings of shared accomplishment and common purpose. Ethnographers who strive to make the experience personally rewarding for participants will facilitate disclosure in on-site visits. Here are some ways to think about structuring the encounter to make it psychically pleasing for respondents.

Expectations. If the ethnographer shares high expectations for the session's outcomes, respondents will follow that lead. There is always a bit of anxiety as the encounter begins. The people involved are new to each other, struggling to define their roles or figure out the right way to behave. Despite all the preparation, the initial encounter may feel forced or awkward. It is the ethnographer's responsibility to take over and fill the vacuum. This section of a transcript exemplifies an actual entry into respondents' lives and shows the importance of setting high goals from the outset.

Ethnographer: Hi Trish!

Respondent: Hello!

Ethnographer: How are you doing? Nice to meet you.

Respondent: I'm fine. How are you? Nice to meet you.

Ethnographer: Oh thanks so much for letting us come in and visit with you this morning.

Respondent: Oh sure!

Ethnographer: We're really looking forward to it.

Respondent: Well, I hope it's successful.

Ethnographer: Uh, looks like, looks like it will be.

Respondent: Of course I'm not quite sure exactly.

Ethnographer: Well let me introduce you to Sean [camera operator]

Respondent: Hi Sean. How are you?

Ethnographer: And, we'll turn off the camera for a minute while we discuss what we're up to . . .

Recognition. Respondents participate in research studies because they seek recognition and validation. They are flattered when major corporations seek their advice. When site visitors show positive regard and treat the respondent as the expert, they build rapport and help respondents demonstrate their regular practices with comfort and confidence.

The following example shows how this was accomplished in a site visit on the topic of bathroom cleaning by reinforcing the participant's expertise through reassurance that "you seem to know a lot about cleaning." This helped her feel more comfortable about being observed and interviewed, and it also stimulated further questions about how she learned about cleaning. The participant was using a razor blade to scrape off some glass shelves, and then sprays them with glass cleaner and wipes them off.

Ethnographer: So you use them together on spots like that?

Respondent: Actually, I keep one [razor blade] in my bathroom because when I put my mascara on in the morning it flakes on the mirror, and you can't just get that off with Windex or any other kind of window cleaner for that matter. So I keep the razor blade and scrape the whole mirror off, and then I go over it with Windex or whatever cleaning products I have.

Ethnographer: That's a really good tip! So mascara is problematic. Are there any other products that are problematic?

Respondent: You know when you get blush and stuff down in your grout, it's very hard to get out.

Ethnographer: What have you tried and what have you . . .

Respondent: Probably just that stuff I showed you . . . I had cranberry juice in the tile in the grout, and I could not get it out so ended up using bleach.

Ethnographer: You seem to know a lot about cleaning!

Respondent: (laughs) Just call me Hazel!

Ethnographer: (laughs) I was wondering, do you look to any particular sources for cleaning tips?

Respondent: No. Again it all goes back to my mother. I think just because our house was always neat and clean and I tried to appreciate that. And then, once I got my own house . . .

Altruism. Participants respond in research studies because they want to make a contribution. They are excited that their responses will impact company policies, help develop new products, and help create new advertising campaigns. Some categories and products are better able to position themselves as responding to respondents' altruistic strivings, those that involve health, education, and social welfare, for example.

Sympathy. Sometimes, people participate in research because they are looking for sympathy. They may have had a negative experience with a product category or a particular brand and are now looking for a receptive listener. The ethnographer may pay attention but ought to avoid making disparaging remarks about competitive brands.

Catharsis. Similarly, some participants just want to get something off their chest. They are encouraged when others hold the same opinion or when they are given a compassionate ear.

Meaning. Respondents appreciate being able to see things in new ways or reflect on their behavior. It is common for respondents to close the visit by commenting, "I never really realized that I go through all these steps" in completing a task.

New experience. An on-site visit can be an exhilarating experience. Novel research techniques are stimulating for the respondent as well as for the researcher. Typically, at the close of the session, respondents will speak enthusiastically about how much fun the experience was for them.

Extrinsic rewards. It would be naïve to believe that respondents are only motivated by intrinsic rewards; obviously, participants are encouraged to follow the rules because they are being paid a generous cash payment at the end of the session. In the United States, research participation is viewed as a form of work with associated norms of commitment, responsibility to employers, and so on. In 2004, a typical payment for cooperating respondents was $200 or more per visit. Nevertheless, researchers should never rely only on the fee to encourage openness, nor should respondents ever be threatened with withholding the fee for any reason whatsoever.

Note

1. Material in this section is adapted from Gorden, 1975.

19

Asking Questions

Asking respondents for information is not a simple process. To collect accurate and reliable data, the researcher must be careful to ask questions fairly. The ethnographer is continuously challenged to maintain rapport and assure honesty and open revelations; consequently, everything about the process—from the stance taken through the forms of the questions, probes, and reactions—must be managed sensitively.

Naïve Outsider Role

Team members should play the role of a *naïve outsider* coming to learn about things from the participant's point of view. This requires them to suspend or suppress their own knowledge and leave the initiative to the respondents. This is difficult because respondents tend to treat visitors as the experts. They will ask, "Am I doing this right?" or similarly betray a lack of confidence in their conventional practices when first confronted by members of the visiting team.

Ethnographers often have to emphasize that they are coming into the setting without assumptions. Here's a helpful example:

> I know it's hard to believe that someone knows absolutely nothing about laundry detergent, but when you're responding, please treat me as though I'm completely ignorant about this product.

Also, prefacing questions by saying, "Can you help me out?" or "I would like to learn about . . . in your own words" places the respondent in an authoritative position and helps with maintaining rapport.

Natural Language

Researchers should learn consumers' natural language and terminology as quickly as possible. This will allow them to call things by their "right" names and avoid imprecision about what respondents mean. Researchers should avoid using business or marketing jargon, even relatively benign usages such as referring to "white goods," which has no meaning to average people. Consumers may be using the "wrong" words from the perspective of the visiting team, but it is not the team's responsibility to share "correct" usages. Instead, observers should focus on how consumers talk about the products and categories under examination.

Researchers also have to be sensitive to cultural, regional, and social class differences in language usage. Certain expressions may have different connotations and meanings, and this could have a broad impact on the implications derived from the research. Observers should choose their words carefully and make certain they fully understand what respondents mean.

Natural language becomes critical in several contexts: when dealing with youth culture, members of ethnic groups, and technically oriented subjects. Youth culture, for one, uses its own language as an identity badge. Reinforced by sources such as hip-hop music and the terminology used in SMS messaging or Internet chat rooms, youth jargon helps to communicate ideas that young people want to keep from the adult world. Its subject matter may be drugs, sexual dalliance, or other forms of rebellion; they may express unique values and aspirations. Once adult culture begins to catch on—as, for example, when the Oxford English Dictionary provides the meaning of *bling-bling* (bright, as in jewelry)—youth culture generally moves on to another set of words.

Members of racial and cultural minorities also use their own argot at times as a symbol of inclusion or exclusion. African-American and Yiddish cultures in the United States have had a strong impact on usages that often defame members of the out-group and assert in-group solidarity. Often, usages are reversed, as when something is referred to as *funky, phat,* or *bad* as a positive indicator, in order to reinforce group spirit and sense of belonging and to further confuse outsiders.

Technical language is pervasive in all types of occupations and professions. Conducting ethnographies in just about any workplace requires you to learn the meaning of the precise terminology used there. Often, technical language creeps into the larger culture as shorthand for new kinds of habits and cultural trends; for example, when we say we want to "google" something as a way of expressing that we expect to use a search engine for executing an Internet search.

Composing a Question

Questions asked in an ethnographic research study should be phrased clearly and precisely. Researchers should also be sensitive to the underlying structure of the questions and watch their tone of voice as they speak.

- *What, how,* and *when* questions about factual matters or opinions encourage respondents to offer explanatory answers.

  "How do you decide whether to use the liquid or the powder?"

  "When do you go to the 'help' function?"

- To encourage elaboration, use active verbs to preface questions: *Describe, explain, tell me,* and *spell out* are good ways to begin questions. Researchers also ask: "Clarify what you mean by . . . ," "Give me details about . . . ," and "Put . . . into plain words."
- Limit questions or probes using *why.* Even though the main objective for qualitative research is to explain why, questions that begin that way tend to stimulate defensiveness. They restrict the range of responses. *Why* puts people on the spot, making them think they have to supply a rational explanation immediately. *Why* questions can be touchy, inflammatory, and threatening if they seem frequent.
- Ask questions in a way that permits a range of opinions. Several types of questions that open options are provided in the next section.

Types of Questions

Questions differ in terms of whether they are asking for something factual or seeking to explore underlying emotions or attitudes behind a behavior or an expressed opinion. In most marketing studies, we ask for statements of fact; for example, "How often to you go to the movies every month?" In marketing ethnographies, on the other hand, we need to resist seeking statements of fact related to behaviors under review until after they have been enacted. Obviously, we need to observe before we ask, and if we solicit information such as "How do you wash your dishes?" or "How do you diaper your baby?" before watching the behavior, we are setting up a set of expectations that will influence what consumers will actually do.

In seeking feelings or opinions, we often have to help consumers frame their responses accurately. Many respondents feel inhibited about expressing negative emotions when a visitor is in their home and need help to reveal themselves. Here are several useful questioning approaches that help consumers frame their attitudes.

- *Two-tailed questions:* This type of question sets up a response framework and validates highly positive or negative opinions. The manner of formulating the question is to state both sides; for example: "Some people would be highly satisfied with this kind of an outcome; others would be very disappointed. Where do you stand?"
- *Prefaces that encourage revelation:* Introducing a question in a manner that encourages respondents to acknowledge negative emotions is often necessary when it appears that the politeness barrier is inhibiting them from revealing themselves. This question takes the form of "Some people feel x if y. How do you feel?" as expressed in the following exchange:

(Respondent is coughing and choking after spraying Product X to clean the ceilings inside his shower.)

Ethnographer: How do you feel about the way the product is working?

Respondent: It's OK, I suppose.

Ethnographer: I suppose it's working to clean up inside the shower, but how are you feeling right now?

Respondent: Could be better . . .

Ethnographer: Well, some people would be feeling upset about coughing like that. How did you feel about it?

Respondent: Yeah, I could do without the coughing.

- *Avoid educating or informing respondents:* Researchers can bias responses by betraying too much of what they are subconsciously or consciously expecting to hear. During the course of natural conversations, we normally are not neutral. We converse to convince, to sell our ideas, to debate, or to dramatize our verbal or conceptual skills. These aspects of natural conversations must be muted during ethnographic site visits lest they offend or inappropriately guide respondents.
- *Avoid leading questions:* Leading questions are those that imply a preferred answer as they are asked. They should be carefully avoided. The worst form of leading question is the one that starts with a declaration and then looks for confirmation; for example, "You want to be more productive, don't you? Do you agree that this would be a good product for us to offer?"
- *Don't inject your own opinions into the discussion:* This has a tendency to lead respondents who may be seeking the approval of an authority figure. At the same time, be sensitive and sympathetic toward what respondents are saying through their body language and give them a chance to express negative emotions.

- *Sequence of questions:* To reduce ego threat, let your question sequence follow the natural stages of the interview described earlier. In the early stages, engage in small talk and ask general questions to get oriented. Save challenging and pointed questions until late in the experience.

REACTIONS, ACKNOWLEDGMENTS, AND REINFORCEMENTS

When somebody provides a response or finishes a task, it is natural for the researcher to punctuate it with a reaction, acknowledgment, or reinforcement. However, it is very important to avoid judgmental responses that are common in natural conversation like, "That's good," or "That's too bad."

The observer should react with emotionally neutral reinforcements, if any; for example, "That's interesting to see" or "That's new to me" or just, "Uh-huh." Nonverbal reinforcements are also important. A smile, a nod, or widening your eyes demonstrates interest and encouragement without leading respondents in particular directions.

ACTIVE LISTENING

Ethnographers must be active listeners, continuously analyzing the discussion in their own minds and seeking the larger meanings and implications of behaviors that are being enacted. Participants also need frequent evidence that the observer is being attentive and empathizing with respondent concerns. Sometimes, ethnographers may rephrase a participant's remark or summarize the drift of the discussion to demonstrate their understanding of the issues that concern respondents.

When ethnographers are listening actively, they should avoid making respondent's feel as though words are being put into their mouths. Do not declare or interpret "what respondents really mean" during the course of an interview because it will make them feel disempowered. If a respondent's remark is paraphrased, the ethnographer should always double check with the respondent to make certain that his or her voice is represented authentically.

THE SPECIFIC QUESTIONS AND ACTIVITIES STAGE

The specific questions and activities stage normally begins about 30 to 45 minutes into the on-site visit. If things have been going well, the ethnographer has cultivated rapport with the respondents, and they have developed a comfortable behavior and discussion pattern.

The interview is now ready to move into a higher risk mode:

- to delve into emotions
- to probe more intensely
- to discuss sensitive issues

20

Expanding Your
Understanding of Respondents

This chapter describes additional strategies for gathering information from respondents.

Probing

There's always more to learn after a task has been observed and a question has been answered. Good researchers want to understand salience, implications, and emotional resonance. Furthermore, because of time pressures or ego threat, respondents may be offering less than a full response. That's where probing becomes important. The observer may ask for clarification, elaboration, a definition, a comparison, or a context.

Sometimes, the most effective probe is what is known as the silent probe, in which interviewers simply use body language, such as raised eyebrows, to communicate that they expect more than the respondent has proffered.

Probing has many important functions:

- to check for thoroughness
- as a validation technique
- to demonstrate active listening
- as a starting point for analysis

A sophisticated repertoire of probes distinguishes an effective ethnographic interviewer. Here are some techniques and examples of probing.

- Remember to limit using *why* in probes because overuse of *why* questions tends to make respondents feel uncomfortable and defensive.

- Make effective use of nonverbal probes such as the following:

o Silent probe (the interviewer just keeps listening and expecting more)
o Hand gestures
o Inquisitive or puzzled eyebrows
o Smiling
o Request for elaboration, clarification, definition, context, conditions as in:

Tell me more about that.

What does ___ mean to you?

Do you always do it that way or only sometimes?

Give me an example of ___.

When was the last time you saw/felt/thought ___?

What/who/anything else?

Give me another word for that.

What were you thinking when you ___?

- Add some reflective probes to your repertoire.

o *Echo probe* is a fairly exact playback of what the respondent has said.
o *Summary probe* reduces what the respondent has said to key points and then reflects the content back to make certain that the summary represents the respondent's feelings.
o *Interpretive probe* rephrases what the respondent has said.

When using reflective probes the interviewer should make sure that respondents don't feel that words are being put into their mouths.

- Use confrontational probes only when a high level of confidence and trust has been established. These tend to challenge words or assertions that the respondent has made. For example, "You don't really believe that."

- Use creative probes—imagination, projections, and similar tools—to elicit further feelings from respondents. Here are some examples:

If you were 20/70/90 years old, what would your opinion be?

If I wanted to discourage you from buying the product, what should I say?

If money was no object, which ___ would you choose?

What would you say to someone else about ___?

Interpreting Body Language

Understanding body language while conducting ethnographies is very important on several levels: Being there and paying close attention to respondents' behaviors provides an opportunity for interpreting their inner feelings. Attitudes that participants may not wish to discuss openly can become apparent when their faces contort in anger or express disappointment when they are engaging in a product-usage process.

Researchers also need to be aware of the potential impact of their own nonverbal communication. Ethnographers' feelings of boredom or disgust may be communicated by gestures and expressions as well. These cues may disorient participants and lead to distortions of their own behavior. Thus, the ethnographer needs to maintain a neutral stance to maximize rapport and to control projecting negative attitudes.

Body language and nonverbal communications can be expressed through a variety of channels that are reviewed here.

Facial expressions. The muscles of the face communicate expressively. Paul Ekman (2003) argues that we have inherent ways of exhibiting emotions to the outside world and that educated observers can do a highly reliable job of interpreting these emotional messages. Ekman asserts that facial signals are hardwired into the structure of our brains and are essentially the same whether our emotions take place in Brooklyn, Berlin, or Borneo. Whether or not facial gestures are universal remains a fairly controversial question. Other theorists of body language such as Edward Hall (1959, 1977) and Ray Birdwhistell (1970) emphasize the cultural grounding of both displays and interpretation of outward signals of the inner experience. In contrast, Ekman argues that although the gestures of emotion, such as shaking one's head to say no, are patterned by one's culture, the facial expression of emotion is physiological and, therefore, consistent across cultures.

Ekman (2003) insists and proves that reading the facial expression of emotion is something that can be learned and mastered at high levels of reliability. Basic to the author's approach is understanding that subtle facial expressions of emotion are more common than demonstrative gestures. Emotional signals usually register as microexpressions lasting one fifth of a second or less. There are unconscious, culturally based display rules that require us to suppress, mask, or exaggerate what we are really feeling. We all know how difficult orderly social life would be if people displayed their real feelings in all situations. Language has only a limited capacity for communicating underlying emotions. Consequently, Ekman insists that words cannot be fully trusted as communicators of emotion. We need to look at faces carefully as well as listen to what people are saying.

Body movements and characteristics. Various parts of our bodies in addition to the face convey information: body posture, hands, legs. For example, by maintaining eye contact, smiling appropriately, leaning forward while listening, and acknowledging respondents as they speak, researchers quietly communicate that they are open, honest, and authoritative. Command of a situation is also expressed by an upright posture and assertive hand gestures to emphasize points. Some other examples of body language that you may observe among participants include the following:

- Tightly crossed arms or legs indicate a defensive stance and may represent discomfort or the need to mask an underlying feeling.
- A hand-to-mouth gesture, hands over the eyes, or breaking off eye contact are often used to disguise feelings of doubt, deceit, or exaggeration.
- Open palms facing the listener typically indicate honesty and openness.

Nonverbal aspects of speech. Voice volume, intonation, pitch, and other non-verbal aspects of speech are clues to underlying feelings. Some examples include:

- An increase in pitch often indicates deceitfulness, nervousness, or tension.
- Lowering the volume of speech can indicate doubt or insecurity.
- Hurried or unclear speech, sounding as though the informant is trying to get through with a statement as fast as possible, can indicate deceitfulness or self-doubt. Similarly, very slow speech may indicate that respondents are being exceptionally thoughtful or, conversely, that they are making things up as they go along.

People in space and in relation to each other. Hall (1959) has demonstrated that the manner in which territory and space are manipulated and managed provide clues to inner feelings. Think of the way family members arrange themselves around the dinner table or the way managers take their places around a conference table. Each says a great deal about the authority relations, hierarchy, and power of the particular individuals taking their places. For example, in Western cultures, the most authoritative person is at the head of the table.

In addition, the way personal space is manipulated speaks loudly. We all have culturally produced zones of intimacy. Rules of politeness and discretion maintain strict limits on who may enter these areas. Normally, people who are intruding into someone else's intimacy zone will create discomfort or present themselves as rude because they are not following clear cultural rules for allowing others to come close.

Time. How we use and manipulate time is another dimension of nonverbal communication. People's rate of speech, how quickly they complete an activity, whether they are late or on time, and the rate at which they interrupt can communicate a great deal about relative power, interest, and insecurity about completing a task and many other feelings. It is not uncommon during ethnographic observations in the home-cleaning category, for example, to see consumers wiping or polishing things up very quickly with little regard for the actual outcome. We have referred to these as "get-it-done cleaners" because completing the task quickly ranks higher on their scale of priorities than the actual cleaning outcome.

It is easy to be aware of nonverbal cues but hard to interpret them. Dishonesty or guilt typically cannot be inferred from a single gesture. On the contrary, reading body language requires a careful study of people's individual natural patterns of nonverbal communication as well as breaks or disruptions that may occur when specific questions are asked. Any individual gesture must be interpreted in the context of what else is going on at the moment, not in isolation.

Nonverbal communication is also highly variable across cultures. Consequently, this factor should be taken into account when making interpretations. For example, slowness in reacting to a question may signal evasiveness in most Western cultures; however, in Asian cultures, it may indicate deliberateness. The cultural patterns associated with body language should also be accounted for when making assumptions about respondents' natural patterns because there will be cultural variability based on regional, ethnic, racial, and other demographic differences.

Body language interpreters look for "leaky channels"; that is to say, inconsistencies between words, eyes, hands, and so on. The logic behind this is that it may be possible for a liar to control one or several communication channels but hard to manage them all at once. Thus, if a respondent indicates that he or she likes a product but handles it with minimal affect or eye contact, it may be a clue that the words are false.

Reflecting body language. Skilled interviewers maintain rapport and intimate contact by trying to mimic the respondent's body stance, pace of speech, level of eye contact, and other communications characteristics. This communicates similarity, compassion, solidarity, and other emotions that are useful in the interviewing situation.

Participants will also naturally reflect the ethnographic observer's body language. If the ethnographer is "up" and enthusiastic, respondents are likely to follow that cue. If the ethnographer is dull and speaks in a monotone, it will have a negative impact on the experience and may result in invalid observations.

21

Managing and Closing the Visit

This chapter discusses how to deal with potential obstacles to the site visit and how to close it effectively.

Time Pressures and Contingencies

Ethnographers conducting site visits are subject to a variety of real world pressures that are likely have an impact on their ability to collect useful data:

When outside matters intrude into the site visit. It is difficult to stay on track and not allow the visit to get derailed when other matters interrupt. Phone calls, social visits from family and friends, and intrusions by children are among the personal issues that can cause delays if not total stoppages. If the performance of some task is critical, respondents must be informed that provisions need to be made for care of children or pets while this activity is taking place. Most of the time, however, ethnographers have to be flexible and allow some diversion to private matters and be sensitive to the respondent's personal concerns. After all, we are observing consumers in real time and in their own space, so, predictably, some degree of natural disruptiveness must be expected.

When participants want a non-household member present. We have found that lately, owing to general societal concerns about safety and security, respondents are requesting that non-household members be present during site visits. This concern seems to be particularly prevalent among single women and young mothers. For the most part, we find this practice to be acceptable as long as the guests are treated as such and not incorporated into the observations. If they are present, guest protectors need some degree of orientation about the need to maintain the authenticity of the respondent's behavior.

Scheduling enough time. Visits must be scheduled for a time slot that is long enough to allow for the completion of relevant tasks. Make sure that respondents are not forced to change their routines or habits for the benefit of the research team. Placing time or performance pressures on the respondent destroys rapport and open disclosure. If there are significant time pressures, such as the need to meet travel arrangements, these limitations should be described to respondents well in advance of the visit.

Make sure respondents feel they are being heard. Sometimes, it is necessary to move the visit along. Respondents can become verbose or drift into areas that are not central to study objectives. Also, the real world can get messy, and, owing to lateness, intrusions, and interruptions, the visit's schedule may get disrupted. If researchers need to press for completion, they must make sure that the respondents feel they are being heard and not cut off. Nothing can break rapport as quickly as being rushed to complete tasks.

Determining relevance. At every stage in the visit, the observer will have to make decisions about how relevant and salient a particular remark or behavior may be. Should the researcher pursue an issue by probing? Should he or she take notes on a particular action or statement? For the most part, observers should avoid behaving as though they are in control of the situation. Let the respondents stay in charge and try to understand why things are important to them.

Redirecting the discussion. Researchers should be polite and positive when they have to redirect the discussion, doing this in a spirit of completion and accomplishment and never lack of interest; for example: "I'm glad we finally finished the bathroom; let's move on."

Managing contingencies. Problems have some probability of occurring in all research situations. The observation team can be met by hostility or lack of seriousness. Some respondents may be unable to articulate their attitudes and feelings, or they may be dishonest or highly emotional. The best approach for dealing with contingencies is to remain positive and professional. Researchers should always try to re-establish rapport by emphasizing the positive purposes of the study. It is wrong to threaten to withhold payment or to leave abruptly.

Threats to the researcher. One reason for completing ethnographic site visits as teams is that every once in a while, there may be some threat to the researcher's safety or dignity. We have encountered respondents who were visibly inebriated when the visiting team arrived. In one case, a prospective respondent appeared at the door without clothing. In no case should ethnographers enter a household if they feel that common decorum is not being followed.

Some tips for dealing with common contingencies follow.

- *Lagging interest:* If the energy level and interest at the site start to die down, pay close attention to your own and the team's actions, body language, and energy level. What could you be doing differently? Perhaps, you need to raise your own interest and energy level or manage the encounter differently.
- *Hostility to the interviewer or the research sponsor:* Customers who have had negative experiences with a brand, company, or category may carry a chip on their shoulder, and the observer is the most convenient target for their hostility. In fact, some participants agree to take part in research studies in order to "send those bums a message." To manage this contingency, you should not deny the validity of the criticism or try to defend the company. It will only make matters worse. Instead, acknowledge the problem, get feedback, and move on. Here's one approach:

I understand how you felt to be treated that way by the service department; but research like this is designed to learn how to do things better. What would you have preferred?

- *Emotional reactions.* In the normal course of observation studies, something may trigger a recollection or reinforce some latent emotion that the respondent is feeling. This becomes particularly evident in studies involving health issues, such as diabetes. Suddenly, while discussing a traumatic experience, respondents may react emotionally—with anger, tears or nervous laughter.

Drawing out emotional reactions is actually a sign of success. It indicates that sufficient rapport and confidence have been established between the observer and the observed so that true feelings can be expressed. At the same time, within the situation, it can be experienced as uncomfortable and embarrassing. Here again, the best way to deal with emotional reactions is to show empathy and acknowledge the respondent's special circumstances. Being a good listener without much reaction other than an expression of sympathy and concern is the most effective manner of dealing with this situation.

Closing the Visit

An effective closing is one of the most important parts of the site visit and should not be dismissed as irrelevant. Strong personal feelings often develop as the site visit proceeds, and it can be hard for the respondent to let go of a sympathetic listener. This is particularly true of people in vulnerable social categories, such as the elderly. After a day of observation at her Northern California home, an 87-year-old cancer survivor sharply admitted: "This is the longest amount of time that anyone has listened to me in years. Can you please come back again?"

Protecting the vulnerable is not the only reason to plan for an effective closing. It can have many benefits: It provides a sense of closure and accomplishment for participants. It creates a situation in which respondents may go into a speculative mode to offer projections for the future; for example, do they anticipate changing buying behavior or decision-making habits in any way?

The closing lets respondents offer feedback and may encourage them to suggest ways to improve future site visits. It can also provide a validity check to assess how close to reality respondents' behaviors were while they were being observed.

Ethnographers should initiate the closing about 15 minutes to a half hour before the visit actually ends, with an anticipatory remark, such as, "We need to start winding down now because we only have 29 minutes left."

Closing remarks and questions should stress accomplishment and goal achievement. Participants should be thanked for their cooperation. The researcher should reassure respondents that regardless of their specific behaviors or expressed attitudes, their cooperation will make a difference and contribute to incremental improvements.

Some closing speculative questions may include:

"What concluding advice would you give the company about how to better serve customers?"

"If there was a single word or idea that we should definitely include in an ad campaign directed to you, what would it be?"

"How might you want to do things differently, now that you have been through this experience?"

"What kinds of products or what changes should be made to better meet your needs?"

At the conclusion of the site visit, researchers should bid a warm farewell to everyone in the household. Next, they should make certain to offer the incentive payment or at least discuss how the payment will be transmitted. After gathering up all materials and belongings, it's time to say a final thank you and good-bye. Now, you have to focus on the next visit and the upcoming analysis phase.

PART IV

Analysis and Presentation

22

Introduction to Analysis and Presentation

The process of ethnographic data analysis is often quite challenging. After organizing the fieldwork and interacting with customers, researchers have to make some sense of the collected data. Ethnographies can produce huge volumes of information representing consumer behavior that must be made meaningful. Expressions of attitudes toward products as they are experienced, descriptions of usage processes and outcomes, physical traces of product usage results, and debriefing notes all contribute to the mountain of information that collects at the end of fieldwork. To turn this information into knowledge and action, researchers must become consultants and make certain that research efforts are matched with marketing insights. Ethnographic data must be turned into solid recommendations for marketing strategies and tactics in order to have any productive meaning.

Four steps are essential to move from raw observations to fully processed insights while making certain that the conclusions are not half-baked:

- *Compiling the data:* Make certain that everything is systematically organized so that nothing important escapes attention.

- *Reviewing the data:* Examine the full record systematically to seek out inherent meanings. The review process is continuous following the initiation of fieldwork because conditions in the field may require adaptation and modification of research tactics.

- *Decoding the data:* Determine what is going on in the visual and verbal record so that it all makes sense. Explain what is being reviewed through concepts, generalizations, and metaphors that delineate the inherent meanings that reside in the record of observations. This process also starts at the beginning because hunches and hypotheses based on observations become apparent from the earliest encounters.

- *Making imaginative marketing "leaps" on the basis of the data:* Share insights that influence strategic decision making so that the data collection and analysis delivers its full value to the client. Marketing ethnographies should go beyond simple structured reporting of observations, however valuable these may be; they must produce interpretations of the observations that can drive business decisions.

23

Reporting

Before embarking on the process of analysis, ethnographers should make sure they understand the client's expectations for reporting. Lengthy, highly technical reports, although satisfying to academics, are not necessarily the best means of making ideas compelling to the marketing managers who make decisions on the basis of ethnographic studies.

Researchers working for particular clients for the first time should learn about local traditions for reporting; typically, corporate cultures have unique expectations for report length and media. There is no single standard for optimizing the effectiveness of the information. At the very least, users of ethnography expect the consultant to go considerably beyond describing the data to discuss implications for their business. Nevertheless, some clients expect heavy documentation and support whereas others demand the briefest of summaries featuring primarily conclusions and recommendations.

In addition, some clients demand heavy involvement in the analytic process while others expect the conclusions to be developed entirely by the consultant. Maximizing client service requires researchers to be attentive to client expectations for participation in the analysis as well as their need for particular deliverables.

Developing Deliverables

Following the completion of data collection and analysis, the written report is the final deliverable for the site visits. The report should be composed as the authoritative record of the observations for both immediate and long-term needs. Final reports are both *descriptive* and *prescriptive*, offering rich details about consumer behavior and opinion patterns as well as an extensive discussion of their implications for strategic marketing and new product development.

If a video record of the site visits has been made, it is possible to develop a video report of findings as a supplementary deliverable. This format allows the presentation of excerpts from the video record that illustrate and exemplify points made in the written reports. Preparing a video report requires several additional steps in planning, data review, and script development.

Types of Reports

How the information will be used is often a good guide to the reporting format and type of analysis that will be required. As noted earlier, many ethnographic studies are commissioned primarily to provide corporate managers with a consumer-immersion experience. In this case, offering opportunities for post-fieldwork debriefing and brainstorming of research implications is highly desirable; clients often request nothing more than a review of ideation outcomes.

At the other extreme are clients who expect to create documentary records of consumer behaviors that may be reviewed from time to time after the study's completion. These marketers will sometimes require detailed case reports in addition to a summary report and may benefit from having retrieval tools, such as processing through a qualitative data analysis software package.

Let's review some of the reporting formats common in corporate ethnography.

Ideation summary. Following a consumer immersion experience, the ideation summary is a record of insights, observations, and ideas that were acquired through encountering customers.

Site report. Also called a case analysis, this report is a thorough review of behaviors and attitudes at a single site. It is generally organized against a template or format sheet so that observations can be systematized and made comparable across a range of categories.

Summary reports. These can vary in length from 3 to 15 pages, depending on client expectations, and normally focus on the most important research implications and conclusions. Summary reports either are developed following a review of the ethnographic record or are based on recollections of the visiting team. If significant detail is required, we recommend reviewing the entire collection of site reports across individual topics. Thereby, the modal consensus or range of behaviors across respondents can be reported with a high level of accuracy.

Full reports. These offer a definitive review of study findings, implications, and conclusions by combining interpretive details with an elaboration of characteristic observations and verbatim respondent comments. Full reports may vary in length from about 35 to as many as 100 pages of text. In our experience, full reports are diminishing in popularity on account of increasing corporate pressure for fast delivery of a study's strategic insights and reduced opportunities among marketing managers to lavish time on digesting reports of such length. On the other hand, within organizations that preserve a strong culture of background preparation, we find that full reports are commissioned to provide a training resource for new and current employees.

PowerPoint reports. The growing popularity of presentation software, notably Microsoft PowerPoint, has directed client expectations toward this format, which can be read quickly and managed efficiently on internal Web resources; it easily merges text with sound, images, and animations. The oral presentation of a PowerPoint report is also popular with consultants eager to intensify their level of client service. Presentation software sometimes enforces a kind of rigidity that reduces the subtlety and complexity of ethnographic findings. Nevertheless, it simplifies the communication of research results among corporate stakeholders.

Video reports. The growing popularity of digital video, as noted previously, combined with the proliferation of easy-to-use multimedia creativity tools such as Macromedia Director, has stimulated a variety of alternative reporting formats that have gained favor among ethnographers. The video report created as a CD-ROM, DVD, or video kiosk presentation has the additional advantage of permitting a high level of interactivity among users because information may be accessed in a nonlinear fashion.

Sophisticated video reports require consultants familiar with production tools and a higher than average financial investment; nevertheless, they are very effective in communicating research results across a wide spectrum of stakeholders including senior management, the customer service organization, and the sales force, where this format has been avidly embraced.

24

Compiling, Organizing, and Analyzing Ethnographic Data

As mentioned earlier, the analytic process starts with the very first impressions gained by the ethnographic team. When team members communicate and share observations and hypothetical generalizations from the very beginning, everyone is alerted to potential directions for modifying subsequent site visits. Early encounters also provide the basis for the final analysis, which is a continuous process rather than one that begins only at the conclusion of data collection. Consequently, compiling data and organizing them logically are essential analytic processes. Furthermore, because corporate ethnography is commonly a collaborative endeavor, structuring continuous communication among all team members throughout the fieldwork stage is critical in achieving valid and reliable conclusions.

Debriefing Meetings

Among the site visit team. Debriefing meetings among observers should be conducted as soon as possible after completing a site visit, while impressions are still fresh. Here are some tasks to include in the debriefing.

- Share impressions.
- Make sure that reasonable consensus exists surrounding participants' opinions and resolving discrepancies if they occur.
- Make sure that observers at the sessions do not leave with disputed impressions, if possible.
- Where disputed impressions exist, try to understand their source. In particular, if disputed impressions are somehow related to differential statuses of observers—for example, if male and female ethnographers are leaving

encounters with highly different understandings—the analysis ought to reflect on that divergence.

- Suggest areas of the record that may require additional review during the analysis.
- Share ideas, hunches, and hypotheses about the implications of observations.
- Recommend changes in the approach and conduct of future site visits that will resolve any disputes and lend further substantiation to study conclusions.

Debriefing meetings are usually conducted at the discretion of the research team. If there are no compelling reasons to hold them or if doing so is too inconvenient—for example, if the moderator and observers are fatigued or if there are no disputed impressions—then the meetings may be shortened or eliminated.

Within the research company. It is a best practice to conduct a debriefing or brainstorming session among all researchers involved in a particular project after all the site visits have been completed. This activity can be invaluable in reaching consensus about project findings and conclusions.

Returning to the site: Every once in a while, following a debriefing session, it may become necessary to recontact the respondent or even return to the site to flesh out some detail. If this takes place, we recommend first discussing this with the recruiter, who is normally the primary contact with the respondent, to make certain that the latter is available and willing to cooperate.

Building the Report

CREATING CASE FILES

Before going further, case files should be created and labeled in a consistent manner. Labels should carry a reasonable amount of category information to facilitate faster retrieval. Colored tabs, such as those used in medical records environments, may simplify this process for some ethnographers. Information provided on the label should include date, time, basic demographics such as respondent gender and age, if relevant, and location and usage categories that were used to differentiate participants in the first place.

CREATING CASE ANALYSES AND SITE REPORTS

Site reports are a critical tool used by many ethnographers to code the various elements of the record that need to be included in the analysis. Site reports contain a summary of observations, tentative findings, and verbatim respondent comments, reported in a consistent manner according to a template or site report format developed for each project. Site reports are organized by topic and generally cover all or most of the points covered in the observation guide.

Writing site reports of each visit guarantees that high-priority information needed for analysis and presentation has been extracted from the disorganized data record that emerges from each site. It is a good idea to be thoroughly familiar with the site report format before reviewing the data so that the proper pieces of information can be extracted as they come up while reviewing the entire record.

Because systematic coding of the collected material facilitates the production of site reports, many ethnographers use this secondary record as the foundation of the final report. Going through the collected cases point by point is an efficient way of extracting meaningful conclusions about the range of behaviors, the relationship between particular behaviors or attitudes and various respondent categories, and other useful indicators.

QUALITATIVE DATA ANALYSIS SOFTWARE

The process of ethnographic data analysis can be facilitated through the use of qualitative data analysis (QDA) software. Available packages may be used in various ways for retrieving words, phrases, images, and other documentary elements; for example, the ethnographer may apply the case analysis template through the software and thereby automate the analytic process. QDA software may also be used as a search engine to seek information and build conclusions according to hypotheses. After verbatim quotations are categorized by topic, they can be inserted into reports and presentations by simply cutting and pasting. The software also makes it possible to incorporate video, audio, and laptop notes.

QDA software facilitates teamwork. A single transcript can be split electronically so that more than one person can analyze it at the same time, thereby speeding up the analysis process.

WORKING WITH QDA SOFTWARE

Before using qualitative analysis software, original data or transcripts must be reformatted into a software-compatible format. Because most analysis software currently requires imports to be formatted in plain text or ASCII text, you may have to reformat your original transcripts from Word to ASCII text. This is a simple "Save as" operation.

After importing the data, select key sentences or paragraphs by highlighting them just as you would in the coding process for paper transcripts. These target sentences or paragraphs are then allocated into different topic categories. At this stage, you are building a quotation warehouse, with quotes stored by topic. Auto-coding functions enable you to get a quick clustering of key words from the original transcript by simply selecting meaningful terms. For example, in a home cleaning study, selecting terms for various surface materials such as *wood, ceramic,* and *marble* can automatically help to locate observations about these materials across the entire documentary record.

Currently, about 20 analysis software programs are on the market. William Han (2004) has tested, used, and compared the five most popular programs—NVivo, ATLASti, HyperRESEARCH, MAXqda, and The Ethnograph—and summarized his findings in the chart below. Ratings are based on ease of use and range of features. Prices range from $370 to $745 for a single-user license.

QDA programs can ease some of the more tedious steps associated with data review and summarization, but they cannot be relied on to produce the imaginative leaps required to have a significant impact on client decision making. For this to occur, the analyst must go beyond the current information. Comparing current findings to the context of knowledge about the marketplace and how it is moving is a necessary step. Understanding the client's current and desired business situation are also essential.

Validity and Reliability

The production of knowledge about social phenomena requires that we pay attention to whether our observations are valid and reliable. Reviewing a range of prior authors, Winter (2000) notes that validity can be described variously as "an agreement between two efforts to measure the same thing with different methods," "accuracy," "degree of approximation of 'reality,'" and "are we measuring what we think we are?" Similarly, the range of meanings connected with reliability include: "An agreement between two efforts to measure the same thing with the same methods," "accuracy or precision of a measuring instrument," and "reproducibility of the measurements . . . stability." Overall, reliability is a measure of how *replicable* any set of findings may be.

Validity and reliability in the context of qualitative research do not carry the same meanings as they do in quantitative research. Qualitative methodology is often dismissed as a less-scientific approach to the social sciences. The quantitative model is held to be more scientific because it is

5 Popular Qualitative Analysis Software Programs

Product Name	NVivo 2.0	ATLAS.ti 4.2	HyperRESEARCH 2.6	MAXqda	The Ethnograph v5.0
Company	QSR International	Scientific Software Development	ResearchWare, Inc.	VERBI GmbH Marburg	Qualis Research Associates
Rating	BEST	EXCELLENT	GOOD	VERY GOOD	GOOD
Web-Site	www.qrs.com	www.atlasti.de	www.researchware.com/	www.maxqda.com	www.qualisresearch.com
Price (single user)	$735	$715	$370	$745	$515
System Requirements	PC Only 400MHzCPU 64M RAM Windows2000, XP	PC, Mac, Sun Ultra Pentium/AMD 133 MHz; 32M RAM, Window 9X, 2000, NT, ME, XP, Mac, Sun Ultra	PC, Mac OS 7.6 through 9.2.2, X10.1 Windows 98, 2000, NT, ME, XP	PC Only, Pentium 2 64MB RAM Windows 9X, 2000, ME, Windows NT 4.0	PC Only, 12MB RAM, 12MB Hard Disk Pentium Processor Windows 95 onwards
Transcript Import Format	RTF, ASCII Text	ASC II Text	ASCII Text	RTF	ASCII Text
Code Export Format	RTF	ASCII, RTF	ASCII Text	RTF	ASCII Text

5 Popular Qualitative Analysis Software Programs (Continued)

Product Name	NVivo 2.0	ATLAS.ti 4.2	HyperRESEARCH 2.6	MAXqda	The Ethnograph v5.0
Unique Features	• Strong right-click menu • Auto coding • Convenient browsers • Visualized theory building • Multimedia import • Teamwork setting • Hands-on tutoring	• Drag, drop coding • Auto coding • Detailed right-click menu • The Network Editor • XML data import/export • Multimedia coding	• "Point and Click" interface • Multimedia import • Code Annotation (Memoing) • Case card feature • Expanded Auto coding • Code Mapping • Hypothesis testing	• Online to drag, drop • Word frequency statistics • Coding weight score • Memo Manager • Analytical command • Teamwork Export	• In-text coding display • Memo writing
Support	☐ User group ☐ Global workshop ☐ Email	☐ Workshop ☐ User forum ☐ Email support	☐ Email support ☐ Phone support	☐ Fun tutor Web Site ☐ Email support ☐ Workshop	☐ Basic email support ☐ Online tips

SOURCE: From Han, W., "Automating analysis: Selecting and using qualitative analysis software," in *QRCA Views*, *2*(3), Spring 2004. Reprinted with permission.

195

better focused on formal steps taken to produce certainty and because it uses the standards of validity and reliability to demonstrate the relative quality of research findings. However, these may not be appropriate or desirable for qualitative studies. Numerous philosophers and theorists of science since Kuhn's (1962) work on scientific revolutions have debunked the idea that any single approach can claim greater scientific truth than any other based only on its own principles and methods. Nevertheless, it is necessary to confront contemporary definitions of validity and reliability drawn from the quantitative tradition and demonstrate equivalent criteria appropriate for qualitative research.

For starters, ethnographers must confront the issue of quality. Factors that can inherently bias and thereby reduce the quality of research results must be avoided; these include selecting unrepresentative respondents, conducting the ethnographic encounters in a manner that fails to capture essential facts about specific behavioral processes, failing to gain insight from sufficient respondents that cover the varied consumer segments, and basing interpretations on elements other than direct observation of consumer practices. Nevertheless, preventing the purposeful introduction of bias does not mean we must seek a single, static, or objective truth.

Sanjay (cited in Arnould & Wallendorf, 1994) suggests that there are three criteria for assessing an ethnography:

> theoretical candor, transparent representation of the ethnographer's path through data collection, and accounting for the relationship between ethnographic interpretation and field note evidence. (p. 485)

Investigators need to accept that a degree of subjectivity will pervade all qualitative studies. The fact that multiple observers may learn parallel truths is inevitable; cleansing the data of diversity and multiple perspectives introduces yet another set of biases. In contrast, we need to seek a nuanced understanding of the phenomena we are investigating, subjected to a standard of *substantive validity.* That is to say, a pragmatic approach to validity may be based on whether knowing a particular set of study results truly empowers decision makers to make useful adjustments to marketing strategies and tactics.

25

Interpreting and Drawing Conclusions

Operating within the application framework of market research requires ethnographers to maintain an orientation to knowledge production that differs from academically oriented ethnographers. The client orientation that stimulates and sponsors our work must be honored throughout the analysis process.

Interpreting Ethnographic Data

The analytic focus of a market-oriented ethnography should always be on the decision-making needs of the commissioning user. Detailed reports of observations are not enough, no matter how inherently interesting they may be; the ethnographer needs to go well beyond the information collected in the study. A skilled analyst is necessary to make imaginative leaps that go beyond the findings. As Smith and Fletcher (2004) assert,

> Market research is about helping individuals make informed, evidence-based judgements and decisions. It is about asking intelligent questions of users, and potential users, of products and services about their opinions and experiences, listening carefully to what they say, and then interpreting the implications of the feedback. (p. 2)

Interpreters of ethnographic information also need to understand the context, the internal dynamics of the corporate environment that is spurring the investigation. They must realize that the ethnographic studies are being conducted as but one of many information inputs—less than perfect data sources based in multiple methodologies—that are competing for credibility and influence among marketing stakeholders. Ethnographers are likely to enhance their authoritativeness if they understand and work in a complementary manner with practitioners of other methodologies, such as those producing attitude and usage surveys or focus group studies, to fill out the information picture of consumers that the client is seeking.

Clients are nowadays seeking more originality, innovation, and insightfulness as well. Moreover, they need the material presented in an engaging and attractive manner. Research users are being pressured by their internal clients to deliver clarity and reduce complexity. The information overload is already well under way in the corporate boardroom. Brief and meaningful insights that deliver a high level of benefit are favored over mountains of detail.

The analyst's influence is also likely to be enhanced by a thorough understanding of the client's business. In particular, it is helpful to understand corporate culture, goals, and aspirations and how the company's products are faring in the current business climate.

Making Generalizations

Generalizations about the site are translated into various levels of analysis:

- *Descriptions of potential market segments or types of consumers:* During the course of observations, attention may be directed toward distinct categories of behavioral or emotional connections. For example, in research on home cleaning, QualiData ethnographers found two broad categories of consumers; namely, "get-it-done cleaners," who were oriented toward expeditious and convenient completion of tasks, and "serious cleaners," who cared deeply about outcomes. These broad categories allowed clients to plan products meaningful to either segment.

- *Elaborations of processes or sequences in brand decision making or product usage:* Watching consumers complete a process reveals a series of stages meaningful within that category. For example, constructing a breakfast involves assembling ingredients and foods appropriate to that category and preparing them in a particular manner. Daily breakfasts are occasions for consuming cold foods straight from the refrigerator or toasted ingredients.

- *Descriptions of similarities and differences between demographic or brand preference segments:* We learn a great deal in ethnographies by comparing people: older versus younger, those committed to a particular brand versus the uncommitted, those willing to change versus people who are fixed in their habits. Then, through the method of comparative analysis, we may articulate how different types of consumers might behave differently at home or in the marketplace.

- *Hypotheses about causal relationships or conditions that predispose consumers to particular habits or preferences:* Knowing the impact of these influential variables help marketers learn how to satisfy consumer expectations.

- *Thick description:* Meaningful details about unmet needs, home remedies, product combinations, and other information related to site observations can be very useful. These findings can help marketers pinpoint potential areas for new product development.

Creating Imaginative Interpretations

It is difficult to suggest a systematic process for inducing imaginative reflection. To a large degree, this depends on the analyst's experience, intelligence, and sensitivity to client needs. Regardless, it is worthwhile to review several approaches that have proven to be useful. Seeking principles for analytic guidance, Arnould and Wallendorf (1994) offer several valuable analytic stimuli that are included in this section. The authors warn that analysis is not a linear process and hard to reduce to simple propositions. Nevertheless, their ideas are worth noting.

Theoretical direction: Many analysts, particularly those with strong academic grounding, favor analyzing the data through the prism of social scientific theories (Ezzy, 2002.) Using the logic and principles of symbolic interactionism, Freudian psychology, or postmodern theory, for example, may offer guidance for understanding observed phenomena. However, most of the time, clients are more oriented toward pragmatic analysis that supports decision making and show little regard for how well findings match up with theoretical presuppositions.

Accounting for disjunctures. It is common for ethnographers to find that their observations do not fit neatly into set categories. There are convergences and divergences between respondents' verbal expressions and observed behavior, for example, and the ethnographer can often create insights by accounting for these gaps.

Revelatory incidents. During the course of site visits, something typically happens that demands both explication and contextualization. This is the proverbial "Aha!" moment. In the course of a study of paper towel usage, for example, QualiData ethnographers persistently observed paper towels being used in situations that would normally call for paper napkins. When probed, respondents frequently insisted that this behavior was driven by dissatisfaction with using paper napkins while eating various categories of "finger foods" that were becoming increasingly popular at the American dinner table. These findings suggested a host of new product opportunities that were thoroughly developed in reports to the client. A later section of this book reviews several other potential "Aha!" moments.

Personal interpretation. Analysts can offer clarity by accounting for how people interpret their own behavior and actions observed by the ethnographers. During the course of a study, we may find that consumers make unrealistic claims; for example, they may assert that they use branded products when in fact their choice is off-brand. Probing this kind of attitude-behavior gap can produce insights that clarify the basis for product choice within the category.

Cultural context. Placing observed behaviors within their cultural context can reveal higher levels of meaning that are obscured by simple observation. Grooming rituals, for example, are types of situated behaviors that are occasions for using a wide range of product categories—among them hair care products, toothpaste, and skin cream. Accounting for how these behaviors are linked to larger cultural expectations for self-presentation may reveal levels of meaning that circumscribe choice patterns. For example, using certain creams may indicate concerns about aging in a youth-obsessed society.

Tropes. Arnould and Wallendorf (1994, p. 498) advocate constructing tropes; that is, "meaningful symbolic links between various behaviors or verbal statements" as a means of expanding insights into product usage. Illustrating larger structures of meaning by demonstrating what a behavior "stands for" or "what it is like" potentially offers clues to promotional strategies or further product development. Although the authors describe several categories of tropic relations, the most important in our work has been what they describe as metaphoric.

Metaphors. These are constructed to describe a relation of similarity between an observation and a larger cultural phenomenon or structure of meaning. A stuffed turkey at Thanksgiving, for example, symbolizes the larger significance of the holiday as an occasion for experiencing abundance and freedom from want. Feeling stuffed at the end of the meal is paralleled by what happens to the turkey.

From Ethnographic Data to Marketing Intelligence

How do you know when you have a new product opportunity? Observations can often suggest that new product opportunities are lurking in the collected data. The process of going from observation to insight is not an easy one. It requires a heavy dose of what Edward de Bono (1970) called *lateral thinking*, moving from rational calculation to imaginative leaps to the possible.

Consumers themselves are not always conscious of what new product innovations would actually address their own wants and needs. They often believe that the currently available product offerings are as good as anyone can find. When questioned directly about their wants and needs, consumers tend to offer complacent clichés—lower price, more per package, different colors—that hardly yield conceptual breakthroughs and revolutionary innovations.

This section describes the types of observations that should inspire researchers to think about the opportunities that may be revealed when we watch people in their roles as consumers. It suggests that people's behaviors may be better clues to what they want and need than their expressed opinions. Ten categories of observations or behavioral clues that should set innovators thinking are outlined here.

Observing a pattern of product usage reveals process steps. When ethnographers pay close attention to consumers while the latter are using a product, the researchers can observe the stages through which respondents go from intention to satisfaction. The steps may begin when materials are assembled and homemakers change clothing as they start a household clean-up, and they end as homemakers admire the shiny results of their scrubbing.

The steps consumers go through from beginning to end usually reveal clues to expectations, fears, doubts, and wishes.

Process steps in the laundry are exceptionally revealing. Before using their washing machines, consumers go through the task of sorting clothing according to anticipated problems and wishes. Whites are separated from colored garments because of fears about colors running and ruining the whites or because of expectations that white washables need extra attention with chlorine bleach. Some homemakers remove heavily stained clothing during the sorting process in order to treat them with additional products, such as stain removers or pre-soaks.

Paying attention to the process has certainly yielded more than a fair share of innovations, such as nonchlorine bleach. Continuing to seek possibilities in observations of process can take the category even further. QualiData ethnographers were surprised when a study of laundry practices in Turkey revealed that women, following Islamic custom, separated men's garments from those of women. This observation suggested innovations that could address the needs and expectations of consumers in this market, which were not being met by available brands.

Consumers make mistakes. People tend to blame themselves, Don Norman (1990) has noted, when they make mistakes while using a product. They naively accuse themselves of lacking experience, not reading the directions carefully enough, or just not having enough skill with technology.

Mistakes usually occur when the product does not make itself instantly understandable, when users' stock of knowledge creates contradictory expectations, or when their mental images of the ways things are supposed to work are violated by product operation. These problems with usability and a readable user interface do not happen only with computer programs, cell phones, and VCRs. Consumers make mistakes when they use all kinds of products, and watching these usually provides fuel for new product adaptation and innovation.

Several years ago, when we observed consumers using insecticide baits, we were surprised to watch as they used insecticide sprays at the same time, a huge mistake that in effect deactivated the product. Baits are supposed to work by attracting several ants or roaches to feed in their interior space and then walk out to their nests and contaminate the entire colony with the poisons that adhere to them during their visit to the bait. This operational process confused many consumers whose expectations were for the insects to become trapped inside the bait or to have such a powerful attractant in the bait that many ants and roaches would want to feed within. They also expected that the critters would be dying and injured as they marched back to their nests. The solution was a more easily understandable process for arming the baits.

Consumers combine products in novel ways. When commercially available products do not perform as expected or do not provide desired benefits, consumers adapt on their own by combining products. When smart ethnographers see this happening, they should sense an opportunity for line extensions and product innovations.

When we were watching consumers clean their counters and floors several years ago, we noticed something interesting: Homemakers were adding household bleach to their accustomed cleaning products. One woman combined liquid dish detergent with chlorine bleach to clean cutting boards and tabletops. When ethnographers probed for the respondents' goals and intentions, the response was not surprising, considering the context. Recent news reports had been filled with dire warnings about bacterial contamination of food preparation areas. Chicken infected with *E. coli* bacteria had recently sickened several people, and homemakers were paying close attention to news reports recommending bleach as a way to reduce the possibility of contamination.

The deeper understanding that emerged from these observations made it clear that consumers were seeking antibacterial benefits. Until that point, antibacterial products were a relatively small niche, confined to infant care or associated with sick-room clean-up. A soap marketer had recently introduced an antibacterial product promising enhanced deodorant benefits. Our observations convinced the client that a broad spectrum of products promoting antibacterial outcomes could capture considerable consumer attention. Moreover, the client's brand equity and product formulation already were consistent with the sanitizing benefits consumers were seeking. They had only to remind shoppers that products currently available for cleaning countertops and floors had the antibacterial benefits they wanted.

Consumers use home remedies or create products. If available products do not satisfy consumer needs, some creative homemakers invent their own solutions. They might have some extra facility with wire coat hangers, rubber bands, and folded paper; they are sometimes inventive with cooking ingredients or cleaning solvents. Regardless, they like to show off when ethnographers come to visit, and their products provide clues to imaginative marketers who can commercialize these inventions.

Home barbecuing is a category that seems to release inventiveness. Entire regions of the United States, not to mention the male half of the human species, appear to take unusual pride in their grilling skills.

Ethnographers observing a home barbecue during a lazy summer weekend are usually treated to a host of native inventions: a favorite ingredient such as brown sugar, pickle juice, wine, or Worcestershire sauce in a marinade; special woods, such as mesquite, gathered in the backyard and added to the charcoal for smoking or enhanced flavor. In several homes, we watched men start their fires by placing their charcoal along with some strips of paper into an empty coffee can with holes punched into the bottom. This adaptation appealed to consumers who wished for a safer nonchemical means of starting the fire. Most of the observations reviewed here have been turned into viable and profitable product innovations.

Observing usage reveals benefits you did not know about. The consumer's experience of product benefits is highly subjective, a psychological state shaped by factors as diverse as personal expectations, product features, brand image, and life stage. Like all qualitative researchers, ethnographers are challenged to understand the consumer's personal experience of product usage and to shape innovations around those feelings and emotions that constitute benefits.

Prior to conducting research for the Moen Revolution showerhead, we believed that the benefits consumers seek in the shower were both functional—for example, cleanliness, thorough rinsing, hair and skin care—and psychological—a state of relaxation. Careful observation of showering and extended interviewing about associated feelings added to a deeper understanding of the psychological dimension. We had severely underestimated the emotional benefits sought in the shower. Soaking, interaction with water in isolation, and the state of nakedness were relaxing to some and invigorating to others. Respondents were observed praying, meditating, and inhaling steam deeply as though they were involved in aromatherapy. Despite confined circumstances, they languished in the shower as though they were involved in a purification ritual. The end result of our thinking about what we saw was an advanced showerhead design that appeals directly to the emotional benefits sought in the daily shower.

Observing usage reveals delights, frustrations, or complacency about results. Consumers reveal themselves most acutely sometimes when there is a divergence between verbal expressions and body language or when what is visible to the ethnographer is contradicted by what the respondent says. In either case, we have clues to new product opportunities.

We have seen this repeatedly in observational studies of home cleaning. As a homemaker completes her scrubbing of the bath and shower area, stains and caked-on particles of soap scum remain fixed on the tiles' surface. Her unhappy frown, slumped shoulders, and distracted glance disclose more than what she says: "It's OK; it's done." Putting up with unsatisfactory results suggests that new approaches to solving problems of daily living are warranted. The homemaker may feel that the effort has been committed and that products work as well as can be expected; she may not want to achieve some ideal of perfect cleanliness. Nevertheless, the product innovator should not confuse complacency with delight. Just because complaints are not verbalized does not mean that the customer is satisfied.

Observing usage reveals a division of labor. When the tasks associated with everyday life are divided by social category, we witness some underlying assumptions and attitudes toward those responsibilities. Particular tasks may be assigned to children instead of adults or to men rather than women. Some jobs may be reserved for a professional, such as a plumber or dry cleaner; others may get assigned to someone expected to supply regular services within the household, such as the gardener or carpet cleaner. Whenever we witness this division of labor while visiting a site, the ethnographer's imagination should start exploring marketing opportunities.

When consumers expect that a problem can be solved only by an expert, they are betraying the belief that current formulations do not have the requisite strength or tenacity. Following such observations, some brands have created "professional strength" line extensions. When a father assigns some cooking responsibilities to his son, it often means that they want to share a feeling of mutual accomplishment and shared success, to create common memories along with a meal.

Observations reveal a location for product use. One of the pleasant surprises that greet ethnographers when they visit a home is discovering just where certain products "live" in the household. An indoor product may have moved outside or to the garage. Kitchen products end up in the bathroom and vice versa. Items destined for the playroom end up in the bedroom. Consumers simply defy the rigid confines that marketers often have in mind for product-usage patterns. Observant research innovators should pay close attention to these shifts in location because they betray mind-sets, expectations, and unverbalized needs that can lead to successful new products.

In a recent ethnography regarding paper products in the home, for example, we witnessed that large formal dinner napkins had migrated to the bathroom. Homemakers concerned about spreading germs were avoiding the communal cloth towels of yesteryear, yet paper guest towels were expensive and too inconvenient to purchase. Observations such as these offer rich opportunities for line extensions.

Consumers adapt packaging or shift containers before use. Observations of the ways in which products are manipulated before being dispensed or applied are important indicators of new benefits and uses that consumers are seeking. When consumers adapt packaging formats and materials, designers and developers should be alerted to potential new product innovations.

As they prepare and store meals ahead of time for their highly active and mobile families, homemakers create different-size portions for the various members of their families. Some frozen food manufacturers have appreciated the benefits of offering products that reflect consumer practices of portion control.

Similarly, it is interesting to observe how consumers reuse the various types of squeeze and spray bottles that arrive in their households. In the laundry, they may use an old mustard dispenser for dabbing on bleach in a manner that focuses the product on stains without splashing. They may adapt smaller packages for distributing the giant-size products they buy at warehouse superstores such as Costco; for example, using small plastic baggies to contain workable tabletop supplies of napkins. Astute marketers should always think about the potential for innovations in packaging and dispensing.

Consumers share wishes that they regard as unachievable. Listening to consumers share wishes for the distant future while watching them use currently available products is redolent with promise and opportunity. Somehow, the act of free association while engaged in product use releases imagination and grounded thinking. Consumer wishes may seem utopian and unachievable, but these ideas should point innovators in the right direction.

Watching people with diabetes use blood glucose monitoring devices gives the ethnographer insights into the swirl of emotions associated with the product. Concerns about a potentially debilitating chronic disease, desires to maintain dietary discipline and self-control, worries and inhibitions about the act of pricking your finger to draw blood, anxieties about the capabilities of technology to support health maintenance objectives— all collide as the product is being used. At times like this, it is not unusual to hear patients wishing for "bloodless" glucose monitoring devices or for devices that would operate passively and keep better records. The moment of direct confrontation with a product is pregnant with possibility.

This section has reviewed a series of ethnographic moments that should be of particular interest to new product developers. When consumers are exhibiting a process of usage; when they make mistakes, combine products, or invent new ones on their own; when they reveal new benefits or complacency and apathy about results; when they divide up household responsibilities in curious ways or bring products to an unanticipated location; when they shift packaging or dream about possibilities while stuck in the present—all of these should be clues that alternative solutions, new possibilities, and creative new products can satisfy consumer wants and needs. It takes insight and imagination to go beyond basic observations of behavior, but the effort can be amply rewarding.

26

Quality Review

At the conclusion of an ethnographic study, the entire experience of the project should be subjected to an internal quality review. This can be conducted by directors and managers with or without the participation of other project personnel or input from clients. The purpose of the quality review is to identify strengths and weaknesses in the delivery of services, analyze the effectiveness of each project component, and evaluate the human resources allocated to the project.

We recommend a brief overview of each project component and deliverable using both quantitative (scales) and qualitative measures. The following quality points should be assessed:

- *Project design:* How effective and accurate was the project in addressing client problems?
- *Starting documents:* These include respondent specifications, screener, observation guide, participant information sheet, and contracts.
- *Performance of subcontractors:* Freelancers may be hired to help with parts of the project; for example, video.
- *Recruitment:* The effectiveness of tools, such as the specifications list and screener, should be reviewed, as well as the performance of recruitment personnel.
- *Site visits:* Timing, efficiency, and personnel are some elements of site visits that should be considered.
- *Data collection:* Were data complete and effective? What role did different observers play?
- *Cultural sensitivity:* Did observers pay sufficient attention to cultural factors that may have shaped interaction with respondents and the study's analytic outcomes?
- *Field coordination:* Did field coordination go smoothly?
- *Reports:* Were the reporting formats and content sufficient and appropriate?

- *Client interface:* Clear communication and feedback, on-site cooperation, and satisfaction with deliverables are important facets of the researcher-client relationship.
- *Profitability:* Did fees for the ethnography engagement sufficiently cover all the time spent planning, managing, executing, conducting data analysis, and writing the report?

The quality review is a means to improve the delivery of services to clients and to help generate repeat business.

Record Keeping and Document Storage

It is highly likely that data generated by an ethnography will be subjected to future review and reanalysis. Making additional insights and analyses of the data available to clients strengthens the level of partnership between suppliers and users. A best practice is for all partners and subcontractors to maintain their own complete project records for a period of at least 7 years.

Records kept should include a file for each site that includes all tapes, notes, debriefs, screeners, documents, and other materials compiled during the project. A large manila envelope is usually large enough to contain the complete site file. The collection of all site files should be boxed and stored in a place not subject to extremes of heat or cold, humidity, or moisture.

Furthermore, all general reports and brainstorming notes should also be kept with the project file. Copies of all electronic documents should be backed up on portable media.

For the Love of Ethnography

This text has attempted to offer pragmatic, action-oriented guidelines for the creation and dissemination of corporate ethnography. We have taken the reader from providing a rationale for investing in this form of research to describing steps toward organizing the study. We have also moved from elaborating steps for completing the fieldwork to demonstrating how the data may be productively analyzed for the benefit of the clients who commission studies. Nevertheless, we would be deficient if we closed this book without expressing appreciation for the respondents who cooperate in our studies.

The success of any ethnographic study depends on the voluntary participants who allow us into their homes and workplaces to share their lives and inner reflections. They may be receiving a handsome honorarium to render this service; they may even be gaining some exhibitionistic delight in having their personal affairs aired so publicly. Nevertheless, I have found research respondents to be special people who teach marketers a great deal simply by being themselves.

Over the course of many years, ethnography participants have shared with me and my team many moments of struggle, such as when we watched diabetic patients contend with uncooperative blood glucose-measuring devices, as well as many moments of triumph, as when an unconfident cook prepared a meal to delight her family. The joy of ethnography occurs during those unguarded moments, when all the arrangements have been managed effectively, when we are comfortable in our situations and true human contact occurs. Moments like that yield pleasure and compassion as well as understanding and insight.

So, let me close this text with an expression of gratitude to respondents who accept the invitation to participate, particularly to the hundreds who have helped me and my clients benefit immensely from moments spent in common purpose. Let me thank you for the days I have spent in your company while we shared details of our lives. You are the ones who make this endeavor satisfying and rewarding.

Appendix

Ten Commandments for Great Ethnography

1. **Be an observer first.** We are going to consumers' homes to watch, listen and learn. We aren't there to promote, convince, or change minds. (That comes later.) Let the respondent take the lead. As observers, we need to resist the temptation to act like we're in charge and know more about the product than the consumer does.

2. **Respect the site protocol.** The site protocol and observation guide outline general procedures at the site. Follow the team leader. Be helpful and cooperative.

3. **Be objective.** Don't assume or expect anything about how people actually do things. Keep an open mind throughout the experience. Try to understand things from the consumer's point of view. Use consumer language: no marketing or insider jargon.

4. **Love your respondents unconditionally.** Show respect and consideration. (We're asking respondents to reveal some pretty sensitive stuff.) Be good guests. Be warm and friendly. Don't judge. Be careful of the kinds of reinforcements you use; for example, you might be giving cues to behavior by reacting with, "That's good."

5. **Follow the stages of a site visit.** Let the site visit evolve slowly. Spend the early part of the visit developing rapport and building a comfort level. Move from very general questions to specific questions. Save detailed probes until late in the visit.

6. **Everything counts as data.** As ethnographers, we *look, listen,* and *ask.* That means that potential observation points are unlimited: the way someone does things, the body language that betrays respondents' feelings, the way things look before and after, things that family members say to one another, and also respondents' answers to your questions.

7. **Ask questions fairly.** Pose questions in an open-ended way rather than in a yes/no form. Don't educate or lead respondents with your questions.

211

Use verbs like *explain* and *describe* to preface your questions so that respondents are encouraged to elaborate.

8. **Probe positively.** Probes that are confrontational or use *why* can make respondents feel challenged and turn them off. If you want elaboration or an explanation, ask for it affirmatively: "Can you tell me more?" "Is it always that way or only sometimes?"

9. **Don't change what you're watching.** It's our job to make sure that respondents follow their normal routines in their natural order. Make sure that you are not giving off cues through body language or expectations that make them change anything. Never rush a respondent. Don't help. Don't give advice.

10. **Take good notes.** We will provide you with field notebooks. Record your observations in a clear and methodical manner. Write legibly. Make diagrams. Use symbols. Be sure to fan out and observe different locations if necessary. Help with picture taking and tape recording.

Project Management Diagram

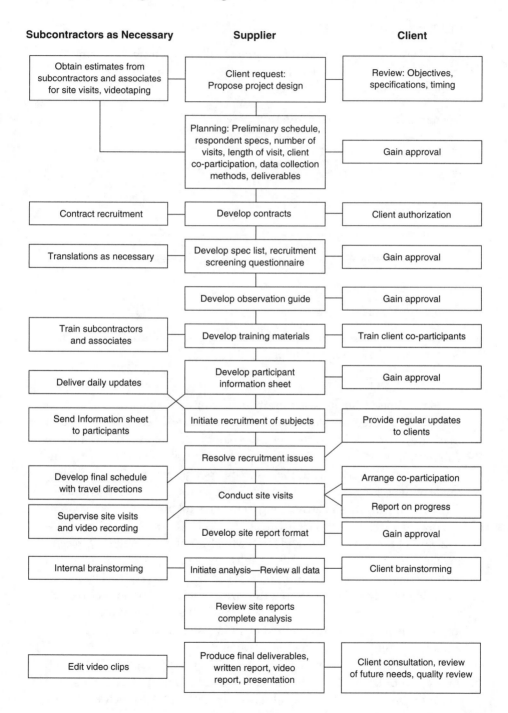

Sample Project Documents

RESPONDENT RELEASE

IMPORTANT: This document is shared for illustration purposes only. We are not offering legal advice. Please discuss this with competent counsel before using any respondent release.

My name (person to be recorded):

_____

_____

My Address:

_____

_____

Age: _____

Recording Means:

Audio and/or video by any means including still photographs, videotape, audiotape, and computer imaging

Project Description:

Recording of me involved in my daily routines which may include—but not be limited to—*[describe main activities to be studied]* for use in marketing research by [your company name], its clients, their respective employees, agents, advertising agencies, photographers, and other technicians making the recording, their successors and assigns. The recording made of me is for use only by the above companies and individuals and not for use of my likeness in advertising to the general public.

By signing this AUTHORIZATION, CONSENT, ACKNOWLEDGMENT RELEASE, WAIVER, and INDEMNITY, I ACKNOWLEDGE receiving the sum of $_____ as the full consideration for my participation in the Project and delivery of this AUTHORIZATION, sufficiency of this sum I knowingly and irrevocably authorize, consent, and permit the recording of me as described in the above Project Description through audio and/or video means by any method including still photographs, videotape, audiotape, computer imaging ("Recording").

I understand that by signing this AUTHORIZATION, CONSENT, ACKNOWLEDGMENT RELEASE, WAIVER, and INDEMNITY, the Recording will be made of me. I knowingly CONSENT to such Recording and fully and without restriction RELEASE QualiData Research Inc., its clients, their respective employees, agents, advertising agencies, photographers, and other technicians making the Recording, their successors, and assigns from all liability in connection with the Recording of me and AUTHORIZE all of them to use such Recording and likenesses of me in the marketing research specified in the Project Description.

I also WAIVE any right to inspect or approve the Recording or receive copies of the Recording, or to object to reasonable uses of the Recording that are within the scope of the marketing research specified in the Project Description.

I also ACKNOWLEDGE that I am over the age of 18 years and have no restrictions which would prevent me from signing this AUTHORIZATION, CONSENT, ACKNOWLEDGMENT RELEASE, WAIVER, and INDEMNITY.

I agree to engage in my normal routine for *[describe main activities to be studied]* in an effort to make the Recording as useful as possible to QualiData and its clients, and refrain from any behaviors that are not part of my daily routine. It is mutually agreed that I will neither be asked to perform nor will I perform any behaviors that might be considered lewd, offensive, indecent, or otherwise inappropriate for research purposes.

I also acknowledge that all companies and individuals involved in this project will be relying on my signing this AUTHORIZATION, CONSENT, ACKNOWLEDGMENT, RELEASE, WAIVER, and INDEMNITY and the statements I have made in it, so I hereby INDEMNIFY and HOLD HARMLESS QualiData Research Inc., its clients, their respective employees, agents, advertising agencies, photographers, and other technicians making the Recording, their successors, and assigns from any and all liability associated with or relating to or arising out of my signing this AUTHORIZATION, CONSENT, ACKNOWLEDGMENT, RELEASE, WAIVER, and INDEMNITY or claims by me or other person(s) claiming that this AUTHORIZATION, CONSENT, ACKNOWLEDGMENT, RELEASE, WAIVER, and INDEMNITY was not properly and knowingly executed by me and/or does not apply to such person(s) including my heirs, spouse (if any), or family members, who will be bound by this authorization.

I ACKNOWLEDGE that I shall maintain in CONFIDENCE all information concerning the project which I obtain by reason of my participation in it and not disclose such information to any other person or company including the name of QualiData or its client.

Date: _____   Signature: _____

Witness: _____

Screener

SCREENING QUESTIONNAIRE
Mexican Food Ethnography

Name _____

Address _____

Phone AM _____ *Phone PM* _____

Cell phone _____ *E-mail* _____

Screener for New York and Chicago Area

REVIEW OF QUALIFICATIONS:
REQUIREMENTS FOR ALL HOUSEHOLDS

- Household is deeply committed to Mexican culture through some combination of travel, cultural commitments, ethnic heritage, etc. However, the household language is English dominant
- A mix of age/household categories
- A mix of children's ages in household (under 11, 11 and over)
- Minimum educational attainment: some college
- All are Heads-of-Households responsible for food purchase and cooking
- Mix of both Working and Nonworking Female Heads-of-Household
- Mix of entertainment, formal and informal eating situations to be observed
- Mix of ethnicity (should not be confined to Mexican Americans)
- Mix of Household Income: Minimum $50,000 per year (pre-tax, all sources)

INTRODUCTORY

Hello, my name is _____ , and I represent _____ . We are conducting a unique market research study of households in the [New York] [Chicago] area for the purpose of better understanding contemporary consumer lifestyles. This study will involve visiting your home and observing you as you conduct your normal food preparation and meal consumption routines. These interviews are likely to be accompanied by videotaping inside your household. The purpose of my call is not to sell or advertise anything to you. We only would like to see if you qualify for inclusion in our study. Are you interested in participating in a study of this type?

Q0. We are hoping to conduct this study with persons and households that have a significant interest in Mexican culture, cuisine, and lifestyles. Does this describe you and your household?

[   ] Yes

[   ] No   (TERMINATE)

SECURITY

Let me start off with a few questions about your work and past research participation:

S1. Do you or does anyone in your immediate family work for any of the following types of companies? (READ LIST AND CHECK AS APPROPRIATE)

    [   ] a bank or brokerage

    [   ] a school or educational institution

    [   ] a manufacturer or distributor of food products   (TERMINATE)

    [   ] an advertising agency   (TERMINATE)

    [   ] a marketing or market research company   (TERMINATE)

    [   ] a retail store   (TERMINATE)

    [   ] a radio/TV/cable company   (TERMINATE)

    [   ] a magazine/newspaper/publishing company   (TERMINATE)

S2. Have you ever participated in a market research study that involved a visit to your home to observe activities in your household?

    [   ] Yes   (TERMINATE)

    [   ] No

S3. When was the last time you participated in a research discussion group or in-depth interview? (DO NOT READ LIST; WAIT FOR UNPROMPTED RESPONSE; CHECK BELOW AFTER RESPONDENT HAS ANSWERED)

    [   ] Less than a year ago

    [   ] A year or more ago

    [   ] Never   (SKIP TO Q1)

S4. What was (were) the topic(s)?

_____

(TERMINATE IF TOPIC WAS FOODS)

QUALIFYING

Let me ask several questions to see if you match our qualifications:

Q1. DO NOT ASK (UNLESS UNCLEAR). RESPONDENT IS

    [   ] Male

    [   ] Female   (WE ANTICIPATE THAT MOST PRIMARY
                              RESPONDENTS WILL BE FEMALES, BUT
                              MALES ARE ALSO ACCEPTABLE)

Q2. What is your age: (FILL IN HERE _____ AND CHECK
                              BELOW)

    [   ] Under 21   (TERMINATE)
    [   ] 21–34
    [   ] 35–54   (OBTAIN A MIX)
    [   ] 55 and over

Q3. Which of the following best describes the composition of your household? (READ LIST AND CHECK APPROPRIATE BOXES)

    [   ] I live with a spouse or   (OBTAIN A MIX)
         life-partner

    [   ] I have one or more custodial
         children *under* 11 at home

    [   ] I have one or more custodial
         children *11 and over* at home

    [   ] I have no custodial children
         living at home

Q4A. Which of the following best describes the highest level of education you have completed? (READ LIST AND CHECK ONE)

    [   ] Postgraduate Degree

    [   ] Some Postgraduate
         Education

    [   ] College Graduate

    [   ] Some College Education   (OBTAIN A MIX OF EDUCATION)

    [   ] Trade or Career School   (TERMINATE)
         Graduate

    [   ] High School Graduate   (TERMINATE)

    [   ] Less than High School Graduate   (TERMINATE)

Q4B. Which of the following categories best represents your total annual income from all sources, before taxes? (INCLUDES WAGES, PENSIONS, INVESTMENTS).

As I read down the list of categories, please stop me when I reach yours.

[   ] A. Less than $25,000   (TERMINATE)

[   ] B. More than $25,000,
       less than $50,000   (TERMINATE)

[   ] C. More than $50,000,
       less than $100,000

[   ] D. More than $100,000,
       less than $200,000

[   ] E. More than $200,000   (OBTAIN A MIX)

Q5. Is your home located in an urban or a suburban area? (DO NOT ASK IF IT IS APPARENT FROM ADDRESS)

[   ] Urban

[   ] Suburban   (OBTAIN A MIX)

Let's go on to employment . . .

Q6A. What is your employment status? Are you . . . (READ LIST)

[   ] Employed full time

[   ] Employed part time

[   ] Retired

[   ] Not employed outside the home/Homemaker

Q6B. What is your occupation?

_____

Q6C. What is the employment status of your spouse or partner? Is she/he (READ LIST)

[   ] Employed full time

[   ] Employed part time   (OBTAIN A MIX)

[   ] Retired

[   ] Not employed outside the home/Homemaker

Q6D. What is his/her occupation?

_____

Q7A. Who is responsible for food purchase for your household?

[ ] I am

[ ] I share the responsibility
    with my spouse

[ ] My spouse or someone else   (TERMINATE)

Q7B. Who is responsible for meal preparation in your household?

[ ] I am

[ ] I share the responsibility
    with my spouse

[ ] My spouse or someone else   (TERMINATE)

Q8. As I said earlier, we are hoping to conduct this study with persons who have a significant interest in Mexican culture, cuisine, and lifestyles. Please let me know what makes you say you belong in this category. (ALLOW RESPONDENT TO DESCRIBE UNAIDED AND THEN PROBE FOR CATEGORIES THAT ARE NOT CHECKED)

_____

_____

(CHECK IF "YES" OR DESCRIBED ABOVE)

[ ] Do you speak or have you studied Spanish language?

[ ] Do you regularly read Mexican newspapers and/or magazines? Which ones?

_____

[ ] Do you frequently cook Mexican dishes? How often _____

[ ] Have you taken courses in Mexican cuisine or culture? Please describe

_____

[ ] Do you travel to Mexico regularly for business or pleasure? How often _____

[ ] Do you own property in Mexico?

[ ] Do you have a personal or professional interest in Mexican music, film, or culture? Please describe:

_____

[ ] Do you have a personal or professional interest in Mexican style or design? Please describe:

_____

(IMPORTANT NOTE: QUALIFYING RESPONDENTS SHOULD HAVE A GOOD MIX OF THESE INTERESTS AND ACTIVITIES. PLEASE CHECK IF IN DOUBT.)

Thank you for all your help so far. These final questions are for classification purposes only.

Q9A. Do you consider yourself Spanish, Hispanic, or Latino?

[   ] Yes

[   ] No   (OBTAIN A MIX)

Q9B. Do you consider yourself to be a Mexican American?

[   ] Yes

[   ] No   (OBTAIN A MIX; MAKE SURE TO
                                   INCLUDE NON-MEXICAN
                                   AMERICANS IN SAMPLE)

Q9C. Which is the dominant language spoken in your household?

[   ] English only   (PREFERRED)

[   ] English mostly   (ACCEPTABLE)

[   ] Spanish mostly   (ACCEPTABLE ONLY IF HOUSE-
                                   HOLD IS NON-HISPANIC)

[   ] Spanish only   (TERMINATE)

Q10. What do you consider to be your racial category? (OBTAIN A MIX IF POSSIBLE)

[   ] Caucasian or White

[   ] Asian American or Pacific
     Islander

[   ] African American or Black

[   ] Native American or American Indian

[   ] Mixed Race _____

[   ] Other _____

INVITATION

Thank you so much for taking the time to answer these questions. Based on your answers, I would like to invite you to participate in a unique and very interesting market research study. This is a rare opportunity for you to take part in helping us learn about the needs and expectations of households like your own.

There will be absolutely no sales presentation or any attempt to sell you anything during these visits to your home. We are only interested in your practices, thoughts, and opinions.

Your participation in this research study will take about 4 to 6 hours of your time. Our research team will visit your household and watch you complete your normal household routines. As a token of our appreciation, you will receive a cash honorarium on completion of your home visit.

One final detail: Your participation in the study depends on our ability to schedule you for particular types of visits: We would like to schedule you on a *[weekday—family dinner* (NY & Chicago)] *[weekend—entertaining guests* (Chicago only)] and observe the following in your household:

[   ] Shopping for ingredients

[   ] Assembling ingredients

[   ] Inventory of foods, utensils, amenities

[   ] Meal preparation

[   ] Meal consumption

[   ] Clean-up and storage

CLOSE

Observation Guide

MEXICAN FOODS STRATEGIC STUDY—ETHNOGRAPHY

1. Introduction
- Introduce team members
- Review ground rules for observational research
- Small talk re: family composition, occupations, hobbies, etc.
- General attitudes and motivations regarding usage of tortillas, salsa, and Mexican meals in general

2. The Context
- Location, streetscape, dwelling type, age, size and number of rooms
- Own vs. rent
- Condition of home
- Structure
- Furnishings/appliances/decorations: How do these (or do they not) reflect Mexican-ness?

3. Participant Characteristics
- Age, gender
- Other demographics
- Household composition
- Health/strength/disabilities
- Self-presentation
- Participant role in meal preparation and grocery shopping; others involved

4. Lifestyle

Explore in-depth to provide a "full-color" picture of households

- Family dynamics; roles in household
- Pets
- Hobbies
- Vacations: where/when/how often
- Computers/video games/technology
- Collections
- Media usage
- Magazines/periodicals
- TV shows
- Internet
- Clothing/footwear: brands, styles, where bought
- Cars: how many, makes/models
- Entertaining: family/friends? what are occasions?
- To what degree do lifestyle choices and activities reflect involvement with Mexico, Mexican culture, and Mexican style?

5. Storage and Purchase Issues

- (Look) Document storage and inventory dynamics of ingredients used in preparing Mexican meals
  - Canned vegetables (including tomatoes, beans, nopalitos, etc.)
  - Prepared sauces (e.g., chipotle, mole, habanero, etc.)
  - Olive oil
  - Seasonings: dry or fresh (e.g., chiles [what kinds, e.g., jalapenos, serranos], oregano, cilantro, garlic, onions, pepper, etc.)
  - Masa/hojas/other dry goods
  - Frozen ingredients and prepared dinners
  - Fresh ingredients
  - Wine, liquors, beverages

- (Ask) What makes something relevant as a Mexican meal ingredient?
- (Look) Where are Mexican meal ingredients stored (cupboards and closets, etc.)? Where are other groceries stored? (NOTE: Conduct inventory of packaged goods at all locations including garage, pantry, basement, etc.)
- (Look) Which brands are regularly used/stored? (NOTE: When documenting store brands, please be specific about quality/grade and imported vs. not imported)
  - Volume
  - Flavor/variety
  - Packaging

- (Ask) What are reasons for storage in particular locations?
- (Ask) What is intended use of each product?
- (Ask) Purchasing dynamics
  - Reasons for buying each product
  - Reasons for buying each brand
  - Reasons for package size choice
  - Multiple-versus single-unit purchases
  - Use of coupons/promotions

- Purchasing decision-making considerations (i.e., price, quality, size, brand, store where purchased, etc.)
- PROBE: Dimensions of quality; what are considerations/meanings?
- Multipacks
- Individually packaged versus bulk packaging
- Single serving versus family size versus other sizes

Shopping

- What are choice criteria?
- What is noticed, influential?
- Are choices habitual or intentional?
- What is considered, rejected? final choice
- What other products, categories are associated with Mexican foods purchase?

6. Mexican Foods Usage Issues

- (Ask, Look) Describe usage occasions and issues around Mexican meals and ingredients.
- Mexican American (Tex-Mex, Cal-Mex) vs. authentically Mexican—does this make a difference
- Do brand, quality grade, etc., change for different usages (side dish vs. ingredient in casserole, recipe, etc.)?
- Do brand, quality grade, etc., change for different occasions (family vs. guests; weekday vs. weekend vs. holiday)?
- Satisfactions, dissatisfactions, frustrations, compromises
- PROBE: Other uses for Mexican ingredients besides usage occasions described above
- (Ask, Look) Impact of children and/or other household members
- (Ask, Look) Impact of health consciousness (calories, fat, salt, sugar, organic ingredients)
- (Ask, Look) Ethical/religious issues (alcohol, vegetarianism, kosher, hallal)
- (Ask) Weekly and monthly frequency of Mexican meal usage
- (Ask) Anticipation/expectations
  - Benefits sought from Mexican food products
  - Importance of brands
  - Importance of sensory dimensions
  - Spiciness versus blandness
  - Label design, information
  - Wishes/unmet needs

7. Observation of Food Preparation/Eating Meal

- Foods to be cooked/meal type
- (Ask) Attitudes toward cooking in general
- Favorite menus and recipes; get two favorite recipes and reasons why
- (Look) Preparation and recipes
  - Source of recipe (e.g., family heritage, magazine, book, product package, etc.)
  - Reasons for choosing particular recipe
  - Products used/brands and forms (can/box/frozen); How does recipe have an impact on choice of ingredients?
  - Combination of products including fresh/instant/frozen/canned vegetables

- (Look) Attitudes/Feelings Communicated During Usage
  - Amount of effort/ease of use/problems
  - Body language reflecting attitudes
  - Joys, pleasures, frustrations, inconveniences

- (Look) Volume prepared, for consumption at meal and leftovers
- (Look) Combination of products/brands used

- (Look) Substitutions; If another item is used, find out reasons
  - (Ask) Results, How to describe results
- How satisfied with results
  - Problems and issues/product satisfaction

OBSERVE EATING OF MEAL

- (Look) Family dynamics during eating
- (Look, Ask) Sensory dimensions of food consumption
  - Flavor
  - Spiciness
  - Color
  - Aroma
  - Texture
- What sensory dynamics are associated with satisfaction, Mexican-ness

8. Packaging

- Important information/not important
- Missing information/copy ideas
- Package size issues
- Package re-use issues
- Convenience of packaging
- Single serve versus family size versus other sizes

9. Wish List/Unmet Needs

- (Ask) What is the ideal way to make products better? (NOTE: Pay particular attention to tortillas, salsas, canned ingredients, frozen entrees and ingredients)
  - Sensory: taste, flavor, color, texture
  - Packaging
  - Product variety, e.g., regional, ingredients
- (Ask) Expected changes in usage over the years.
- (Ask) Parting advice for makers of Mexican food products to make meal preparation easier, better for you and family members.

Respondent Information Sheet

ALL ABOUT THE MEAL PREPARATION HOME VISIT

Dear Participant,

Thank you for your interest in the Meal Preparation Home Visit market research study. This information sheet gives you answers to questions you may have about the project. It also gives you more details on the reasons this research is being conducted and describes how you can be most effective as a participant.

Is this serious?

It's only natural to be skeptical and suspicious about a research project that asks you to invite researchers to your home to observe behaviors that are normally kept private. In truth, this is a serious scientific study being supervised by Ph.D.-level researchers with considerable academic and professional credentials. If you would like more information about the company and people conducting this study, please let us know.

Above all, we want to assure you that volunteers will be treated in a dignified and respectful manner. We want you to be partners in this research process.

Who is conducting the study?

The study is being conducted by QualiData Research Inc. on behalf of a well-known food manufacturer. Project Director is Dr. Hy Mariampolski, Principal of QualiData and a member of the Board of Directors at the Master's of Marketing Research program at the University of Georgia.

Why is the study being done?

Our client is trying to better understand how people behave in relation to food preparation. They have undertaken this research project in order to learn more about the ways in which people interact with and feel about their meals prepared at home. This information will help the manufacturer develop new and improved products. It is also likely to support efforts to communicate with consumers like you.

How is the study being done?

Interviews conducted over the phone or in research laboratories provide only limited information about consumers. That's why we would like to visit with you at home during the time you typically prepare meals for your family. That way we can learn about your way of cooking: your expectations, frustrations, and preferences.

To make sure that we don't miss any valuable details of your behavior, we will, in some cases, videotape the visit, using a small, hand-held video camera. Otherwise, we may use a tape recorder and still camera. Since we will be visiting so many households, videotapes and pictures will allow us to keep a behavioral record and compare the many ways in which different people prepare meals for their household.

What about confidentiality?

The observations and any information you provide in interviews will be strictly confidential. Your name, identity, and area of residence will not appear in any reports based on the research.

How long will it take?

Our visit probably will last between 2 and 4 hours depending on the scope of the visit. We will arrive at the scheduled time to introduce ourselves and meet the members of your household. Then, we will move aside and watch you in the course of your routines. Then, we will conduct some follow-up interviewing with you and other members of your household, if necessary.

Who will be visiting my home?

The people who visit you will be members of the QualiData Research team. We expect that no more than two to three people will visit your home. All visitors have been instructed to be good guests, to stay out of your way and to respect your property.

What will the researchers do?

The researchers will watch you and take notes about how you practice your mealtime routines. Our goal is to observe this process from start to finish. Each person and household we visit will be different. We want to see you in your natural environment, behaving in your routine manner.

How should I prepare for the home visit?

Please don't do anything special to prepare for our visit! Following social convention, people often like to clean up or prepare before guests come over. However, to make this as realistic as possible, please don't clean up or prepare things before we arrive. Please wear the clothes you normally wear when completing household tasks. Please don't dress up for our visit. Also, please do not buy any products that you don't generally use.

We are not coming into your home to make judgments; we only want to get a sense of your normal routines and to learn about how you do things.

Also, please do not prepare any meals for us. We will take care of our own meals and will not be part of your own mealtime or entertaining. We will also not be able to accept any alcoholic beverages during our visit, but please do not hesitate to consume alcoholic drinks yourselves if that is your regular practice.

Will anyone try to sell me something?

Absolutely not. Our purpose is to learn from you, to find out how your tasks are performed and what your needs are.

Will I have to sign anything?

Yes. Before participating in this project, volunteers will be required to sign an AUTHORIZATION, CONSENT, ACKNOWLEDGMENT, RELEASE, WAIVER, AND INDEMNITY form. The purpose of this form is to give us permission to conduct the study according to our specifications and to protect us from any liability that might arise from the research methodology. The letter has several other provisions, and you will be given a copy of it to consider well before the site visit.

Who will be seeing the report?

This study is only for our clients' marketing purposes and not for the public or for use in advertising. Only our clients and our research consultants will see copies of any videotapes, notes, photos, documents, or reports that come out of the study.

Who else is being invited for participation?

We are looking for many different types of individuals, from households with and without children, older and younger people, people living in different types of homes, and those from all different walks of life. Your household is being selected because you qualify as one of these types.

Who else is participating?

Other participants in the study are like yourself. We are visiting homes throughout the country. Our purpose in conducting the study this way is to learn from the widest variety of people.

Will anything happen if I decline?

If you do not wish to participate, you have every right to decline. We won't think any worse of you. On the other hand, if you agree to participate, you are making a commitment to cooperate with all aspects of the research project.

What's in it for me?

At the end of the observation period, in appreciation for your time and cooperation, you will receive the cash stipend promised by the research company that contacted you.

Most of all, this project should be lots of fun for you. And, you will have a chance to offer your advice and opinions so that our client can provide better and new products to households like your own.

If you have any questions or would like more information, please call QualiData Research Inc. at 718-XXX-XXXX or visit our Web site, www .qualidataresearch.com.

Site Report Template

Auto Owners Ethnography: SITE REPORT OUTLINE

INSIGHTS SUMMARY

Please be sure to include the following:

What is the nature of the role the vehicle plays in their lives?

How do they behave with their cars?

How and where do tires come into play concerning their thinking about their car?

What is the interplay between the wheel and the tire?

What's important in a tire for their car?

How are they interacting with auto enthusiast publications?

What are their media habits? (TV, radio, magazines, Internet, etc.)

PARTICIPANT CHARACTERISTICS

Age, gender, other demographics such as: household composition, health/strength/disabilities, and self-presentation:

Lifestyle and hobbies, especially auto club-related interests

Cars: How many do they own, makes/models?

THE CAR: OBSERVED

Location where car is kept: parked on street, in garage, indoors or outdoors; is car a family car or for personal use only?

Make and model of car(s) and condition of car's exterior as well as condition of car's interior

Tires: Make and model and condition of tires

Product Storage for Car Care

Where are car care products and tools stored? What room? Near car or elsewhere?

Conduct inventory at all locations including garage, pantry, and basement to see which products/brands are stored in each place. NOTE: When documenting store brands, please be specific about name/amount/quality/grade.

What is intended use of each product? What are some purchasing decision-making considerations (i.e., price, quality, size, brand)?

Emotions Around Their Car

What is the role the vehicle plays in their lives? Why do they own the car they own? Who or what influenced their purchasing choice?

Does the car fit into their identity? How? Is it a hobby, a passion, a reason for working?

What activities do they do with their car (car shows, etc.)?

How much time do they spend thinking about it? What triggers them to think about their car?

Driving it: favorite times/favorite places to drive

Working on it: time of day, day of the week, season that they work on it the most

FOR PARTICIPANTS WHO HAVE CUSTOMIZED

What is the main motivation for customization: performance or esthetics?

What exactly did they change?

What is intended use of each product/addition?

The Driver OBSERVED

How do they behave with their cars? Where do they go in them (if you go for a ride with them)?

The Tires

What tires do they have now and why?

How and where do tires come into play concerning their thinking about their car? What are their sources of information about tires?

What is important about a tire? What do tires represent or "do" for the car/driving experience?

What role does brand play? What are their brand preferences? What influences their selection of a brand?

What is their take on [Brand q] as a performance tire (perceptions of [Brand q] brands in a competitive context)?

Auto Enthusiast Pastimes

Are motor sports relevant to them? Do they watch/follow motor sports? If so, which ones?

Do they feel that tires are an important element in motor sports competition?

Wish List/Unmet Needs

What is the ideal way to make car customizing product options better? How has usage changed over the years? What future changes are anticipated?

Parting advice for makers of tires products to make usage easier, better for them and their special needs

Observation/Debriefing Notes

ROLE VEHICLE PLAYS

Besides transportation, their vehicle makes them feel good about their lives—successful, safe, secure, and "happening." A nice car raises self-esteem. It can be a fantasy come true, an opportunity to get away from day-to-day troubles. Often used for weekend relaxation/experiences, it brings them great enjoyment and comfort. Some experience this to a greater degree than others. They care about their cars, and, for some, their car can be a big part of their lives.

[Respondent AW]:

Makes me feel great. Boosts confidence and self-esteem. I thought I was THE MAN.

I think it tells a lot about me, about my style, character. It is a representation of me—what kind of person I am.

It's the feeling—I'm free—the weather is awesome, you look to your left is the ocean, the top is down, it is great. You just forget about all your worries, all your problems, you forget about work. You think about YOU. Whether the future or present—issues that have been going on in your life. Talking about issues to yourself.

It does make you feel very confident, very good about yourself. It raises your self-esteem. You drive a nice car.

It does mean image, status, definitely shows success.

Drove it to work when I got it only because I was so excited about it. Best car I have ever owned. I would go to sleep thinking about it—wake up thinking about it. Still is going on but now I control myself. Take it out on weekends. Thought about it all the time—all the time. I was in class and was thinking—oh man I got the Porsche—I can't wait to get out there. Friday and Saturday are my favorite days of the week. Tonight for example, I am going out to a club—will take this car.

When I drive the Porsche, I am happy and excited. It is exciting. I will be honest, you might not be a bigger Porsche but you still get a lot of looks. I got two dates because of the car.

[Respondent BT]:

It is like my office. Don't like to say I am materialistic, but I enjoy having a nice car. Feel better about myself. Like having a nice car. Don't like to think an object could represent me. Always liked this car. Perfect car for my personality. It was between this and Solaro. Felt so much better in Honda—felt more me—liked the dashboard. Feel fun, fast, fly by the seat, exciting but classy. Sporty in a classy sense—sleek. I feel very protected— very secure. Never worry. Don't feel unsafe. Feel secure in the car. Feels strong and sturdy. It is my passion. I am a little protective of it. Rock dings—drives me crazy to look at that. Was rear-ended 6–7 months ago. Bumper fixed and silver doesn't match—drives me crazy. I love my car. Personality—outgoing, fun, and have class.

It is a good feeling to have a nice car. When I got it, people would comment, your car is so nice. Would get looks and smiles. Nice feeling. Especially when guys check out the tires and rims.

BEHAVE WITH CARS:

Appreciate their cars—respectful but enjoy experiencing the performance.

TIRES/INTERPLAY WHEEL TIRE/IMPORTANT IN TIRE:

Respondents seemed less knowledgeable about tires.

I wish there was some way you could test them—drive—I am pretty sure tires makes a big difference on the ride of the car—whether there is a soft nice easy ride or a stiff ride or noise. That would be great. If I were to test these tires that I got on the Navigator [Brand z] I would not have bought them—no way.—Respondent AW

Really good tire. [Brand p] is household name. Comfortable with— don't know that much about them.—Respondent BT

References

Arnould, E. J., & Wallendorf, M. (1994). Market-oriented ethnography: Interpretation building and marketing strategy formulation. *Journal of Marketing Research, 31,* 484–504.

Benedict, R. (1934). *Patterns of culture.* Boston: Houghton Mifflin.

Birdwhistell, R. L. (1970). *Kinesics and context.* Philadelphia: University of Pennsylvania Press.

Bogdan, R., & Taylor, S. J. (1975). *Introduction to qualitative research methods: A phenomenological approach to the social sciences.* Hoboken, NJ: John Wiley.

Bourdieu, P. (1990). *Photography, a middle-brow art.* Pierre Bourdieu with Luc Boltanski . . . [et al.]; translated by Shaun Whiteside. Stanford, CA: Stanford University Press.

Burton, A. (2001, October 2–3). *A brief review of the environment and behaviour underlying trial.* Paper presented at Marketing Week: Creating Product Trial, London.

Corstjens, J., & Corstjens, M. (1995). Store wars: *The battle for mindspace and shelf-space.* Hoboken, NJ: John Wiley.

DeBenedictis, D. J. (1990, March). Automobile intrigue: Suit claims Nissan spy lived with family to observe lifestyle. *ABA Journal, 76,* 28.

de Bono, E. (1970). *Lateral thinking.* New York: Harper & Row.

Denzin, N. K., & Lincoln, Y. S. (Eds.). (1994). *Handbook of qualitative research.* Thousand Oaks: Sage.

Dewan, S. K. (2000, September 19). Washing up is down. *The New York Times,* Section B; 3; column 1.

Dichter, E. (1964). *Handbook of consumer motivations.* New York: McGraw-Hill.

Duggan, P., & Eisenstodt, G. (1990, November 12). The new face of Japanese espionage. *Forbes,* p. 96.

Durkheim, E. (1966). *The rules of the sociological method.* New York: Free Press.

Ekman, P. (2003). *Emotions revealed: Recognizing faces and feelings to improve communication and emotional life.* New York: Henry Holt.

ElBoghdady, D. (2002, February 24). Naked truth meets market research: Perfecting a new shower head? Try watching people shower. *The Washington Post,* pp. H1, H4–H5.

Erard, M. (2004, May 6). For technology, no small world after all. *The New York Times,* p. G5.

Ezzy, D. (2002). *Qualitative analysis: Practice and innovation.* New York: Routledge.

Fox, J., & Fisher, S. (2002, August 5). *Usability testing: Evaluating your websites.* Paper presented at the 4th National Customer Service Conference, Washington, DC. Available at www.epa.gov/customerservice/2002conference/visitorfocus.ppt/

Gans, H. J. (1967). *The Levittowners; ways of life and politics in a new suburban community.* New York, Pantheon Books.

Garfinkel, H. (1967). *Studies in ethnomethodology.* Englewood Cliffs, NJ: Prentice Hall.

Gladwell, M. (2000). *The turning point.* Boston: Little, Brown.

Glaser, B. G., & Strauss, A. L. (1967). *The discovery of grounded theory: Strategies for qualitative research.* Chicago: Aldine-Atherton.

Goffman, E. (1959). *The presentation of self in everyday life.* New York: Anchor.

Goodall, J. (1991). *Through a window: My thirty years with the chimpanzees of Gombe.* Boston: Houghton Mifflin.

Gorden, R. L. (1975). *Interviewing: Strategy, techniques, and tactics* (Rev. ed.). Homewood, IL: Dorsey Press.

Gubrium, J. F. (1975). *Living and dying at Murray Manor.* New York: St. Martin's.

Hall, E. T. (1959). *The silent language.* Garden City, NY: Doubleday.

Hall, E. T. (1977). *Beyond culture.* Garden City, NY: Anchor.

Han, W. (2004). Automating analysis: Selecting and using qualitative analysis software. *QRCA Views, 2*(3), 30–34.

Hirschmann, E. C. (Ed.). (1989). *Interpretive consumer research.* Provo, UT: Association for Consumer Research.

Humphreys, L. (1975). *Tearoom trade: Impersonal sex in public places.* New York: Aldine De Gruyter.

Kanter, R. M. (1977). *Men and women of the corporation.* New York: Basic Books.

Kornblum, W. (1974). *Blue collar community.* Chicago: University of Chicago Press.

Kuhn, T. (1962). *The structure of scientific revolutions.* Chicago: University of Chicago Press.

Lester, S. (1999). *An introduction to phenomenological research.* Stan Lester Developments Home Page. Retrieved June 1, 2002, from http://www.devmts.demon.co.uk/resmethy.htm

Levitt, T. (1983). *The marketing imagination.* New York: Free Press.

Lewis, O. (1965). *La vida; a Puerto Rican family in the culture of poverty—San Juan and New York.* New York, Random House.

Liebow, E. (1967). *Tally's corner; a study of Negro streetcorner men.* Boston: Little & Brown.

Malinowski, B. (1922). *Argonauts of the western Pacific.* London: Routledge.

Mariampolski, H. (1988, January 4). Ethnography makes comeback as a research tool. *Marketing News, 22*(1), 32.

Mariampolski, H., "Ethnography as a Market Research Tool: Why, how, where and when." In Peter Sampson (ed.) *Qualitative Research: Through a Looking Glass.* New Monograph Series, Volume 4. (ESOMAR, 1998).

Mariampolski, H., "The Power of Ethnography." *Journal of the Market Research Society.* January, 1999.

Mariampolski, H. (2001). *Qualitative market research: A comprehensive guide.* Thousand Oaks, CA: Sage.

Merton, R. K. (1987). The focused interview and focus groups. *Public Opinion Quarterly,* (51), 550.

Merton, R. K., Fiske, M., & Kendall, P. L. (1990). *The focused interview: A manual of problems and procedures* (2nd ed.). New York: Free Press.

Mestel, R. (1998, March). Avarice. *New Scientist,* 28th March, 38–39.

Meyerhoff, B., & Ruby, J. (1982). Introduction. In J. Ruby (Ed.), *A crack in the mirror: Reflexive perspectives in anthropology.* (pp. 1–35). Philadelphia: University of Pennsylvania Press.

Mills, C. W. (1967). *The sociological imagination.* Oxford, UK: Oxford University Press.

Murphy, E., & Dingwall, R. (2001). The ethics of ethnography. In P. Atkinson, A. Coffey, S. Delamont, J. Lofland, & L. Lofland (Eds.). *Handbook of ethnography* (pp. 339–351). London: Sage.

Nielsen, J. (2000). *Designing web usability: The practice of simplicity.* Indianapolis, IN: New Riders.

Nielsen Marketing Research. (1993). *Category management.* New York: McGraw-Hill.

Norman, D. A. (1990). *The design of everyday things.* New York: Currency/ Doubleday.

Ozanne, J. L. (1989). Exploring diversity in consumer research. In E. C. Hirschmann (Ed.), *Interpretive consumer research.* Provo, UT: Association for Consumer Research.

Pink, S. (2001). *Doing visual ethnography.* London: Sage.

Plummer, K. (1983). *Documents of life: An introduction to the problems and literature of a humanistic method.* London: Unwin Hyman.

Powdermaker, H. (1966). *Stranger and friend: The way of the anthropologist.* New York: Norton.

Rogers, C. (1951). *Client-centered therapy.* Boston: Houghton Mifflin.

Rogers, C. (1961). *On becoming a person.* Boston: Houghton Mifflin.

Rothenberg, R. (1997, June). How powerful is advertising? *The Atlantic Monthly,* pp. 113–120.

Rothenberg, R. (2003, August 13). Speak, O muse, of strategic synergy. *The New York Times,* p. A25.

Rydholm, J. (2002, June). The revolution is at hand: Moen designs new showerhead after ethnographic research uncovers host of innovation opportunities. *Quirk's Marketing Research Review,* pp. 24–25, 82–83.

Schutz, A. (1970). *On phenomenology and social relations* (H. R. Wagner, Ed. and Introduction). Chicago: University of Chicago Press.

Sella, M. (2000, May 21). The electronic fishbowl. *The New York Times Magazine,* p. 50.

Skeggs, B. (2001). Feminist ethnography. In P. Atkinson, A. Coffey, S. Delamont, J. Lofland, & L. Lofland (Eds.), *Handbook of ethnography* (pp. 426–442). London: Sage.

Smith, D. V. L., & Fletcher, J. H. (2004). *The art and science of interpreting market research evidence.* New York: John Wiley.

Spradley, J. P. (1979). *The ethnographic interview.* Austin, TX: Holt, Rinehart & Winston.

Spradley, J. P., & Mann, B. (1975). *The cocktail waitress: Women's work in a man's world.* New York: John Wiley.

Stanley, L., & Wise, S. (1993). *Breaking out again: Feminist ontology and epistemology.* London: Routledge.

Taylor, S. J., & Bogdan, R. (1984). Introduction to qualitative research methods: The search for meanings (2nd ed.). Hoboken, NJ: John Wiley.

Tse, D. K., Belk, R. W., & Zhou, N. (1989, March). Becoming a consumer society: A longitudinal and cross-cultural content analysis of print ads from Hong Kong, the People's Republic of China, and Taiwan. *Journal of Consumer Research, 15,* 457–472.

Underhill, P. (2000). *Why we buy: The science of shopping.* New York: Simon & Schuster.

von Oech, R. (1983). *A whack on the side of the head: How to unlock your mind for innovation.* New York: Warner Books.

Weber, M. (1949). *The methodology of the social sciences.* Glencoe, IL: Free Press.

Whorf, B. (1956). *Language, thought, and reality: Selected writings of Benjamin Lee Whorf.* Cambridge: MIT Press.

Whyte, W. H. (1980). *The social life of small urban spaces.* Washington, D.C.: Conservation Foundation.

Winter, G. (2000). A comparative discussion of the notion of "validity" in qualitative and quantitative research. *The Qualitative Report, 4*(3 & 4). Retrieved June 20, 2004, from http://www.nova.edu/ssss/QR/QR4–3/winter.html

Wirth, L. (1956). *The ghetto.* Chicago: University of Chicago Press. (Original work published 1928)

Wong, S. M. J. (1993, December). The importance of context in conducting Asian research." *Quirk's Marketing Research Review.* Retrieved June 20, 2004, from https://www.quirks.com/articles/article.asp?arg_ArticleId=182

Wylie, L. (1976). *Village in the Vaucluse* (3rd ed.). Cambridge, MA: Harvard University Press.

Zorbaugh, H. W. (1976). *The gold coast and the slum.* Chicago: University of Chicago Press. (Original work published 1929)

Index

About the Author

World-Class Snooper Shares His Secrets

Hy Mariampolski, the leading worldwide corporate voyeur, finally shares his tools and techniques with corporate managers and product developers in *Ethnography for Marketers: A Guide to Consumer Immersion*.

For nearly 20 years, Mariampolski has exposed and explained people's everyday lives—with their explicit cooperation and consent, of course—in order to help leading corporations come up with ideas for new products, services, and communications. He has watched shoppers make decisions in stores and has stood by their side as they try navigating new computer software. Mariampolski has led Fortune 500 executives into kitchens to watch consumers cook family meals; he has gone into people's bathrooms to watch them clean toilets and, in a well-known study for Moen Corporation, even videotaped people while they were showering to help his client develop a new shower fixture.

As a rejoinder to telephone pollsters and those who stay within the walls of market research laboratories, Mariampolski asserts, "If you really want to get to know your customers, you need to eat with them in front of the TV set, hang out with them in bars, sit alongside them through health management routines—yes, even get into the shower with them."

Since he started using the well-established tools of cultural anthropology and qualitative sociology—doing what some practitioners call *observational studies* and *contextual research*—his ideas have caught on among innovative corporations. In the 1920s, Margaret Mead used ethnographic methods to learn about sex in Samoa; Mariampolski has adapted these approaches to learn about laundry in Istanbul and barbecues in Boston.

Now, Mariampolski's book has codified the rules of engagement. The best practices and numerous examples he describes can serve as a guide for corporate executives eager to engage in "consumer safaris" to watch customers use their products. *Ethnography for Marketers* may also be used by students and marketing research practitioners as a training resource and reference guide.

Hy Mariampolski was a college professor before he founded his consulting firm, QualiData Research Inc., and embarked on a corporate snooper career. He has become well-known for developing and teaching *QualiData Worldwide Ethnography for Marketers* workshops, delivered everywhere from Berlin to Budapest, Sydney to Shanghai. His advice is straightforward and practical rather than theoretical and complex. He constantly insists that corporate ethnographers need to respect cultural sensitivities and ethical requirements to gain the deepest insights possible while watching and videotaping consumers just being themselves.

Like his first book, *Qualitative Market Research: A Comprehensive Guide* (Sage, 2001), a textbook and reference for organizing and conducting focus groups and using other qualitative strategies, this one contains insights that are sure to attract attention among leading-edge corporate managers. In this highly competitive consumer marketplace, creativity and innovation are the engines for growth. *Ethnography for Marketers* brings the boundaries of imagination forward and stimulates thinking about new possibilities to better meet the needs and expectations of fickle consumers worldwide.